The Consortia Century for Impact

The Consortia Century breaks new theoretical ground by going beyond standard individual or organizational levels of analyses to make a strong case for building and sustaining multi-party institutions capable of tackling the major challenges of the 21st century. The authors then provide well-researched and tested roadmaps for guiding the next generation of institutional entrepreneurs in leading and governing these consortia. Bravo to this creative consortium of authors.

Thomas A. Kochan, Professor Emeritus, Sloan School of Management and Institute for Work and Employment Research, MIT

The world's complex problems, from health, environment, social media, technological change, and social justice cannot be resolved by any one nation, organization, individual, or even social movement. This book presents an important flexible, adaptable, and agile form of organized "aligned impact"—consortia of interests, seeking to work through coordinated action with horizontal, lateral intergroup forms of problem solving. This is a blueprint for a different kind of organizational structure between top-down or bottom-up patterns. A must read for those interested in social change, public policy, and organizational leadership.

Carrie Menkel-Meadow, Distinguished and Chancellor's Professor of Law and Political Science, University of California, Irvine

The Consortia Century documents early signs of what could be a much-needed transformation in the institutional arrangements of the 21st century. The book focuses on lateral alignment across diverse stakeholders in order to better address societal challenges, including the advances in artificial intelligence, human health, and climate change. Learning to think laterally, not just top down or bottom up, will be an essential skill if institutions are to successfully co-evolve with accelerating technological change.

Ray Kurzweil, inventor, author, and futurist

The Consortia Century is a momentous book, documenting a rich tapestry of consortia. In this tapestry, Ikamva Labantu stands as a beacon of collaboration and community-led empowerment. Through nurturing the next generation and addressing the enduring challenges of South African society, Ikamva Labantu exemplifies the essence of purposeful collective action. We are honored to be a leading example of the transformative power of consortia in establishing social institutions where hope thrives.

Ishrene Davids, Director, Ikamva Labantu

Consortia are everywhere and this book explains why and how these uniquely focused constructs coalesce around common goals and interests without losing the individuality of their components. The concept is ancient. Think multicellular plants and animals and the United States for examples of consortia with a purpose. This book puts a new lens on a venerable phenomenon.

Vint Cerf, internet pioneer

In a society of heightened polarization, dis and misinformation and interdependency for our existence, *The Consortia Century* offers principles, examples, and inspiration for addressing some of our greatest challenges by forming and advancing together as consortia. With an urgent need for dialogue and shared vision among disparate types of organization whose knowledge and experience impacts both local and global outcomes, this book offers insights into an essential construct in a complex world.

Mary Lee Kennedy, Executive Director (retired), Association of Research Libraries

In our rapidly evolving era of molecular medicine, collaborations across the biomedical research ecosystem have become essential in driving innovation in patient treatment and care. Advancing the frontiers of biomedicine can often be achieved most effectively through partnerships that integrate valuable scientific resources and insights from industry, government, universities, and patient groups. As *The Consortia Century* documents, these multi-stakeholder consortia are and will continue to be vitally important to achieving breakthrough advances in human health.

David Wholley, President and Executive Director (former), Foundation for the National Institutes of Health

The Consortia Century highlights the utilization of multi-stakeholder consortia in many environments, including labor relations. In labor-management relations and other domains, *The Consortia Century* guides us in both expanding the proverbial pie as well as dividing it. Engaging in labor relations without a labor-management partnership is like operating with one hand tied behind your back.

**Dennis L. Dabney, Senior Vice President (retired),
National Labor Relations, Kaiser Permanente**

Thriving in Games Group (formerly the Fair Play Alliance) empowers game developers worldwide to create safer, more inclusive gaming experiences. We achieve this through a consortium of developers, researchers, and more, all united in a shared mission to help people thrive in today's online world. *The Consortia Century* rightly emphasizes that caring for our digital worlds requires a shared effort at a global scale. They are to be commended for highlighting the importance of social systems and collaborative action in fostering digital well-being.

Kimberly Voll, Co-Founder, Thriving in Games Group

The thousands of fab labs in the world have been growing through consortia of many kinds – the Fab Foundation, the Fab Academy, the Fab Cities initiative, the Fab All In initiative and various regional consortia. *The Consortia Century* documents this underlying way of operating, enabling social systems to keep pace (barely!) with accelerating technological change.

Sherry Lassiter, President, The Fab Foundation

The Consortia Century

The Consortia Century

Aligning for Impact

by

THE STAKEHOLDER ALIGNMENT
COLLABORATIVE

Joel Cutcher-Gershenfeld,
Ken Anderson, Karen S. Baker,
Nicholas Berente, Helen M. Berman,
Alan Blatecky, Christine L. Borgman,
Patrick Canavan, Bobby Clark,
Yaminette Diaz-Linhart,
Alysia Garmulewicz,
Alyson Gounden Rock,
Michael Haberman, Phyllis D.K. Hildreth,
Ron Hutchins, John Leslie King,
Christine R. Kirkpatrick, John C. Klensin,
Kimberlyn Leary, Spencer Lewis,
W. Christopher Lenhardt,
Michael Maffie, Lauren A. Michael,
Barbara B. Mittleman, Rajesh Sampath,
Sarah Soroui, Namchul Shin, Miya Ward,
Susan J. Winter, and Kimberly E. Zarecor

OXFORD
UNIVERSITY PRESS

Oxford University Press is a department of the University of Oxford.
It furthers the University's objective of excellence in research, scholarship,
and education by publishing worldwide. Oxford is a registered trade mark of
Oxford University Press in the UK and in certain other countries.

Published in the United States of America by Oxford University Press
198 Madison Avenue, New York, NY 10016, United States of America.

© Oxford University Press 2025

All rights reserved. No part of this publication may be reproduced, stored in
a retrieval system, transmitted, used for text and data mining, or used for training artificial
intelligence, in any form or by any means, without the
prior permission in writing of Oxford University Press, or as expressly permitted
by law, by licence or under terms agreed with the appropriate reprographics
rights organization. Inquiries concerning reproduction outside the scope of the
above should be sent to the Rights Department, Oxford University Press, at the
address above

You must not circulate this work in any other form
and you must impose this same condition on any acquirer

Library of Congress Cataloging-in-Publication Data
Names: Stakeholder Alignment Collaborative, author |
Cutcher-Gershenfeld, Joel, contributor.
Title: The consortia century / the Stakeholder Alignment Collaborative.
Description: New York, NY : Oxford University Press, [2025] |
Includes bibliographical references and index.
Identifiers: LCCN 2024039693 (print) | LCCN 2024039694 (ebook) |
ISBN 9780197761649 (paperback) | ISBN 9780197761632 (hardback) |
ISBN 9780197761663 (epub) | ISBN 9780197761670
Subjects: LCSH: Consortia. | Institutional cooperation.
Classification: LCC HD2963 .S73 2025 (print) | LCC HD2963 (ebook) |
DDC 021.6/5-dc23/eng/20241021
LC record available at https://lccn.loc.gov/2024039693
LC ebook record available at https://lccn.loc.gov/2024039694

DOI: 10.1093/oso/9780197761649.001.0001

Paperback printed by Marquis, Canada
Hardback printed by Bridgeport National Bindery, Inc., United States of America

To the inspiring leaders and members of consortia addressing societal challenges, small and large.

Contents

List of Figures	xiii
List of Tables	xiv
Acknowledgments	xv
About the Authors	xvi

Prologue	1

PART I CONSORTIA

1. Consortia and Global Challenges	7
2. A Gathering of Destinies	30
3. Barriers to Collective Action	49
4. Agile and Adaptive Consortia	68

PART II ALIGNING STAKEHOLDERS

5. Managing and Engaging (But Not Aligning) Stakeholders	93
6. Scoping: Specifying Stakeholders and Identifying Interests	112
7. Structuring: Forging a Shared Vision, Drafting a Charter, and Agreeing on Metrics	132
8. Sustaining: Delivering Results, Adjusting, and Adapting	160

PART III LOOKING FORWARD

9. Storm Clouds on the Horizon	181
10. A Vision of Consortia for a Complex World	195

Epilogue	213
Acronyms	214
Glossary	217
Index	219

List of Figures

1.1.	UN Sustainable Development Goals (SDGs)	11
2.1.	Research Computing and Data Consortia 1950–2020	33
2.2.	Illustrative Example of a Matrix of Stakeholders and Interests	41
4.1.	Stakeholder Alignment Model: Aligning and Advancing Stakeholders in a Consortium	76
4.2.	A Landscape of Stakeholders and Interests	83
5.1.	Sample Stakeholder Management Grid with Support and Influence	96
5.2.	Kotter Model for Leading Change	97
5.3.	Model for the Impact of Change	101
5.4.	Deming Continuous Improvement Model	102
6.1.	Stakeholder Alignment Model—Scoping the Landscape of Stakeholders and Interests	115
6.2.	Illustrative Example of a Matrix of Stakeholders and Interests	122
7.1.	Stakeholder Alignment Model—Structuring a Shared Vision, Charter, and Metrics	135
7.2.	Visualization of a Shared Vision by Kaiser Permanente	139
7.3.	Visualization of Collaborative Work by Aviation and the Environment	140
8.1.	Stakeholder Alignment Model—Delivering Results, Adjusting, and Adapting	162

List of Tables

1.1.	A Spectrum of Institutional Arrangements	13
2.1.	Guiding Principles for Stakeholder Alignment	40
3.1.	Key Barriers to Collective Action	51
4.1.	Key Characteristics of Consortia	70
5.1.	Contrasting Stakeholder Management, Engagement, and Alignment	94
7.1.	MS-CC Key Performance Indicators	155
8.1.	Example Pulse Survey Ranking Potential Programming Topics for MS-CC	171
9.1.	Storm Clouds on the Horizon	184

Acknowledgments

This work was made possible with support from the National Science Foundation, including "EAGER: Democratizing the Use of Advanced Computational Resources" (NSF OAC 21-27459); "EAGER: Supporting and Learning from Principal Investigators 'Making the Leap to Large'" (NSF CNS 21-29177); "Collaborative Strategies for Successful Large-Scale, Distributed Science and Engineering Projects" (NSF CNS 19-39224); "Geosciences EarthCube Community Office" (NSF GEO 19-28208); EarthCube Test Enterprise Governance, "Targeted Chartering and Stakeholder Alignment Data Feedback" (NSF); I-Corps grant on "Stakeholder Alignment for Public-Private Partnerships" (NSF I-Corps 13-13562); INSPIRE/CREATIV grant on "Enabling Transformation in the Social Sciences, Geosciences, and Cyberinfrastructure Through Stakeholder Alignment and New Institutional Theory, Methods, and Analytics" (NSF GEO 12-49607); "Envisioning Success: A Workshop for Next Generation EarthCube Scholars and Scientists" (NSF OCI 12-56163); RAPID grant on "Stakeholder Alignment for EarthCube" funded by NSF Program on Virtual Organizations as Sociotechnical Systems (NSF OCI 12-29928); EAGER grant on "Stakeholder Alignment in Socio-Technical Systems" funded by NSF program on Virtual Organizations as Sociotechnical Systems (NSF-VOSS 09-56472).

We appreciate the many individuals who have commented on aspects of this book, including: Steven Barley, Sam Barratt, Paul Arthur Berkman, Fran Berman, Dana Brunson, Vint Cerf, Michael Daniels, Ishrene Davids, Ali Farid, Maurizio Floris, Jon Gant, Alan Gershenfeld, Neil Gershenfeld, Brandon Grant, Ann Greiner, Steven Hoffmann, Zachary Hylton, Thomas Kochan, Deborah Kolb, John Kotter, Jeanette Kruger, Ray Kurzweil, Sherry Lassiter, Helen Lieberman, Greg Martin, Matthew Mayernik, Charles McElroy, Carrie Menkel-Meadow, Akiko Otani, Jim Pruitt, Hal Ruddick, Patrick Schmitz, Mark Servilla, Douglas Stewart, Kimberly Voll, Ian Waitz, David Wholley, Scott Yokel, and Eva Zanzerkia. While the many inputs are deeply appreciated, we bear full responsibility for the material.

About the Authors

Joel Cutcher-Gershenfeld, Professor and Florence G. Heller Chair, Heller School for Social Policy and Management, Brandeis University

Ken Anderson, Principal Engineer, Research and Experience Definition (RED) Client Computing Group, Intel Corporation

Karen S. Baker, Research Scientist, School of Information Sciences, University of Illinois, Urbana-Champaign

Nicholas Berente, Professor of IT, Analytics, and Operations, Mendoza College of Business, University of Notre Dame

Helen M. Berman, Professor Emerita, Department of Chemistry and Chemical Biology Rutgers University; Research Professor, University of Southern California

Alan Blatecky, Visiting Fellow, RTI-International

Christine L. Borgman, Distinguished Research Professor, Information Studies, University of California, Los Angeles

Patrick Canavan, CEO, WayMark Analytics; Retired SVP, Global Governance, Motorola Corporation

Bobby Clark, Director, CCIT Procurement & IT Vendor Management, Clemson University

Yaminette Diaz-Linhart, Postdoctoral Scholar, Institute for Work and Employment Research, MIT

Alysia Garmulewicz, Associate Professor, Faculty of Management and Economics, University of Santiago of Chile, Chile

Alyson Gounden Rock, Doctoral Candidate, Desautels Faculty of Management, McGill University, Visiting PhD student at Institute for Work and Employment Research, MIT (Summer and Fall 2023)

Michael Haberman, Senior Software Engineer, Energy Sciences Network

Phyllis D.K. Hildreth, Associate Professor of Conflict Management, American Baptist College

Ron Hutchins, CTO, Golden State Net

John Leslie King, Professor Emeritus of Information, School of Information, University of Michigan

Christine R. Kirkpatrick, Division Director, Research Data Services, San Diego Supercomputer Center, University of California, San Diego

John C. Klensin, Consultant; Internet Hall of Fame Pioneer Member

Kimberlyn Leary, Executive Vice President, Urban Institute, and Associate Professor, Department of Psychiatry, Harvard Medical School; Associate Professor in the Department of Health Policy and Management, Harvard T.H. Chan School of Public Health

Spencer Lewis, Doctoral Student, Brandeis University

W. Christopher Lenhardt, Senior Research Scientist, Renaissance Computing Institute (RENCI), University of North Carolina at Chapel Hill

Michael Maffi, Assistant Professor, SC Johnson School of Business, Cornell University

Lauren A. Michael, Consultant, Research Engagement, Internet2, Principle Consultant, Lauren Michael Consulting, LLC

Barbara B. Mittleman, Chief Strategy Officer, WayMark Analytics; Retired Director, Public–Private Partnerships, National Institutes of Health

Rajesh Sampath, Associate Professor, Heller School for Social Policy and Management, Brandeis University

Sarah Soroui, Visiting Scholar, Heller School for Social Policy and Management, Brandeis University

Namchul Shin, Professor of Information Systems, Seidenberg School of Computer Science and Information Systems, Pace University

Miya Ward, Consultant, Nexight Group, Washington, DC

Susan J. Winter, Associate Dean for Research, College of Information Studies, University of Maryland, College Park

Kimberly E. Zarecor, Professor of Architecture, College of Design, Iowa State University

Prologue

On June 1, 2017, then US President Donald Trump announced that the United States would withdraw from the Paris Climate Accord. For proponents of progress against climate change, it was a shocking and discouraging development. Chicago Mayor Rahm Emanuel responded that day by committing to honor the Paris Climate Accord. To the surprise of many, five weeks later on July 10, 2017, 350 additional US mayors announced that their cities were also joining the Climate Accord. These mayors represented 65 million of the 325 million US citizens. In the space of about one month, leadership of American foreign policy on climate change had briefly shifted from the US president to a distributed network of mayors.

In this case, there was sufficient alignment among the mayors and their constituents as stakeholders for them to act together. What made the alignment possible was less visible. When the 350 mayors made their announcement, they were building on earlier decisions by 20 mayors in 2013–2014 to join the Natural Resources Defense Council (NRDC) and the Institute for Market Transformations (IMT) Energy Project. Further, they were building on a coalition called Climate Mayors that came together in 2014, which was followed by a series of clean energy commitments in major cities across the United States. Today, Climate Mayors describes itself as a "bipartisan, peer-to-peer network that has mobilized more than 750 U.S. mayors who demonstrate climate leadership through meaningful actions in their communities. Representing 48 states and nearly 60 million Americans, the Climate Mayors coalition reflects U.S. cities' commitment to climate progress."[1] This coalition spans cities that are large and small, led by different political parties, and covering diverse regions across the United States.

The unheralded work of aligning the common and competing interests of hundreds of mayors to form the Climate Mayors coalition is a critical part of the story of how these diverse stakeholders were able to play a role in US foreign policy. Mayor Emanuel's 2017 announcement and the

> mayors' collective embrace of the Paris Climate Accord was not just a spontaneous action. It was a bold move that would not have been possible without the Climate Mayors coalition.

When diverse individuals, groups, and organizations come together to form a consortium, they are doing something remarkable—establishing a social institution where none existed previously. This is different from assembling a group or forming an organization. It is a particular type of institutional arrangement that operates as a coalition, collaborative, consortium, partnership, or other entity signaling the assembly of independent individuals, groups, and organizations that are interdependent and working together purposefully. We use the term "consortia" and include in the analysis these many collaborative arrangements, which are not identical but operate in comparable ways.

Today, many types of consortia are forming to lead change, as in the case of the Climate Mayors coalition, and are also formed to build community, set standards, launch initiatives, conduct research, promote fairness, and address global challenges. Such consortia do not replace existing institutional arrangements. Instead, they enable existing groups, organizations, and institutional actors to collaborate on issues or challenges that no one group or organization alone can address in the same way. We argue that it is this core capability that is driving the expanding role of consortia in today's world.

This book operates at the institutional level of analysis, which is different from individual or group or organizational levels of analysis. Institutional arrangements reflect particular patterns of interaction that constitute the social order in society. Collaborative institutional arrangements don't happen just with good will—they require sufficient stakeholder alignment to enable collective action.

In this book, we share examples and lessons learned from a variety of consortia focused on societal challenges such as biomedicine, climate change, health care, labor and employment relations, science infrastructure, and technology. Many of these consortia have adopted working practices that allow them to be agile and adaptable, with relatively little structure and formality. As we will see, however, such arrangements bring both advantages and limitations. These consortia are flexible, but many are also fragile.

Further, not all consortia are beneficial to society. Some are set up with the intent to undercut the social order. Some consortia operate as monopolistic cartels, others promote terrorism, insurrections, and various forms of extremism in society. These extractive and destructive consortia are not our focus, but their presence does need to be acknowledged.

Our focus is on the two foundational considerations with any institutional arrangement—how to create value and how to mitigate harm. Both are essential in our approach and both raise an underlying question—creating value and mitigating harm for whom?[2] In this context, the process of stakeholder alignment is needed since the "for whom" question spans diverse stakeholders.

We began our research by documenting the increasing formation of consortia to enable the open sharing of data and computing capabilities in science. We extended our focus to a variety of consortia in other sectors—seeing many of the same patterns repeated. In the process, we operated ourselves as a consortium—meeting weekly for dialogue and writing with shared documents. We found that conducting research, writing articles, and now writing this book collectively is also a case of doing together what we couldn't do separately.

There some key new terms introduced, such as "lateral alignment," so a glossary is provided. As well, we span many technical domains, each with their own array of acronyms, so an acronym listing is also provided.

The accelerating formation of consortia leads to our book's claim that we are living in what is becoming the consortia century. This form of collaboration, enabled by advances in digital technologies, is worthy of and requires further exploration, evaluation, and guidance. This is why we wrote this book.

Notes

1. See "Demonstrating Leadership on Climate Change through Meaningful Actions in Our Communities," Climate Mayors, accessed on June 14, 2023, https://climatemayors.org/.
2. In one study of 100 years of labor and employment policies in Australia, it was found that both dimensions—creating value and mitigating harm—were present in different degrees at different times. Most often, new institutional initiatives were justified on the basis of mitigating harm; additional modifications centered on creating value came later. See Joel Cutcher-Gershenfeld and Joe Isaac, "Creating Value and Mitigating Harm: Assessing Institutional Objectives in Australian Industrial Relations," *Economic and Labour Relations Review* 29, no. 2 (2018): pp. 1–26, https://doi.org/10.1177/1035304618767263.

PART I
CONSORTIA

Chapter 1
Consortia and Global Challenges

In just over a decade, one of the oldest pharmaceutical companies in the world, Takeda, has grown from being a member of just one public-private partnership to now being a member of approximately 100. These types of consortia, involving diverse public and private stakeholders, are rapidly transforming how research and development (R&D) happens in medical science.

Founded in Japan in 1781, Takeda is one of the 20 largest pharmaceutical companies in the world and one of the oldest companies still in operation. In order to advance the frontiers of science in today's world and solve complex challenges, Takeda recognizes that it needs to collaborate with partners. Around 2009, Takeda began participating in R&D public-private partnerships (PPPs), which typically feature large pharmaceutical firms, smaller biotech firms, government regulatory agencies, patient advocacy organizations, healthcare providers, and university researchers. These PPPs are in therapeutic areas of strategic importance to the company.

Today, just over a decade later, Takeda is now participating in approximately 100 PPPs globally (the exact number is always evolving) and has a specialized team dedicated to PPPs. This team is led by Akiko Otani, senior director of PPPs and global science policy. The company's website states that its interest in PPPs is to be at the frontiers of knowledge: "Our Public-Private Partnerships extend beyond traditional biological approaches and integrate the latest technological advances, such as artificial intelligence and machine learning. Our Global Science Policy work helps identify and focus on which PPPs to engage with to help us understand, anticipate and influence future scientific trends and policies better."

The rapid expansion of the global PPP portfolio in just over a decade reflects what these PPPs enable that would otherwise be more difficult for the company to do alone. As Akiko Otani observes, "The complex scientific challenges we face today can potentially be more effectively and efficiently tackled by sharing knowledge and expertise, pooling resources and de-risking investments. These pre-competitive, multi-sectoral, multi-stakeholder collaborations strive to advance the leading frontiers of science in areas of strategic importance to the company." She adds that "all partners of a PPP have opportunities throughout the duration of a project, on average about five years, to strengthen collaboration and relationships at the core of which is trust."

Akiko Otani reports that the collaborations enable the company to gain important insights from patient groups, for example, about their experiences (challenges and needs they face) with a particular disease and insights from regulatory authorities about what they are looking for regarding novel therapies. She also reports that PPPs offer opportunities for companies large and small to learn more about their respective capabilities, which can lead to future bilateral collaborations. Finally, representing the company in a PPP offers a valuable career development opportunity especially for early and midcareer scientists. On this last point, Otani comments, "our scientists really find the experience exciting and inspiring, and value the opportunity to directly engage with the leading experts in their field and contribute to shaping the ecosystem around them as they push the boundaries of their field so that better treatments can reach patients faster."

Akiko Otani further observes that, "with each passing year, we have observed how quickly technology advances and realizing the increasing risk of not being part of those efforts at the leading edge of science." She concludes that "some of the most innovative approaches to tackling some of the most challenging scientific hurdles are being developed by PPPs. Those that have successfully delivered impactful outputs that everyone can utilize demonstrate the power of PPPs to move that needle so novel treatments can reach patients faster."[1]

Although there are considerable mutual gains at individual and organizational levels driving the growing engagement with consortia in the pharmaceutical sector, it is important to recognize that this is happening with concurrent competing interests. Pharmaceutical companies have business models that don't always align with patient or public interests. What is important in this case, however, is that the work through consortia has the potential for movement toward increased alignment between public and private interests in ways that might not happen otherwise.

Decades from now, historians will celebrate consortia as a defining feature of the 21st century. These self-governing collaborative arrangements, which may also operate under names such as alliances, collaboratives, coalitions, councils, or public-private partnerships (PPPs), will come to the forefront since the many challenges facing the world today do not fit neatly within existing organizational boundaries. No one organization will prevail in addressing climate change, accelerating technological change, food insecurity, global pandemics, gender and ethnic violence, eroding privacy, digital divides, supply chain crises, and countless other challenges that require a long-term vision and an inclusive approach. It is not just that the challenges are vast and complex (though they are); it is that our dominant mechanism for tackling big challenges—the public or private hierarchical organization with clear lines of authority and responsibility—are an incomplete match for these challenges.

Consortia enable many individuals, groups, and organizations to accomplish together what they cannot do separately. At a time of accelerating technological change,[2] which is itself a challenge, consortia have the flexibility to coevolve with technical systems. It is these capabilities that make consortia an essential institutional arrangement for the 21st century.

In this century, consortia will play a defining role, much as guilds played a defining role in the 18th century, industrial production played a defining role in the 19th century, and multinational corporations played a defining role in the 20th century.[3] Consortia will not replace government agencies, multinational corporations, private foundations, local and international nongovernmental organizations, professional societies, universities, unions, and other parts of the institutional landscape. Indeed, people in these various types of organizations are typically the ones forming consortia. These individuals and groups are drawn to consortia that can be agile and adaptive, crossing institutional and organizational boundaries and providing a form of self-governance that is matched to the emergent and complex natural, social, and economic ecosystems in which the challenges reside.[4]

Why Now?

Consortia have long been at the heart of social movements and social change. The draw has always been the underlying assumption that the perspectives of multiple parties are all important—what social scientists term a pluralist assumption. The interests of the diverse stakeholders are all seen as sufficiently legitimate to work together—even if some are in tension with others. Today, three broad societal forces are increasing the importance of consortia.

First, we face societal challenges from local to global scales which it is increasingly clear that no one organization or institutional actor can sufficiently address. Many of the challenges have geologic, biologic, sociologic, technologic, and other dimensions, all intertwined. A half century ago it was thought that the United Nations (UN) could be an institutional actor commensurate with global challenges. Yet, when in 2015 the UN listed its 17 sustainable development goals (SDGs; Figure 1.1), and specifically included "Strong Institutions" as SDG 16, it was not referring only to the UN. The challenge of SDG 16 is to "Promote peaceful and inclusive societies for sustainable development, provide access to justice for all and build effective, accountable and inclusive institutions at all levels." The UN also included "Partnerships for the Goals" as SDG 17: "Strengthen the means of implementation and revitalize the Global Partnership for Sustainable Development." Both SDG 16 and 17 signal that social systems are needed and indicate that progress on the goals is beyond the scope of even an institution as large as the UN.[5] Thus, the need for consortia is great for all of these deeply challenging issues.

Second, digital technologies are advancing at an accelerated rate. This includes social media, asynchronous communication platforms, and other technologies that facilitate lateral communications. These technologies enable the formation and sustainment of consortia across time and space. The technologies also bring new challenges—such as weaponized social media, threats to privacy, digital divides, ethical issues associated with artificial intelligence, and more—that can't be fully addressed by any one organization or institutional actor. Thus, emerging technological capabilities for collaboration enhance the potential impacts of consortia and at the same time illustrate why the need for them is growing.

Figure 1.1 UN Sustainable Development Goals (SDGs)

Third, societal challenges are dynamic—solutions advanced today may not be sufficient or effective in the future. Commercial organizations, government agencies, not-for-profit and nongovernmental organizations, universities, and others all have key roles to play in society and all contribute by being stable entities. Yet their very stability also makes change difficult. This is where consortia can play a key role. Consortia have the ability to bring together diverse stakeholders relative to a given issue or challenge, with progress toward shared interests becoming feasible in agile and adaptive ways.

What Is a Consortium?

We use the word "consortia" to encompass a wide variety of collaborative institutional arrangements, including alliances, collaboratives, councils, public-private partnerships, and others. Our focus is on consortia that operate as self-governing collaborative arrangements among independent organizations and other stakeholders, accomplishing together what they cannot do separately. We see rapid growth in consortia defined in this way, spanning institutional boundaries and often including organizations in both the public and private sectors.

It is helpful to unpack the above definition of consortia in a few ways. Our focus is on consortia that bring together many different types of stakeholders or interested parties. There is a point at which a group of people acting together is no longer a crowd or social movement and instead takes the form of a consortium. The indicators of this shift include a shared vision statement, a charter, a process for identifying leaders and members, and other artifacts that signal the underlying acceptance of shared governance. While they are connected by a shared vision or sense of urgency to address a given challenge, these parties are independent for other purposes. Otherwise, they would just be an organization. In a consortium, there is always a tension between the interdependence and the independence of the parties. As a result, there is invariably a mix of common and competing interests, which is where self-governance comes in. While there are partnerships and collaboratives that operate within narrowly defined domains, it is consortia that cross boundaries—locally, regionally, or globally—that are particularly important today since, as we have noted, the challenges we face don't fit within existing organizational boundaries. Finally, the definition signals that consortia are purposeful and only formed when there doesn't appear to be an alternative. The parties would operate on their own to address a given challenge if they could achieve the same or better results separately, since there are transaction costs, autonomy considerations, and other constraints to working together (elaborated in Chapter 3).

Note that the noun "consortium" (Latin consortium, plural consortia) in basic form refers to a partnership, association, or collection of individuals or groups (e.g., organizations).[6] Some names contain the word (e.g., the Microelectronics and Computing Consortium). Others do not and need additional context to see where the consortium comes in. For example, the nonprofit University Corporation for Atmospheric Research (UCAR) is a consortium, even though the name does not use the word. Many long-standing organizations are structured as consortia, such as professional societies, associations, sports leagues, and others. Although they have multiparty structures, they operate largely as unitary commercial or nonprofit organizations. At the other end of the spectrum, there are consortia-like entities that operate laterally but are not fully instantiated as multistakeholder consortia. For example, a cross-university research team may have some similar properties as a consortium. While many of our findings will have relevance for these organizations and entities, particularly if they seek to scale while remaining agile and adaptive, our primary focus is on emergent and evolving consortia that are establishing new forms of self-governance to address pressing societal challenges. In this context, we focus both on consortia as a lens into the collaborative work taking place in complex ecosystems and as institutional entities that serve as a type of "boundary object," helping parties to bridge across boundaries in order to have collective impacts.[7] Our approach is what has been termed "institutional work," which has been defined as "creating, maintaining and disrupting institutions."[8]

Among institutional arrangements, we locate consortia between social movements and organizations, as illustrated in Table 1.1. We see these institutional arrangements as conceptually distinct, although there are various ways that they interact. On the one hand, social movements can drive the formation of consortia (drawn by their formalization and inclusive structure) that then become formal organizations. On the other hand, organizations can drive the formation of consortia (drawn by their flexibility and inclusive structure) that then become social movements. From a social movement perspective, consortia represent much-needed formalization (while still being diverse and inclusive). From an organizational perspective, consortia represent much-needed flexibility (because they are diverse and inclusive).

We come to this formulation in two ways. First, inductively, we observe that consortia are often emergent out of some form of social movement or collective action and then progress to incorporate as a formal organization. For example, the Minority Serving Cyberinfrastructure Consortium (MS-CC) mentioned throughout this book is the product of a growing movement to advance representation of underserved groups and underresourced universities in advancing the frontiers of science, social science, and the humanities. Now MS-CC has a formal board of directors and is in the

Table 1.1 A Spectrum of Institutional Arrangements

Social Movement	Consortium	Organization
Connected individuals and groups with a shared vision and a commitment to action	Connected stakeholders (individuals, groups, and organizations) operating within a formal pluralist structure guiding action	Individuals and groups operating within a formal unitary structure guiding action

process of incorporating as a formal organization. In this case, there is a movement toward more formalization that goes from social movement to consortium to organization.

Second, organizations are unitary actors with a defined mission, which contrasts with consortia, which have what is termed a pluralist structure—spanning across organizations (as well as interest groups, individuals, and others). Pluralist consortia may expand in scope to become social movements in society. For example, the Biomarkers Consortium (a case considered throughout this book) was formed by organizational leaders in major pharmaceutical companies (PHARMA), the US National Institutes of Health (NIH), and the US Food and Drug Administration (FDA) in order to carve out a precompetitive space to collaborate and openly share data on projects that identify and qualify biomarkers, which are indicators of disease and health. The Biomarkers Consortium has become part of a broad social movement around open science. In this sense, there was a progression from formal organizations toward a more flexible and more broadly inclusive arrangement that goes from organizations to consortia to social movement.

We use the term "stakeholder" to describe the parties who form a consortium, and this needs special consideration. Stakeholders are individuals, groups, organizations, and other parties with substantive interests in a given issue, initiative, or organization. On the one hand, the term has a progressive connotation in the business context, where corporations must increasingly attend to a greater breadth of stakeholders (employees, customers, suppliers, shareholders, regulators, collaborators, and communities) as opposed to a narrow focus on shareholders. This is often referred to as stakeholder capitalism, which is promoted as an advance over shareholder capitalism. In that sense, the term "stakeholder" is inclusive and progressive.

At the same time, the term "stakeholder" also has historical baggage,[9] since the concept of a "stake" has roots in colonizing forces where land was given away at the expense of first nations (often with an additional aim of eradicating the cultures of first nations)—literally putting a stake in the ground to claim what was already occupied by others. In that sense, the term "stakeholder" has been criticized as having an expropriating connotation. To counteract this historical connotation, first nations have been given unique standing, for example, in negotiations in the Polar regions.[10] They are not seen as one more stakeholder, but are appropriately accorded higher status as "rights holders," while those designated as "stakeholders" in these negotiations have a higher status than "interested parties." In this book we will use "stakeholder" as an overarching term—there is no better alternative, and it has some positive connotations. Where appropriate, we will also make distinctions among "rights holders," "stakeholders," and "interested parties."

The consortia we have studied are dynamic, and it is possible that in a few decades from now this institutional arrangement will have evolved in ways that will require adjustments in the definitions of terms offered here. What is clear now and will likely be clear in the near future, is that consortia are different from hierarchies, markets, and regulatory control. They are a distinctive institutional arrangement that tends to be nonbureaucratic, adaptable, and able to work at local or global scales as needed. It is these properties that are behind both the growth in the formation of consortia and the impacts they are having.

It Takes Stakeholder Alignment

Consortia require stakeholder alignment—lateral connections across stakeholders sufficient to enable collective action. Stakeholder alignment is the underlying theory that guides our understanding of consortia. Stakeholder alignment is different from top-down or bottom-up alignment; it involves a different, lateral way of thinking.

Top-down alignment typically involves a hierarchical organization.[11] It is a dynamic, iterative, negotiated process by which sufficient understanding or agreement is reached around the goals set by the leaders.[12] Regulation can be imposed with the aim of achieving top-down alignment, although the result may just be compliance, rather than greater degrees of alignment.

Bottom-up alignment is typically associated with self-organizing forms of collaboration in the absence of hierarchies and can include market-based coordination and collective action.[13] It is a dynamic, iterative, negotiated process by which sufficient understanding or agreement is reached around the goals from distributed individuals and groups to enable coordinated action toward achieving common goals. Markets may be intended to achieve bottom-up alignment, although the result may just be unconstrained, rather than greater degrees of alignment.

In contrast to top-down and bottom-up alignment, stakeholder alignment involves the lateral or horizontal collaboration among parties who come together, typically (but not always) with more equal standing than would be the case in a market, hierarchy, or regulatory situation. We define lateral alignment as the dynamic, iterative, negotiated process by which sufficient understanding or agreement is reached across individuals, groups, and organizations to enable coordinated action toward achieving common goals. It is the process by which independent parties who are also interdependent operate horizontally to accomplish together what they can't do separately.[14] Our definition of consortia is echoed here in our definition of lateral alignment, since that is how consortia operate. Our approach is similar to the collective impact model, which emphasizes a common agenda, shared measurement, mutually reinforcing activities, continued communication, and a backbone organization.[15] We give more emphasis to the competing interests and the associated dynamics needed for alignment as well as the features of a consortium as an agile and adaptive institutional arrangement. Still, our stakeholder alignment model and the collective impact model are both among the few examples of middle-out, lateral models.

Stakeholder alignment is also different from stakeholder management and stakeholder engagement (covered in more detail in Chapter 5). When people call for stakeholder management, it is typically expressed by one party looking out and seeing stakeholders who may be opposed or present complications that need to be managed. When people call for stakeholder engagement it is typically expressed as the need for one party to engage stakeholders who may be supportive or who would have important inputs to be taken into account. In both cases that focus is on viewing stakeholders from one party's perspective. By contrast, stakeholder alignment takes the vantage point of the system as a whole, with alignment being an inclusive process in which all involved stakeholders are seen as having agency to join in.

There will, of course, be power differences among stakeholders as they seek sufficient alignment for action. Even with power differences among members of a consortium, there is typically some parity in the opportunity to have a say in what the consortium does and some parity in how each contributes. For example, we have mentioned the Biomarkers Consortium, which was formed in 2006 as a precompetitive space where pharmaceutical and biotech companies could work together with government agencies (FDA and NIH), universities, and patient advocacy organizations to discover and qualify the indicators of healthy and disease states. While there are many different types of power differences among these parties (financial resources, regulatory authority, research expertise, moral authority, veto power, etc.), the steering committees and project teams launched by this consortium mostly operate on a consensus basis, with each party contributing based on its knowledge, expertise, and capacity. The contributions of each type of stakeholder are not identical, but they are collectively seen as appropriate and necessary for each project launched by the consortium.

What brings a consortium together are common interests, but the parties invariably have other competing interests as well. The mix of common and competing interests can be difficult to navigate. As a result, stakeholder alignment is dynamic, continuous, and complex. Results are achieved through influence and persuasion rather than authority. Actions taken by consortia are typically preceded by negotiations that take into account both the common and competing interests. Indeed, not attending to the competing interests can be fatal for consortia. For example, even though the Biomarkers Consortium operates in what it calls a precompetitive space, some projects are in domains that are competitive for some biotech companies. As a result of these competing interests, it is essential that they can opt out of these projects and work independently in order to preserve their separate intellectual property. They can still stay in the consortium and contribute to other projects where their interests are shared. What is precompetitive for some turns out to be competitive for others. The consortium structure has to be flexible in dealing with these types of complications.

Because consortia are focused on a particular purpose, but involve independent stakeholders, they utilize relatively lightweight organizing and governance structures. Many of us have facilitated the chartering of new consortia and one of the first issues raised is a reluctance to create anything complex or entangling. This led to our 2022 call in the *Stanford Social Innovation Review* for a "minimum viable consortium," much like a minimum viable product for entrepreneurial initiatives, to allow for learning and adjustment.[16] This approach makes consortia well-suited for making progress on broad societal challenges. Consortia can adapt to dynamic changes in agile ways because their formation and operation does not usually rely on rigid or long-standing structures, protected turf, or bureaucratic procedures—all of which limit action. Further, most consortia incorporate diverse capabilities and interests that typically exceed those contained within any one organization. Together these combined capabilities and interests, including taking into account the competing interests, create new opportunities.

For leaders and members of private corporations, government agencies, universities, and nonprofit organizations, the rising importance of stakeholder alignment and consortia is both enabling and complicating. This is because these lateral arrangements cross organizational and institutional boundaries. Crossing boundaries is challenging for those used to exercising their role within the stability and predictability of a traditional hierarchy or regulatory domain. Alternate patterns of organization and influence emerge over time in a consortium—exciting for people who are themselves agile and adaptable, and challenging for those who are not.

Ultimately, consortia enable new possibilities, providing combinations of stakeholders with agency in advancing common interests and addressing competing interests.

Boundary Spanners Are Required

Boundary spanners—people who connect one stakeholder group to another—are at the core of consortia. All boundary spanners face a dilemma. If they become too aligned with the consortium, they can be accused of having forgotten where they came from. If they do not become aligned enough with the consortium, they will have limited influence and can be rejected as not fitting in. In order to address the dilemma, boundary spanners must do two things: educate constituents in their home organization on what they are learning in the consortium and educate the others in the consortium on the priorities and concerns of their constituents.

Boundary spanners serve in what Kimberlé Williams Crenshaw termed "intersectional" roles, that is, roles in which individuals simultaneously have multiple identities.[17] Crenshaw documented how the intersection of race and gender drove multiplicative disparities. In the context of consortia, intersectional identities have the potential to also be valued as uniquely matched to bridging across boundaries of one kind or another.

Where boundary spanners are successful, innovations can spread. In his seminal research on the diffusion of innovation, Everett Rogers documented how new ideas, new products, and other innovations spread through human interactions and communication channels.[18] In this context, boundary spanners and consortia play a key role. For example, in a study of the diffusion of workplace innovations (such as employee involvement systems, workplace safety training, and other related innovations) in the

Jamestown, New York, Area Labor-Management Committee, Robert Keidel found that innovation did not typically diffuse from part of one organization to the whole organization. Rather, innovations diffused from part of one organization to parts of another organization.[19] The community Labor-Management Committee, a type of consortium, provided a forum through which the boundary spanners in each of the member organizations (most of the employers and unions in the Jamestown area) were connected in ways that otherwise would not have happened. Keidel termed this as "theme appreciation," in which the consortium structure enabled "themes" to cross organizational boundaries.

In addition to enabling members to serve as boundary spanners, consortia also serve as what are termed "boundary objects."[20] They sit at the boundary of different stakeholder groups and enable cross-boundary connections that might not otherwise occur. In this sense, the consortium itself is an actor in a given ecosystem, changing the patterns of interaction.

The Combination of a Social Movement, a Consortium, and an Organization

The documentary film *Brave Hearts* celebrates the founding of a consortium, Ikamva Labantu in South Africa, which is composed of women caring for children among the ravages of apartheid. It is a story that begins with an informal consortium, which becomes a social movement, and then a formal nonprofit organization. Throughout the journey, this collaborative arrangement crossed geographic and embattled cultural boundaries.[21]

> During apartheid in South Africa and in the years since it was replaced with a democratic government in 1994, there has been a continuing challenge in providing childcare for orphaned and vulnerable children as well as those whose parents must travel from the townships using public transport for multiple hours to get to work. Beginning in the 1960s, women who had raised families of their own began to take in children. Referring to themselves as "Mamas," some came to care for as many as 50 or 100 children, who would come into their homes (moving furniture aside) or into spaces that they were able to set up. As Tutu Gcememe, one of few

early Mamas still living recalls, "There was concern from those we worked with. We just worked, not expecting anything in return."

Helen Lieberman, a White speech pathologist, was concerned about a child who had serious oral swallowing issues and was discharged from the hospital clinic prematurely; she chose to follow up with a home visit. During this visit and others, she saw how the women were providing shelter to children in need. These were townships such as Langa and Gugulethu, created by the National Party's apartheid system for Xhosa migrants from the Eastern Cape who came to find work. As Helen put it, "I would say to one that there is another lady doing similarly." The women were interested in talking with each other, but there were restrictions on travel and group meetings. Groups of the women would gather secretly in open fields, often traveling considerable distances and at great risk. Food and ideas were shared. "It would always be with food," Helen recalls, "breaking bread is central. We would bring food for them and then they could bring food back to the children. More and more people came; each told another." The women traveled on trains, buses, and by foot, all coordinating by word of mouth. As Helen notes, "there were no cell phones."

At this point, they were coordinating with each other informally in what we would term a consortium-like arrangement. Most of the initial Mamas are no longer alive. In signaling the scale of the early efforts, we also honor the memory of the early Mamas and other early leaders by listing them here:

Sophia Benge, Maggie Buqa, Gerty Chetu, Mama Dado, Mama Dukashe, Florence Dlamhla, Angelina Gumla, Nokia Hobe, Ellen Kozwayo, Ivy Makosana, Miriam Makosana, Maisie Manata, Linda Mapolongwana, Zora Mashlemakulu, Nomsa Pelem, Mildred Rayi, Ruth Sokeyeka, Joyce Serokie, and Flora Siyatula.

As Tutu Gcememe commented, "People need to know what happened. Maybe they can also learn from it because Black people are often not recognized for the role they played." Tutu herself championed the expansion from childcare to elder care and ultimately set up 20 senior community day care and activity centers. The initial challenges were many. There were arrests for violating group meeting laws, but the women persisted. Once, Helen recalls, "Tutu Gcememe heard from her drunk husband that I would be murdered and walked many miles to warn me."

In the 1980s, the government began to understand that some changes were needed with respect to social services. Beginning in 1984 the women were able to be more open, but there were still challenges. In 1986 bulldozers came to take down many of the dwellings in an informal settlement called Crossroads. Maggie Buqa, a Black nurse who was an early leader in the movement, said to Helen, "lie down in front of the bulldozer" and then joined Helen. The newspapers focused on Helen, a White woman, blocking the bulldozers. Helen comments, "it should not have been about me."

The full story is about the many brilliant, devoted, and tough women who were all working together against pervasive challenges. The coverage and the increased awareness of the full story brought attention from donors in South Africa and abroad who indicated they wanted to help fund what had become a social movement. In 1992 Ikamva Labantu was founded as a non-profit organization. Ikamva Labantu means "The Future of the People" in isiXhosa. It was organized by sectors—early childhood, children with disabilities, elder care, youth activities, income generation, and others.

Ishrene Davids joined the organization in 2000 as the field manager and she later became the director. As she recalls, "the founders were activists, not managers. We worked with an external consultant to transform the organization with systems for governance and accountability, which is the structure we have today." Ishrene adds that "at first it was hard to even get government officials to meet with us. Helen was seen as being on the edges and many of the community structures were assessed as not meeting the required government standards for childcare centers. Today, we are an effective organization sought out by government. Our model programs are implemented across South Africa." Helen adds that "Ishrene brings calming wisdom. I am 82 and know I won't always be around. I am at peace that Ikamva Labantu is in good hands."

Around 2010, South Africa began to set standards for licensing of home childcare facilities, each called an Educare. Once an Educare is approved, government payment per child can be applied for. In this way the provider can become an independent small business. Ikamva has set up resources

> including a registration help desk and other forms of assistance, guiding individuals to meet the required conditions for licensure as childcare centers. The efforts of the women of Ikamva Labantu have recently been celebrated in a documentary titled, *Brave Hearts*.
>
> As one of the few early Mamas still living, Vivian Jojoba recalls, "When I started this children's project, I didn't expect it to come to this. Apart from the way the Black race is still being treated, it shows me that we are moving forward. So, it gives me hope that the next generations will have a different experience from what we had."

When viewed through an organizational and institutional lens, the first lesson from Ikamva Labantu is that the consortium arrangement emerged from a network of women who had independently responded to a crisis. The consortium arrangement was needed so they could accomplish together what they could not do separately. As stakeholders, they all had relatively similar interests and identities. Facilitation, provided initially by Helen Lieberman, brought people together. Then, leaders emerged. The evolution into a formal nonprofit organization was needed as they began to seek funding from within South Africa and abroad. In many ways, Ikamva Labantu has also become a social movement. As Jeannette Kruger, a South African social worker now living in the United States observes, "Ikamva Labantu is promoting the idea of women taking action and creating services, not waiting for the system to take care of the needs of pre-school children and the elderly." In this regard, Ikamva Labantu is today, all at once, a consortium, an organization, and a social movement.

In comparison, the Takeda case at the beginning of this chapter illustrates the rapid formation of consortia in biomedicine that span a range of different types of stakeholders and that focus on a range of issues. Most of these consortia focus on time-bound research problems, with Takeda's connection to a given consortium typically being 3–5 years. What is remarkable about this case is the degree to which managing as many as 100 consortium memberships is now a standard part of the company's business model, yet very few of these consortia existed a decade ago.

While these two cases illustrate contrasting pathways to consortia, they have in common diverse stakeholders creating a form of self-governance that crosses organizational, institutional, and geographic lines, enabling them to accomplish together what they cannot do separately.

Additional Illustrative Cases

For this book, we draw on many additional cases that are illustrative of three dimensions of stakeholder alignment—the stakeholders, the interests, and the time frame involved.

In some instances, we will just reference one aspect of a case to illustrate a point. For example, in Chapter 6, when we talk about the power of stakeholder alignment, we will briefly discuss how some of the over 3,000 fab labs around the world (community centers where people can use digital fabrication technologies to make almost anything) came together during the global COVID-19 pandemic to produce personal protective equipment (PPE) when supply chains broke down.[22] In other instances, we will do a deep dive to illustrate interrelated aspects of a given case. In Chapters 6 through 8 we will track two cases—the Biomarkers Consortium and the Minority Serving Cyberinfrastructure Consortium (MS-CC) step-by-step from formation to operations. Altogether, we will draw on cases from the biomedical sector, research computing and data, societal infrastructure, employment relations, and engineering innovation—a deliberately diverse set of domains.

Biomedical Cases

Among the cases in this book are three in the biomedical sector. The Protein Data Bank (PDB), a long-standing consortium (founded in 1971), began with a relatively homogeneous mix of stakeholders (university, government, and industry researchers) and a narrow focus on curating shared experimental data on the structures of biological macromolecules.[23] Today, the stakeholders are heterogeneous and include the pharmaceutical industry and computational modelers who are using deep learning techniques to predict protein structures. The Biomarkers Consortium (BC) is more recent, but is well past the decade mark (founded in 2006) and features a heterogeneous mix of stakeholders (pharmaceutical industry, biotechnology sector, government regulatory agencies, government research labs, university researchers, and patient advocacy organizations), with a relatively broad focus on the discovery and qualification of biomarkers or indicators associated with a wide range of human diseases. Takeda Pharmaceuticals is a single firm, but we focus on the company because it set up an office to coordinate memberships in approximately 100 PPPs. In all three cases, the span of stakeholders includes public, private, and nonprofit sectors, with an overriding set of missions centered on human disease and health.

Healthcare Cases

In the healthcare sector, we trace the professionalization of community health workers (CHWs), which began with the emergence of a consortia arrangement that led to an affiliation with the American Public Health Association. This is a case where the alignment was around a new form of professionalization that is inclusive and oriented around social impact. An additional case is the Primary Care Collaborative (PCC), which spans diverse stakeholders in advancing innovative payment and delivery models for primary care with a focus on what they term the "medical home." We also note work by the Patient Centered Outcomes Research Institute (PCORI) on stakeholder engagement, which is distinct from stakeholder alignment. In this case, however, PCORI describes a spectrum that goes from unidirectional engagement to two-way exchanges between patients and researchers that can include shared decision-making and even shared leadership.

Research Computing and Data Cases

Three cases involving research data and computing are introduced. The Research Data Alliance, founded in 2013, encompasses a relatively broad mix of stakeholders (researchers, data and computing professionals, librarians, government officials, publishers, and others) with a relatively broad focus on the curation, preservation, sharing, and reuse of research data. The MS-CC, founded in 2018, encompasses university executive leaders, researchers, students, research computing and data professionals, and others at historically Black colleges and universities (HBCUs), tribal colleges and universities (TCUs), Hispanic serving institutions (HSIs), and other minority serving institutions (MSIs). The MS-CC case is interwoven with a recent report to the US National Science Foundation (that a number of us contributed to) on the "missing millions" who are not represented in the research computing and data workforce. All three cases illustrate the important and growing work with research computing and data in society, which is an underappreciated yet essential element needed to address any global challenge. The Campus Research Computing Consortium (CaRCC), founded in 2019, is dedicated to developing, advocating for, and advancing campus research computing and data, with a particular focus on professionalization and capability.

Geoscience Cases

The Long-Term Ecological Research Network (LTER) was founded in 1980 by the National Science Foundation "with the recognition that long-term research could help unravel the principles and processes of ecological science, which frequently involves long-lived species, legacy influences, and rare events."[24] The Council of Data Facilities (CDF), founded in 2014, is a group of facilities that house and share earth and space science research data. It was spun off from the US National Science Foundation's EarthCube initiative, which has been transforming the conduct of geosciences research by advancing "access, sharing, visualization, and analysis of data and related resources."[25]

Societal Infrastructure Cases

We draw on three cases involving societal infrastructure initiatives. The first involves a 2002 MIT project and report to the US Congress on aircraft noise and emissions.[26] This involved a highly diverse set of stakeholders (aircraft manufacturers, aircraft engine manufacturers, airports, airlines, regulatory agencies, communities, and others) with a relatively narrow focus that has now been incorporated in the FAA's NextGen Air Transportation Initiative. We also draw on a 2013 initiative to bridge digital divides in Dodge City, Kansas, which also involved diverse stakeholders (city government, a community college, K–12 schools, a hospital, the library system, and others) with a relatively narrow focus on Internet access—bridging what is termed the "digital divide." There are additional current efforts along these lines in Alaska and other places on which we will also draw. Turning to large-scale aspects of infrastructure, we discuss the complex mix of stakeholders associated with the Environmental Impact Statement (EIS) of

Australia's Olympic Dam. This case is introduced to illustrate stakeholder management and stakeholder engagement, which are distinct from stakeholder alignment. In all these infrastructure cases, the role of public-private partnerships is indispensable in ensuring effective infrastructure in society.

Employment Relations Cases

In employment relations, there is a long history of labor-management partnerships. We draw on one of the world's largest and most successful partnerships, begun in 1995 by Kaiser Permanente, and what are now two sets of multiple unions operating as the Alliance and the Coalition. Both are focused on enabling the work of over three thousand unit-based teams. They provide needed training and development support, engaging new technology, and other matters of mutual interest for over 100,000 employees. At the other end of the spectrum, we will also draw on a newly emerging "alt labor" initiative by rideshare drivers for Uber and Lyft to reverse engineer the digital platform that governs their work. The Ikamva Labantu case from South Africa presented earlier in this chapter represents an emergent work and social services arrangement centered on child care and elder care. At stake in these cases are the many challenges in today's workplaces and new forms of alignment needed to address them.

Digital Fabrication Cases

We have a set of cases in digital fabrication ecosystems that first emerged in 2002 and that have evolved to include the Fab Foundation, the Fab Cities Initiative, and a Fab All-In initiative fostering diverse and inclusive community building associated with fab labs. All involve relatively similar organizations—fab labs—that are found in community centers, libraries, community colleges, K–12 schools, universities, and entrepreneurial incubators. These multistakeholder efforts foster design thinking, digital literacy, and, increasingly, self-sufficient productive capability in society.

Video Games Cases

Around the planet, video game players engage in billions of hours of entertainment every week. This broad engagement is driving increased interest in harnessing the unique power of video games as a force for good in society. In the last chapter we highlight two relatively recent consortia formed with social impact objectives. One, the Playing for the Planet Alliance, is a broad coalition of game developers, device manufacturers, and others harnessing the broad reach of video games to advance environmental matters. The second, the Fair Play Alliance, features a diverse array of game developers and platform providers focused on reducing toxic behaviors in online playing communities.

Note that there are a number of cases that we have not included because they were at pivotal points in their evolution and there was concern about freezing their stories at this particular juncture. We have honored these requests. Indeed, the requests are illustrative of the evolving and often fragile nature of consortia.

As well, there are other developments documented that are illustrative of key points, such as the climate mayors in the prologue, the responses in Liberia to the Ebola outbreak at the top of Chapter 5, efforts under the US Executive Order 14901 advancing racial equity and support for underserved communities, and other illustrative cases. These illustrate a range of collaborative dynamics.

Our aim is to offer a sufficiently diverse mix of cases so we can generalize to many different contexts, while also providing enough detail on a few cases to fully appreciate the complex dynamics, challenges, and opportunities.

Summing Up

In societies around the world, as well as for the planet as a whole, we face challenges that are beyond the scope of any one organization or institutional actor. We see the growing formation of consortia, achieved through stakeholder alignment, as essential to meeting these challenges and, as a result, playing a defining role in the 21st century.

Forming and sustaining consortia involves thinking laterally, rather than from the top-down or the bottom-up. It involves seeing systems as a whole, rather than viewing things from one party's perspective. The range of illustrative cases spans biomedicine, scientific computing and data, social infrastructure, employment relations, digital fabrication, and other domains.

Building on this foundation, Chapters 2 through 4 in Part I provide more detail on the key principles and organizing frameworks to more fully understand what consortia are (and are not), as well as the underlying theory of stakeholder alignment. Part II provides supporting tools and methods, while Part III is a look ahead at what we anticipate will be the consortia century.

Notes

1. We thank Akiko Otani and Ali Farid for their insights as we developed this vignette, June 6, 2023. Of course, the responsibility for the text is entirely ours as coauthors. The website quote is retrieved from: https://www.takeda.com/science/research-and-development/partnerships/public-private-partnerships/
2. For more on accelerating technological change, see Ray Kurzweil's 2005 book, *The Singularity Is Near* and his 2024 book, *The Singularity is Nearer,* (both New York: Viking Books), updated from his 1992 predictions in *The Age of Intelligent Machines* and other scholarship by Kurzweil.
3. This argument echoes the analysis in Michael Piore and Charles Sabel, *The Second Industrial Divide: Possibilities for Prosperity* (New York: Basic Books, 1984). The Piore and Sabel argument appears in Chapter 2 in more detail.
4. The term "ecosystems," coined by Arthur Tansley more than a century ago, is used in this book to describe natural phenomena that interact together as complex systems within a geographic area. See A.G. Tansley, "The Use and Abuse of Vegetational Concepts and Terms," *Ecology* 16, no. 3 (July 1935): pp. 284–307. At the time, this article challenged the prevailing focus in the field of ecology on well-defined species and other biological classifications. Today, the term also encompasses economic, social, and other complex, interdependent arrangements that may or may not be geographically defined.
5. For more information on the UN SDGs, including tracking of associated events and actions, see "The 17 Goals," The United Nations, Department of Economic and Social Affairs, accessed June 6, 2023, https://sdgs.un.org/goals.
6. "Consortium, n.," *OED Online*, Oxford University Press, March 2023, https://www.oed.com/view/Entry/39,740.
7. For more on boundary objects, see Susan Leigh Star and James R. Griesemer, "Institutional Ecology, 'Translations' and Boundary Objects: Amateurs and Professionals in Berkeley's Museum of Vertebrate Zoology, 1907–39," *Social Studies of Science* 19, no. 3 (August 1989): pp. 387–420.
8. On institutional work, see Thomas B. Lawrence and Roy Suddaby, "Institutions and Institutional Work," in *The SAGE Handbook of Organization Studies*, 2nd ed., edited by Stewart Clegg et al. (London: SAGE Publications, 2006), ch. 6; Thomas B. Lawrence, Roy Suddaby, and Bernard Leca, eds., *Institutional Work: Actors and Agency in Institutional Studies of Organizations* (Cambridge: Cambridge University Press, 2009).
9. See this critique, for example: https://www.fasttrackimpact.com/post/why-we-shouldn-t-banish-the-word-stakeholder.
10. We thank Paul Arthur Berkman, an earlier participant in the Stakeholder Alignment Collaborative, for his observations on the structure of Polar negotiations. See also, Sabaa Ahmad Khan, "Legally Sculpting a Melting Arctic: States, Indigenous Peoples and Justice in Multilateralism," in *Changing Actors in International Law*, edited by Karen N. Scott, Kathleen Claussen, Charles-Emmanuel Côté, and Atsuko Kanehara (Leiden, Netherlands: Brill, 2020), pp. 130–157.
11. For a leading example of top-down alignment in organizations, see Robert Kaplan and David Norton, *Alignment: Using the Balanced Scorecard to Create Corporate Synergies* (Boston: Harvard Business School Press, 2006). In this case, balanced scorecards are the vehicle for top-down alignment.
12. Top-down alignment is a form of top-down change, which is discussed in more detail in Chapter 5. Top-down change involves centralized initiatives operating within the authority and responsibility of a hierarchical structure to achieve a desired aim by an acting party or parties. Organizational leaders (who can be at different levels in an organization) formulate goals and make decisions to achieve those goals.

13. Bottom-up alignment is a form of bottom-up change, which is addressed in more detail in Chapter 5. Bottom-up change involves decentralized initiatives operating without depending on a hierarchical structure to achieve a desired aim.
14. This definition of stakeholder alignment evolved from earlier definitions such as in Joel Cutcher-Gershenfeld et al., "When Launching a Collaboration, Keep It Agile," *Stanford Social Innovation Review* 20, no. 2 (2020): pp. 40–47.
15. See John Kania and Mark Kramer, "Collective Impact," *Stanford Social Innovation Review* 9, no. 1 (Winter 2011): pp. 36–41.
16. See Cutcher-Gershenfeld et al., "When Launching a Collaboration, Keep It Agile."
17. See Kimberlé Williams Crenshaw, "Demarginalizing the Intersection of Race and Sex: A Black Feminist Critique of Antidiscrimination Doctrine, Feminist Theory and Antiracist Politics," *University of Chicago Legal Forum* (1989), Article 8: p. 139.
18. Originally published in 1962, this book has since been updated to a fifth edition. See Everett M. Rogers, *Diffusion of Innovations*, 5th ed. (New York: Free Press, 2003).
19. See Robert Keidel, "Theme Appreciation as a Construct for Organizational Change," *Management Science* 27, no. 11 (1981): pp. 1261–1127, https://doi.org/10.1287/mnsc.27.11.1261.
20. As noted earlier, the lead study introducing the term "boundary objects" is Star and Griesemer, "Institutional Ecology, 'Translations' and Boundary Objects."
21. We thank Ishrene Davids, Jennette Kruger, and Helen Lieberman for their insights as we developed this vignette. Of course, the responsibility for the text is entirely ours as coauthors.
22. Fab labs are community centers with equipment for digital fabrication (e.g., laser cutters, 3D milling machines, 3D printers, 3D scanners, digital sewing machines, etc.) where people can literally make almost anything. The first two fab labs were established in 2003, in Boston, Massachusetts, and the Vigyan Ashram in Maharashtra State in India. For more information on fab labs, see Neil Gershenfeld, Alan Gershenfeld, and Joel Cutcher-Gershenfeld, *Designing Reality* (New York: Basic Books, 2018).
23. See Helen Berman, Kim Henrik, and Haruki Nakamura, "Announcing the Worldwide Protein Data Bank," *Nature Structural and Molecular Biology* 10, no. 12 (December 2003): p. 980, https://doi.org/10.1038/nsb1203-980.
24. Retrieved from: https://lternet.edu/about/#:~:text=The%20LTER%20Network%20was%20founded.
25. Retrieved from: https://www.earthcube.org/info.
26. Ian Waitz et al., "Aviation and the Environment: A National Vision Statement," Report to the United States Congress (Cambridge: Massachusetts Institute of Technology, 2004), http://web.mit.edu/aeroastro/sites/waitz/publications/aviationandtheenvironment.pdf.

Chapter 2
A Gathering of Destinies

For two days in June, 2018, a group of chief information officers (CIOs), computer science faculty, and others from historically Black colleges and universities (HBCUs) gathered to discuss the current state of infrastructure for research computing and data on their campuses—what is often called "cyberinfrastructure." Going into the meeting, one idea on people's minds was the potential to form a consortium so that they could, as the facilitator put it, "accomplish together what they can't do separately."

The HBCU participants responded in a few different ways. One participant, reacting to a presentation on the transformative potential of research computing and data technologies, commented, "You are trying to teach us to fish, but we don't yet even know what fishing is." CIOs and other campus leaders at these historically underfunded institutions didn't have the resources to be current on what was meant by "DMZs for data" (a way to protect sensitive information when it is shared digitally), "containers for software" (a way to exchange code for use on different computing platforms), or "Jupyter notebooks" (an open source, cloud-based application commonly used to record the results from lab experiments in a way that facilitates combination, analysis, and storage of experimental data).

For any collective effort to go forward, the people at the meeting would need to be able to go back home and explain to local stakeholders in nontechnical language just what was possible with increased support for research computing and data. Further, related to institutional culture, many of the participants observed that HBCUs love each other but have historically operated independently and, in some cases, competitively. Certainly, they often compete for students, faculty, and resources, as well as in sports teams, debate teams, and other extracurricular activities. The idea that they might work together on research infrastructure would require a culture change for many of the schools.

Data from a 2018 stakeholder survey of 24 HBCU campuses motivated the workshop. The surveys showed a clear consensus that stakeholders at minority serving institutions (MSIs) saw benefits from collaborating around research cyberinfrastructure, though all saw it as hard to achieve. After acknowledging the challenge and mindful of the needed work on cultural change, the group drafted a vision statement and empowered a working group to draft a charter (a document outlining conditions for collaboration) for what would become the Minority Serving Cyberinfrastructure Consortium (MS-CC). From the start, the group envisioned participation not just from HBCUs, but also from tribal colleges and universities (TCUs), Hispanic serving institutions (HSIs), and other Minority Serving Institutions (MSIs). With support from the National Science Foundation (NSF) and a partnership with Internet2, a nonprofit consortium of leading research universities, MS-CC now has over 100 participating colleges and universities, with an expanding program of workshops, services, and capacity-building initiatives. This includes a special focus on climate change research and health disparities research on issues that are disproportionately impacting the communities where HBCUs and TCUs are located. Together, these minority-serving campuses are working to advance the interests of students, faculty, staff, and the surrounding communities in new and innovative ways, accomplishing together what they cannot do separately.

Consortia will be a defining institutional arrangement of the 21st century because they are fit for purpose—well-matched to the challenges faced by societies around the world. As we have noted, consortia do not replace other institutional arrangements—multinational corporations, constitutional governments, nongovernmental organizations, universities, unions, professional societies, and others. Instead, consortia enable combinations of these stakeholders to accomplish together what they cannot do separately.

The origin of the word "consortium" has elegant implications. "Consortium" derives from the Middle English term "consort" or companion, which comes from the French and Latin "consors"—a combination of the term "con" for "together with or gathering" and the term "sors" for "lot or destiny." In this sense, the roots of the term "consortia" can be thought of as "gathering destinies together" or a "gathering of destinies."

Collaboration happens under many terms and banners, including partnerships, alliances, collaboratives, initiatives, councils, and others. Further, specialized versions of these terms exist that include public-private partnerships, labor–management partnerships, community collaboratives, and others. Examples presented in this book feature many of these terms. We use "consortia" as the overarching term for these institutional arrangements, and the principles that we present apply across these many examples. In the United States, registration of a consortium is only required at the point when it needs to operate as a for-profit or nonprofit organization, such as when it takes in money or hires staff. In Europe, registration is required for any association working on fundamental rights, which includes nongovernmental organizations; trade unions; employers' organizations; relevant social and professional organizations; churches; religious, philosophical, and nonconfessional organizations; universities; and others.[1] Similar rules for voluntary associations vary around the world, with additional severe restrictions common under authoritarian regimes.

Although consortia are not new, the current digital era enables unparalleled capabilities for people to connect and share information, data, and lived experiences over time and space. With these digital capabilities, some barriers to operating laterally are lowered. At the same time, the need for distributed governance of digital resources increases. This is one reason why there has been a substantial increase in the formation of consortia in a growing array of sectors and domains. For example, we have been studying and working closely with consortia associated with the open sharing of data in science, some of which were formed between 1950 and 2000. Yet, in the two decades since 2000 we have seen a 10-fold increase in the formation of consortia with this focus. Some are short-lived and others are long-standing. In the pharmaceutical sector, the rapid increase in the use of consortia for the sharing of R&D data has led leading companies to establish formal departments, as we saw in Chapter 1, in order to support memberships in dozens of public–private partnerships and other types of consortia.

The underlying theory we are advancing is based on what are termed "weak signals." This approach is highlighted in the business strategy literature as a way of seeing what is "around the corner," is not yet widely visible, but will be consequential.[2] It is an approach that is also used with respect to quality, safety, and more broadly in healthcare when tracking low-frequency indicators of what will be high-consequence events when they occur. Although we present a wide variety of illustrative examples throughout the book, and go into considerable depth on a few, it is only when we began looking for them that we began to see the increasing presence of consortia. The variety of forms makes a complete census difficult to assemble. In the case of research computing and data in science, we have tabulated a chart of the consortia we were able to identify between 1950 and 2020 (Figure 2.1).

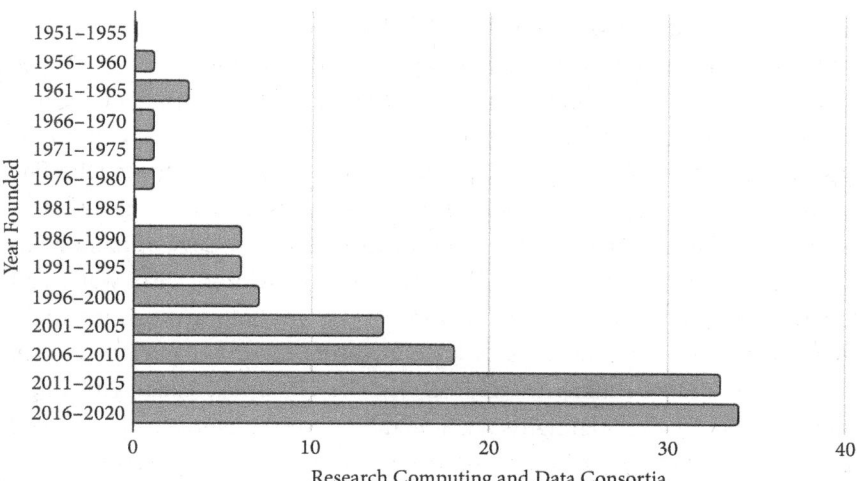

Figure 2.1 Research Computing and Data Consortia 1950–2020

Although the numbers are still small for an ecosystem that includes all universities as well as private and public research labs, it is illustrative of a weak signal that is increasing at an astounding rate (a ten-fold increase in the last twenty years compared to the prior fifty). It is not easily visible if you don't know where to look, but an important signal when you see it. Interestingly, this would suggest that there are just over 100 consortia in this ecosystem, which has several thousand relevant organizations. In this context we speculate that we may come to look back on the 21st century as having a number of sectors or ecosystems, each with some number of consortia that will be at least an order of magnitude less than that number of relevant organizations and groups who might be members.

Lateral Governance

Consortia depend on there being sufficient alignment laterally among rights holders, stakeholders, and interested parties for collective action to be taken. The skills to operate laterally do not come naturally for all leaders. These skills, which center on influence, persuasion, negotiation, collaboration, and shared responsibility, run counter to many organizational cultures that emphasize control and individual accountability. Organizational and institutional theorist Elinor Ostrom observed in *Governing the Commons* that there are many shared resources, such as water, that require some form of shared governance.[3] She found that neither markets nor regulations alone were as effective as various forms of collaborative structures that were then able to balance competition, regulation, and collaboration.

Consortia are an approach to the shared governance that Ostrom encouraged us to use to address urgent global challenges. This is a pluralist approach, spanning many parties, rather than a unitarist approach. The United Nations highlights this by listing "partnership for the goals" as a key global challenge included among the 17 sustainable development goals (SDGs) such as poverty, hunger, literacy, health, education, clean water and energy, inequality, climate, and so forth.[4] The goal of partnerships highlights how enabling mechanisms for addressing the other goals is critical (which we discuss further in Chapter 4). The National Academy of Engineering (NAE) also highlights such enabling mechanisms. In their list of 14 global challenges, including solar energy, virtual reality, reverse engineering the brain, health informatics, secure cyberinfrastructure, preventing nuclear terror, and others, the NAE includes "engineer the tools for scientific discovery."[5] We see consortia as one of these enabling tools, since most scientific discoveries are problem-driven, span fields and disciplines, and operate within time constraints. Thus, they require sufficient alignment across stakeholders to achieve desired results.

Thinking laterally—across stakeholders and interested parties—is different from thinking vertically. For organizational leaders, top-down change models are key for getting alignment throughout levels and functions within an organization. These models are often joined by bottom-up change models to ensure broader input and voice. For social change leaders, bottom-up change models are also key for building momentum around an idea or goal that is designed to reach up and achieve change in the established order. Both top-down and bottom-up changes are important in countless ways. To this conversation, we add additional, lateral sets of tools, methods, and ways of thinking that can cross organizational and institutional boundaries. Some people instinctively think like this; others may initially think in top-down or bottom-up ways, but can build capability for lateral alignment as well.

Many of us have been working with consortia and facilitating stakeholder alignment for multiple decades. We have been studying them intensively for over a decade. Although consortia sidestep existing hierarchies, we have been surprised to find that leaders of many existing organizations and institutions encourage participation in consortia. They do this precisely because they realize that their own organization can't accomplish what is needed on its own.

Historical Eras

Our prediction of consortia as defining institutional arrangements for the 21st century rests, in part, on a historical argument. For three centuries there have been various defining institutional arrangements for a given era.

In the 18th century, the defining institutional feature was organizations for craft production and self-governing guilds. These were effective when transportation limited most communities to local product and labor market dynamics. Concurrently, experiments with constitutional democracies were begun in a number of nations.

The 19th century saw constitutional democracies move into center stage as defining features of this era. Concurrently, this era saw the rise of mass production within hierarchical corporate and industrial organizations. These were matched by industrial labor unions, which were more hierarchical than their craft union predecessors. For example, when the Erie Canal opened in New York State in 1825, long-distance transport of goods at a relatively low cost was suddenly widely available. This disrupted craft and guild structures, and prototypes for regional corporations and industrial unions emerged in their place.[6]

As markets expanded in the 20th century, multidivisional and multinational corporations emerged globally in capitalist countries. Amalgamated unions also emerged in the United States, though they were not able to match the multidivisional and multinational structures of the private sector. In Soviet-style planned economies, such as those in the Soviet Union and Eastern Bloc, the Communist Parties used their authoritarian power to organize economies into integrated, multidivisional, multisector systems that functioned autonomously within their national boundaries, and then later attempted (and largely failed) to coordinate top-down international economic cooperation among the member states through COMECON (Council for Mutual Economic Assistance).[7]

The wake of World War II saw the rise of R&D consortia in the United States. R&D consortia are a class of consortium intended to build national capabilities in fields with rapid technological advancement to support industrial competitiveness, including aerospace, semiconductors, and plastics.[8] R&D consortia typically involve private corporations, universities, and other institutional stakeholders, yet operate outside the bounds of any of the member organizational hierarchies. They are voluntary, and they produce public and private goods. Many are quite successful and have persisted for decades, such as the successful semiconductor consortium, SEMATECH.[9] Others were successful for a time, but terminated for various reasons, including loss of government funding. Research has emphasized the role of R&D consortia and how they have proven to be an effective way for member corporations and universities to advance their separate and shared interests and advance national priorities. These consortia are an important precursor to the consortia we highlight here. There are also state-level or regional higher education systems, athletic conferences, and others. In many cases, these collaborative institutional arrangements have become institutionalized to the point that they no longer fully fit the agile and adaptive model that we highlight here. Indeed, we have argued that some of these more formal consortia would benefit from a return to their roots, when there was more flexibility and a greater range of strategic choices in play.[10]

In global diplomacy, collaborative arrangements are also a long-standing form that is still very relevant. For example, the Indo-Pacific Economic Framework for Prosperity, which promotes economic cooperation among Australia, Brunei Darussalam, Fiji India, Indonesia, Japan, the Republic of Korea, Malaysia, New Zealand, Philippines, Singapore, Thailand, and Vietnam;[11] the Americas Partnership for Economic Prosperity, which includes Barbados, Canada, Chile, Colombia, Costa Rica, the Dominican Republic, Ecuador, Mexico, Panama, Peru, and Uruguay;[12] the US-EU Trade and Technology Council; and the United States' trilateral coordination with Japan and Korea. While the increased prosperity through trade is the stated and important reason for these arrangements, the counterbalancing of political influence by China and Russia is equally important. The coalition of nations that joined in support of Ukraine following Russia's invasion in 2022 is a vivid example of alignment around a mix of economic, political, and military objectives. In some ways, these coalitions, councils, and frameworks are subject to long-established and highly structured norms that govern international relations, but we see in these cases the potential to bring in the agile and adaptive lessons from the lighter-weight consortia we highlight here.

In the 21st century, digital technologies are disrupting markets in countless ways at the same time as global challenges are crossing political and geographic boundaries in numerous additional ways. Many scholars point to the current, postindustrial digital era as a fundamental shift for societies. For example, when Michael Piore and Charles Sabel wrote *The Second Industrial Divide* in the 1980s, they focused on regional agglomerations, such as the textile sector of northern Italy. They emphasized how new technologies were enabling an era of "flexible specialization." They noted that in the regions they studied, the craft and mass production arrangements of the earlier eras did not disappear with the emergence of new arrangements. Craft skills were still needed to make and maintain the mass production equipment. Mass production equipment and hierarchical organizations still had a role to play for high-volume operations. Their point, however, was that the more flexible, specialized approaches were moving to the foreground as the defining features of the postindustrial era, even as the earlier arrangements persisted. But shared prosperity from these flexible arrangements was not assured nor was it evenly distributed.[13] This is a reminder that all institutional arrangements have the dual function of creating value and mitigating harm. With any new institutional arrangements, it is incumbent to ask for whom value is being created and who is in harm's way. This is certainly the case for so many challenges in the current postindustrial, digital era.[14]

Since Piore and Sable's seminal work, many have observed that ubiquitous digital technologies have ushered in an "information age" or "digital economy" that necessitates and enables a variety of postindustrial organizational forms.[15] This involves a succession of digital revolutions in communication, computation, and fabrication. Each of these digital revolutions had transformational impacts, with common underlying logics rooted in the modularity of digital technologies. Each also had unintended consequences that could have been mitigated with more complete attention and earlier application of stakeholder alignment tools and methods.[16] For example, increased stakeholder alignment in the 1990s around the potential impacts of social media might have anticipated some of today's challenges with weaponized uses of these media. It is in this context that we see the rise of many different types of consortia as characteristic of and important to the functioning of societies in a postindustrial, digital era.[17]

Stakeholder Alignment for Transformational Change

Consortia are only possible with sufficient multistakeholder alignment for collective action. In Chapter 1, we defined stakeholder alignment as the dynamic process by which diverse stakeholders advance common interests and resolve conflicting interests sufficiently to accomplish together what they cannot do separately. Implicit in this definition are five characteristics of consortia (which may be composed of individuals, groups, or organizations):

- Being independent and interdependent
- Having common and competing interests
- Achieving sufficient alignment for action
- Engaging in dynamic and continuous interactive processes
- Addressing together what cannot be accomplished separately

While there are always alignment challenges within any organization (a robust literature describes financial and reporting processes with balanced scorecards as key to internal alignment, for example),[18] our focus is on the alignment processes that cross organizational boundaries. Stakeholder alignment is a continuing accomplishment, not a one-time event. It is a verb, not a noun—parties are never done aligning. Often there is a pivotal moment in which it becomes clear to some stakeholders that they can do more together than separately. As they collaborate, they invariably build on shared interests while acknowledging conflicting interests. Indeed, one of the major strengths of consortia is that committed stakeholders will vigorously advance and negotiate from their interests within the consortium, rather than outside the common forum. Alignment does not imply uniformity or perfect agreement or concurrence. Consortia necessarily involve a diversity of interests. The key is that there be sufficient negotiated alignment for specific issues. This typically involves some compromise and may involve creativity in generating new, integrative options. Sufficiency as a goal for alignment avoids gridlock (while still enabling accountability) and creativity provides the possibility of something new emerging.

Stakeholder alignment is distinct from the related concepts of stakeholder management and stakeholder engagement. When people use the term "stakeholder management" the focus is on top-down change processes— "managing" stakeholders who might be in opposition. This typically involves leaders from one organization looking out at a range of stakeholders responding to an initiative by the organization. The focus in stakeholder management is particularly around mitigating the risk of opposition from influential stakeholders who may oppose a given initiative or change agenda. Generally, the goal is not to turn them into supporters, but just to neutralize the opposition. Stakeholder management involves top-down change processes.

When people use the term "stakeholder engagement," the focus is still from one party's perspective looking out. Of course, those identified as influential and supportive may be engaged immediately, but engagement activities often deploy town halls, open comment periods, dialogue, and other ways to engage stakeholders seen as potentially supportive. Thus, stakeholder engagement can involve either "top-down" or "bottom-up" change processes, which are outlined in additional detail in Chapter 5. These contrast with stakeholder alignment, which involves "middle-out" change processes that are lateral and span individuals, groups, and organizations, which are developed more fully in Chapter 4.

Importantly, as captured in the five defining elements above, stakeholder alignment is not as seen from the perspective of any one party, but rather from the perspective of the consortium, typically in the context of an ecosystem. Arthur Tansley introduced the term "ecosystem" in 1935 at a time when the field of ecology was dominated by experts in individual plant or animal species. The idea that you study the interactions of many plants, animals, and other elements was radical in two ways. First, it suggested that the whole could be greater than the sum of the parts. Second, it acknowledged that though all elements of the system might not be fully cataloged, a study could still consider the system as a whole. It is in the same spirit that our focus on stakeholder alignment shifts the conversation from individuals, groups, and organizations to the full array of independent, yet interdependent, parties. In the process, this approach acknowledges that alignment will invariably be dynamic and incomplete. For example, unborn generations are key stakeholders on many global challenges. Those not currently (or yet) employed are key stakeholders in the conversation about work. Such stakeholders are relevant from an ecosystem perspective, but are not easily identified and included.

Guiding Principles

We simultaneously seek to advance theory and practice for stakeholder alignment. There are seven guiding principles that are advanced in multiple places in this book. We introduce them here (Table 2.1) and develop them more fully, in Chapters 6 through 8. Underlying the principles is the view that stakeholder alignment is an iterative, dynamic, and interactive process—and that it is negotiated, not imposed. This reflects the underlying reality that stakeholders are independent and interdependent, and that they have both common and competing interests.[19]

The first two principles, specifying stakeholders and identifying interests, involve scoping the landscape for collaboration.

Table 2.1 Guiding Principles for Stakeholder Alignment

Principle	Motivating Questions
Specify Stakeholders	What individuals, groups, or organizations have relevant rights or interests?
Identify Interests	What are the interests that are at stake (as well as underlying rights)?
Build a Shared Vision	What would success look like for all relevant rights holders, stakeholders, and interested parties?
Ensure Internal Alignment for Lateral Alignment	What internal differences within each consortium member must be taken into account?
Achieve Sufficient Alignment for Action	How much alignment is needed for the members of the consortium to act together?
Establish a Minimum Viable Consortium	What is the minimum viable structure for the consortium (and nothing less than that)?
Sustain Agile and Adaptive Governance	How can we ensure that the consortium is able to adapt as circumstances change?

Specify Stakeholders

When seeking to align stakeholders with respect to a given initiative or issue it is rarely known in advance who all the stakeholders are. As a result, the first principle involves an iterative series of discussions around what are the relevant stakeholder categories that are to be aligned. Sometimes what is initially thought to be one stakeholder is revealed to be two or three different parties. At other times two or three stakeholders can be usefully treated as a single party. Over time, the mix of stakeholders often changes, so the principle needs to be applied on a continuing basis.

Identify Interests

The work of consortia centers on interests. In negotiations, a key distinction is made between "positions" and "interests." Positions are what one party or more states as what it wants or does not want. Interests are the underlying reasons why it is important, which may include hopes, concerns, values, and assumptions.

When facilitating stakeholder alignment, it is important to surface underlying interests, which are often met with expressions such as, "Oh, if that is what is important then what if we were to consider this?" In most cases, a given stakeholder has more than one interest with respect to a given issue or initiative. Across all stakeholders there may be a dozen or more interests that are "at stake" with respect to a given issue or initiative. The second guiding principle is to identify these interests, which together with the set of stakeholders can be thought of as a matrix, with stakeholders on one side and interests on the other. The combination of the two represents the landscape on which stakeholder alignment takes place, as is illustrated in Figure 2.2 (with four interests and five stakeholder categories) in the case of a hypothetical community initiative to bridge digital divides.

In this hypothetical case, there is a broad consensus on increasing access to the Internet, so this would indicate general support for a community initiative on this issue. Training and privacy are issues in this hypothetical on which there is a mix of people who feel positively and others who are neutral. This suggests a need to better understand the mix of views in order to see

	Interest 1: Expanding access to the Internet in the community	Interest 2: Increasing the speed and quality of Internet connections	Interest 3: Ensuring privacy with health data on the Internet	Interest 4: Funding the expanded Internet access – whether through taxes or user fees
Stakeholder 1: Gov't. Leaders	+	0	+	+
Stakeholder 2: Church Leaders	+	+	+	0
Stakeholder 3: Retirees	+	0	0	−
Stakeholder 4: College Students	+	+	0	−
Stakeholder 5: Medical Leaders	+	+	+	0

Key:

Positive	Neutral	Negative
+	0	−

Figure 2.2 Illustrative Example of a Matrix of Stakeholders and Interests

which may be more promising as an initial focus for such a community initiative. The issue of taxes going up to support access is one on which there are strong positive and negative views. This indicates that it may be a barrier facing the consortium. In fact, a community initiative on bridging the digital divide that a number of us supported had early successes and then was undercut on this issue.

Note, for clarity the interests here are just rated on positive, negative, or neutral views. In many of the stakeholder mapping projects that we have conducted, they are rated on two dimensions—importance and difficulty. This distinction helps to reveal early priorities (important and not that difficult), as well as major challenges (important and difficult), and potential stumbling blocks (a mix of positive or negative views on importance). Also, they are rated on a 10-point scale rather than a 3-point scale in order to see more subtle differences. Further, we use a multicolor visualization (not easily represented here) so that the contrasts are even more visible.

In addition to interests, the landscape for consortia also includes rights. Rights are legally specified and must be taken into account. Of course, legal systems represent the primary venue in which rights claims are adjudicated. Consortia cannot substitute for courts, but they do need to be mindful of rights that are relevant. Underlying the rights are various interests, which is where most of the work of consortia takes place.

The next three principles, shared vision, internal alignment, and sufficient alignment for action, involve the structuring and functioning of a consortium.

Build a Shared Vision

Virtually all change models involve a vision of success, and for good reason. Knowing "true North," or the overall direction in the long run, enables agreements and action in the short run. Here, however, it is not just the vision of a senior leader. When it comes to aligning stakeholders for action, it is key that the vision be widely shared. This invariably is an iterative process where some stakeholders suggest what they think could be a shared vision, others indicate points of agreement and possible adjustments, and a negotiated process ensues in which the resulting shared vision may be broad or narrow. Whatever it is, that is what guides and sustains the alignment efforts.

Building a shared vision is an interactive process, as is illustrated by the formation of the Research Data Alliance in 2013:

> A diverse mix of research computing professionals, librarians, research faculty, administrators, and others all agreed that they should work together to launch the Research Data Alliance (RDA), but they and others in their home organizations had different views on just what the RDA should or should not be.
>
> Some felt that the primary focus should be on shared data from government agencies, each of whom should set standards and regulations for the use of their data. Others observed that most government agencies were not taking sufficient responsibility around the sharing of their data—so there was a need for the RDA as an independent body.
>
> Some challenges came from groups who did not see the need for the consortium at all (as also happened with the case of the geoscience Council of Data Facilities [CDF]—see the beginning of Chapter 7). They felt that existing organizations were adequate to do the work. These groups saw the establishment of a consortium as a threat to the resources needed for work that they were already doing. They encouraged their own members and institutions to lobby RDA members to cease and desist.
>
> Two groups wanted to fold the consortium into their organization; in effect, each organization would take over the vision, goals, and so forth, and do the work. The RDA, in this scenario, would become a new division or a focus area in their organization.
>
> Sorting out these competing and contending interests took approximately 15 months. Government agencies with public data were supportive of the formation of the RDA, since it would help with their public duty to share their data. Some of the individuals who were being pressured by their organizations to oppose the formation of the RDA pushed back on their organizations and advocated for the need of such an alliance. Others, seeing that they couldn't prevent the RDA from moving forward, pulled back from the efforts. Groups that had wanted to subsume the RDA instead became organizational partners and sponsored joint events, indicating that the RDA had gained sufficient momentum on its own. Achieving sufficient alignment for action on issues of what is termed FAIR data (data that is findable, accessible, interoperable, and reusable) ultimately moved forward.

Ensure Internal Alignment for Lateral Alignment

There is a common expression in labor negotiations, which is that it takes three agreements to get one—one within the union, one within management, and one between the two. Most experienced labor and management negotiators will say that the internal agreements are often more difficult to achieve than the agreements between the two parties. When it comes to stakeholder alignment, the same principle applies, only now there are not just two parties, but "n" stakeholders. We refer to this as the "n+1" rule, which is that an agreement among "n" stakeholders will take "n" internal agreements in order to achieve one across the stakeholders. Of course, if there are coalitions (groups of stakeholders acting together) it is even more complicated, but the guiding principle is that there needs to be sufficient internal alignment within each stakeholder in order for there to be lateral alignment across the stakeholders.

Achieve Sufficient Alignment for Action

It is never possible for all stakeholders to be fully aligned on all dimensions. Even one person may be internally conflicted on a given issue. It is possible, however, to achieve sufficient alignment for some steps to be taken in service of the shared vision. This then begins a virtuous cycle where some progress reinforces discussions on additional next steps. At the same time, some actions surface new disagreements among stakeholders who may have agreed in principle to certain steps but shift their views once they see what is happening. Achieving sufficient alignment for action is essential for progress, with actions invariably prompting continued alignment efforts—sometimes going further and deeper on a given issue or initiative and sometimes backing away or pivoting in one way or another.

Alignment includes areas where action is agreed on as well as areas that will not be pursued by the consortium. This is illustrated by the Primary Care Collaborative:

> Founded in 2006, the Primary Care Collaborative (PCC) is a consortium focused on the quintuple aim of: "better care, better health, lower costs, greater joy for clinicians and staff, and greater health equity."

> The PCC describes itself as "a not-for-profit multi-stakeholder membership organization dedicated to advancing an effective and efficient health system built on a strong foundation of primary care and the patient-centered medical home." Its structure and mission are summarized as follows: "Representing a broad group of public and private organizations, the PCC's mission is to unify and engage diverse stakeholders in promoting policies and sharing best practices that support the growth of high-performing primary care that treats the whole person."[20]
>
> Although the members are aligned overall on the mission, there are issues in which the competing interests of different stakeholders limit what the PCC can do. For example, there are what are termed "scope of practice" differences among registered nurses (RNs) and physician assistants (PAs) when it comes to primary care. Since both RNs and PAs are important stakeholders for the PCC, the Collaborative presently stays away from these scope-of-practice issues. In time, the PCC may be an appropriate forum for dialogue and action on scope of practice.

The final two principles, a minimum viable consortium and agile/adaptive governance, center on evolving and sustaining a consortium.

Establish a Minimum Viable Consortium

There is a point at which collective action transitions into an organizational form or institutional arrangement. As we noted, it could be called a partnership, alliance, collaborative, initiative, council, project, or something else. We use "consortium" as the overarching term here. Typically, a charter or a set of terms of reference, or a governing document such as a memorandum of agreement is generated. Our guidance is modeled on the concept of a "minimum viable product" for an entrepreneurial organization. We suggest setting up a minimum viable consortium so that it can be agile and adaptive with input from stakeholders over time and as circumstances change. In some cases, the "minimum viable" involves very little structure and can happen in a matter of days or weeks; in other cases, even the minimum is complex and can take months or years to establish.

Sustain Agile and Adaptive Governance

Because stakeholders and interests are dynamic—due to changing circumstances or even just new learning about existing conditions—the way the alignment functions, including how things are governed, must be flexible and responsive. Becoming agile and adaptive requires beginning with a "minimum viable consortium," so there is enough structure to deliver results, but no more. This allows for flexible adjustments initially, and then the "minimum viable" approach needs to be sustained. Agility and adaptation are particularly important in an era where there are accelerating rates of change with many technologies. Indeed, because stakeholder alignment is capable of being agile and adaptive, it is an organizational or institutional form that is capable of coevolving with accelerating technologies. In this sense, the seventh guiding principle, sustaining agile and adaptive governance, is also a key virtue of the approach.

Summing Up

Consortia will not replace commercial, regulatory, and nonprofit organizations. Indeed, they are typically composed of representatives from these types of organizations and other groups in society.

Key guiding principles highlighted here include:

- Specify stakeholders
- Identify interests
- Build a shared vision
- Ensure internal alignment for lateral alignment
- Achieve sufficient alignment for action
- Establish a minimum viable consortium
- Sustain agile and adaptive governance

Taken together, these principles provide a foundation for consortia that complement, rather than replace, more traditional, hierarchical organizations.

Notes

1. On the registration process, see " How to Register," European Union Agency for Fundamental Rights, accessed June 6, 2023, http://fra.europa.eu/en/cooperation/civil-society/how-to-register.
2. See, for example, Igor Ansoff, "Strategic Issue Management," *Strategic Management Journal* 1, no. 2 (1980): pp. 131–148, https://doi.org/10.1002/smj.4250010204.
3. Elinor Ostrom, *Governing the Commons: The Evolution of Institutions for Collective Action* (New York: Cambridge University Press, 1990).
4. See "The 17 Goals," The United Nations, Department of Economic and Social Affairs, accessed June 6, 2023, https://sdgs.un.org/goals.
5. See "14 Grand Challenges for Engineering in the 21st Century," National Academy of Engineering, accessed June 6, 2023, http://www.engineeringchallenges.org/challenges.aspx.
6. The Erie Canal is what today would be called a disruptive technology, prompting a shift from craft unions to industrial unions, see John R. Commons, *The History of Labor in the U.S.* (New York: Macmillan, 1918).
7. See Michel Christian, Sandrine Kott, and Ondrej Matejka, eds., *Planning in Cold War Europe: Competition, Cooperation, Circulations (1950s–1970s)* (Berlin and Boston: Walter de Gruyter, 2018).
8. See William M. Evan and Paul Olk, "R&D Consortia: A New US Organizational Form," *Sloan Management Review* 31, no. 3 (1990): pp. 37–46; Howard E. Aldrich and Toshihiro Sasaki, "R&D Consortia in the United States and Japan," *Research Policy* 24, no. 2 (1995): pp. 301–316, https://doi.org/10.1016/0048-7333(93)00768-O.
9. See Robert D. Hof, "Lessons from Sematech," *MIT Technology Review*, July 25, 2011, https://www.technologyreview.com/2011/07/25/192832/lessons-from-sematech/.
10. See the Stakeholder Alignment Collaborative, Joel Cutcher-Gershenfeld et al., "Lessons from Multi-Stakeholder Consortia for Public Higher Education Systems," in *Recreating Multi-Campus University Systems*, edited by Jim Johnsen (Baltimore: Johns Hopkins University Press, forthcoming).
11. See:https://www.dfat.gov.au/trade/organisations/wto-g20-oecd-apec/indo-pacific-economic-framework.
12. See: https://www.state.gov/americas-partnership-for-economic-prosperity/.
13. See Michael Piore and Charles Sabel, *The Second Industrial Divide: Possibilities for Prosperity* (New York: Basic Books, 1984).
14. Joel Cutcher-Gershenfeld and Joe Isaac examined 100 years of labor legislation in Australia, finding that all of the acts can be classified with respect to a focus on mitigating harm, creating value, or a combination of the two. See Joel Cutcher-Gershenfeld and Joe Isaac, "Creating Value and Mitigating Harm: Assessing Institutional Objectives in Australian Industrial Relations," *Economic and Labour Relations Review* 29, no. 2 (2018): 143–168, https://doi.org/10.1177/1035304618767263.
15. See George P. Huber, "The Nature and Design of Post-Industrial Organizations," *Management Science* 30, no. 8 (August 1984): pp. 928–951, https://www.jstor.org/stable/2631586; John Child and Rita Gunther Mcgrath, "Organizations Unfettered: Organizational Form in an Information-Intensive Economy," *Academy of Management Journal* 44, no. 6 (2001): pp. 1135–1148; Erik Brynjolfsson and Brian Kahin, eds., *Understanding the Digital Economy: Data, Tools, and Research* (Cambridge, MA: MIT Press, 2000), https://doi.org/10.7551/mitpress/6986.001.0001.
16. See Neil Gershenfeld, Joel Cutcher-Gershenfeld, and Alan Gershenfeld, *Designing Reality: How to Survive and Thrive in the Third Digital Revolution* (New York: Basic Books, 2017).
17. See Anders Ørding Olsen, Wolfgang Sofka, and Christoph Grimpe, "Coordinated Exploration for Grand Challenges: The Role of Advocacy Groups in Search Consortia," *Academy of Management Journal* 59, no. 6 (2016): pp. 2232–2255, https://doi.org/10.5465/amj.2015.0730; Deborah Dougherty and Danielle D. Dunne, "Organizing Ecologies of Complex Innovation," *Organization Science* 22, no. 5 (2011): pp. 1214–1223, https://doi.org/10.1287/orsc.1100.0605.

18. See, for example, Robert S. Kaplan and David Norton, "The Balanced Scorecard: Measures That Drive Performance," *Harvard Business Review* 70, no. 1 (January–February 1992): pp. 71–79.
19. These ideas draw on principles in the 2017 article by members of the Stakeholder Alignment Collaborative, see Joel Cutcher-Gershenfeld et al., "Five Ways Consortia Can Catalyze Open Science," *Nature* 543 (2017): 615–618.
20. Retrieved from: https://thepcc.org/.

Chapter 3
Barriers to Collective Action

In 2013, a trio of civic leaders, a librarian, a city council member, and a community college professor in Dodge City, Kansas, launched an initiative to bridge what was seen as a digital divide. Many citizens did not have affordable, high-speed access to the Internet, which limited the availability of healthcare information, employment opportunities, educational offerings, civic engagement, commerce, entertainment, and more.

In order to assess the landscape of stakeholders and interests on this issue, a stakeholder survey was conducted, reaching over 100 community leaders. For those without access to the Internet, public data collection sessions were held in the community's main library. The majority of respondents were positive about bridging digital divides so that all citizens could have access to the Internet (65% said access in the home was "very important" or "essential," while just 3% said it was not important). There were many supportive open-ended comments such as, "digital inclusion is absolutely essential in today's world. You're left behind without it" and "We recognize that digital communication is absolutely essential. We communicate digitally and are frustrated when government, health and community organizations aren't sufficiently digital. We support access for everyone, including those with disabilities and whose first language is not English." Also in the open-ended responses were a very small number of respondents who expressed strong opposition, such as "I think that internet access is still a privilege, and I am not willing to pay more for my access just so lower-income families and such do not have to pay or get a reduced cost for theirs."

The overwhelming support was sufficient to launch a consortium involving local government, K–12 schools, the library, the community college, and a local hospital. This earned the community an innovation grant from the state government. People worked together for a few years, but the arrangement was never fully instantiated as an ongoing

> consortium. Critical in the collapse of this collaborative effort was the vocal opposition of a small number of citizens opposed to an initiative that would raise local taxes or increase the cost of their cable bills. Today, with various public and private initiatives, access to the Internet has expanded to reach about 95% of the city's residents, but it has taken far longer than it might have.

Here's the thing about consortia—they involve people. People bring aspirations, common interests, and good will. People also bring biases, frailties, and conflicting interests. Of course, consortia involve more than people since they coevolve with technology and are embedded in both the built and natural environments. In order to have the desired impacts on social, technical, and natural systems, there are barriers to collective action that must be understood and addressed.

Modern social sciences—sociology, psychology, political science, management science, industrial relations, institutional economics, and other fields and subfields—emerged within the past two centuries and all have wrestled with one form or another of what is termed the "collective action" problem. The traditional Western view of the collective action problem centers on a core tension between individual self-interests and collective interests. This is a core tension for consortia, but the challenges go further to include Eastern views on the tension between harmony or balance and disharmony or unbalance, which are also central challenges for consortia with respect to social, technical, and natural systems. Consortia, in their form and function, must wrestle with these long-standing challenges.

We will not review all barriers to collective action—there are many and new barriers arise. We will review major arguments around collective action problems (see Table 3.1). Note that the items in Table 3.1 are illustrative of intellectual insights that have emerged over decades, centuries and, in a few cases, millennia. This list of challenges is not exhaustive. What is offered here is indicative of the complex, human-created dynamics that consortia face.

The barriers to collective action are organized into four categories. The first category, "incentives," draws on the work of economics, game theory, and related disciplines. The second category, "power dynamics," draws on sociology, social philosophy, and related disciplines. The third category, "social groupings," draws on social psychology, group dynamics, and related disciplines. The fourth category, "combinations of incentives,

Table 3.1 Key Barriers to Collective Action

Incentives

Issue	Tangible and intangible incentives undercut collective action
Examples:	*Tragedies of the Commons*: Self-interest alone will deplete shared resources.
	Principal/Agent Dilemmas: Representatives may have self-interests different from the interests of those they represent

Power Dynamics

Issue	Entrenched power, control, privilege, and elitism run counter to collaboration
Examples:	*Iron Law of Oligarchy*: Once established, organizations tend to perpetuate those in power at the cost of other goals
	Tokenism: Symbolic or performative gestures do not represent real sharing of power

Social Groupings

Issue	Different groups have different priorities, assumptions, worldviews, and rationales for action.
Examples:	*In-Group/Out-Group Bias*: Humans have a tendency to discriminate in favor of their group and against other groups.
	Knowledge Boundaries: Knowledge and expertise stay within domains even when cross-domain sharing is needed.

Combinations of Incentives, Power, and Social Groupings

Issue	Incentives, power, and social groups combine together in constraining ways
Example:	*Fissurization*: Fragmentation of the social order in ways that serve some interests over others.
	Dominant Worldviews: Incentives, power structures, and social groups reinforce dominant worldviews that undercut collective action.

power dynamics, and social groupings," draws on integrative domains such as organizational behavior, industrial relations, institutional theory, and related domains.

What is interesting about all of these challenges is that efforts to mitigate the barriers don't just lower the barriers. As social theorist Kurt Lewin observed, as the barriers are addressed, they typically turn into drivers.[1] At the end of each section we will provide a few illustrative suggestions on how to lower the barriers, mitigating the risks to collective action and creating new drivers. Later, in Chapter 9, we document emergent and now only partly understood barriers to collective action, using the same four major categories.

Incentives: Tragedies of the Commons

A classic formulation of the collective action problem is known as the "tragedy of the commons." Classically this is a situation where common land is overgrazed by sheep or cattle compared to privately held land. The concept was first signaled by economist William Forster Lloyd in 1833 and popularized by ecologist Garrett Hardin in 1968 in the journal *Science*. The tragedy of the commons is rooted, in part, in the "free rider problem." In 1965 Mancur Olson wrote in *The Logic of Collective Action* that the free rider problem is a major disincentive—people can often enjoy the benefits of collective action without having to contribute their time, energy, and resources.[2] Further, he observed that there are often incentives that reward individual interests over group interests. Incentives that reward inaction or individuals at the expense of groups are both barriers to collective action. These incentives can encourage individuals to exhaust shared resources without contributing proportionally.

All consortia must face the challenges of a small number of volunteers who carry a disproportionate amount of the work, as well as overutilization of other common resources. Elinor Ostrom earned a Nobel Prize in economics for making the case that neither markets nor regulation could effectively govern common pool resources.[3] Instead, she pointed to public-private partnerships (a form of consortium) as having the greatest potential for success. Even as we build on Ostrom's work, we note that preventing tragedies of the commons is a constant struggle for multistakeholder consortia.

Scholarship on common resources has evolved from its early roots in addressing the physical common-pool resource dilemmas documented by Garrett Hardin and Elinor Ostrom to more recent scholarship in understanding what are termed "knowledge commons." Information resources are also subject to social dilemmas in that they are collectively produced and accessed through the use of distributed digital technologies such as the Internet.[4] Knowledge as a shared resource is inherent to the phenomenon of multistakeholder consortia—both as a strength of consortia and as a risk where some bear unequal burdens in contributing to the knowledge commons. The knowledge commons in the context of any specific consortium must grapple with the actors, institutions, and action situations particular to the knowledge resources being shared.[5]

Although competition has limits when it comes to common pool resources, another aspect of collective action is a bias in market-based economies for competition. Individual action (by entrepreneurs, firms, and other entities) is prioritized over collective action. Indeed, certain forms of collaboration are seen as anticompetitive and are illegal in most market-based economies. As we will discuss in more detail in Chapter 4, there are examples of competitive firms and regulators carving out what are termed "precompetitive" domains, which are characterized by open sharing of information and other resources. This is the case with the Biomarkers Consortium, which we introduced in Chapter 1 as having carved out a precompetitive space for data on the identification and qualification of biomarkers that serve as key medical indicators, such as whether a patient is or is not in a disease state. One lesson from this case is that research identifying and qualifying biomarkers may be precompetitive for some (such as large pharmaceutical firms) even as it is competitive for others (such as various small biotech firms). As a result, the concept of a precompetitive space is not absolute and requires continuing mechanisms for governance.

To the extent that consortia can identify potential tragedies of the commons there is at least the potential to reduce the risk. For example, when contributions to the collective effort are unequal and there is the risk of free riders, this at least can be discussed and decisions made. That does not mean that such "tragedies" are always bad. Returning to the Biomarkers Consortium, all of its data is open to the public—not just to members of the consortium. For the pharmaceutical and biotech industry members of the consortium, the open sharing of the results of considerable financial investments runs counter to their norms around protecting information that could provide a competitive advantage. Their instinct is to not make the result of their projects available to free riders outside the consortium. Yet, for the government members this is essential—they have a public mandate to advance public goods. For academic and patient advocacy members the open sharing is welcome as it advances science and the prospects for new therapies. Even the industrial partners ultimately benefit from the accumulated open data. Ultimately, the sharing in this case does benefit free riders, but it is not a tragedy. The bug is actually a feature when there is sufficient value in the commons.

Incentives: Principal/Agent Dilemmas

Although there are many reasons for stakeholders to work together, there are also many incentives that undercut collective action. The classic incentives dilemma is that agents may have different motivations and face different incentives than those they represent.[6] A representative serving as a member of a consortium will learn things as an agent that others in their home organization, principals, will not know. As the representative behaves in new ways, based on what is learned, those back home will begin to question whether their interests are still being advanced. This is a core dilemma—if an agent only advances the expressed priorities of the home organizations, they may be less effective in the consortium. But if they work together with others in the consortium in new ways, they may be less trusted back home.

In a 1996 article, Julia Adams argues that a network structure—both economic and political—maintained control by the Dutch East Indies Company over its distributed agents and colonial forces. The company deteriorated as this network broke down.[7] We make an argument in the other direction here, which is that the emerging network structure of consortia weakens the influence of principals—raising trust issues by the principals. Trust issues with agents are not new—they are even documented in popular culture, such as in depictions of sports agents.[8] Members of consortia must be mindful of their role as agents on behalf of constituents, which is what motivates our principle, advanced in Chapter 4, that internal alignment is needed for lateral alignment.

Beyond the ways that the principal/agent dilemma impacts consortia, there are many other related issues around incentives. And the issues can be combined, for example, principal/agent dilemmas can be combined with free rider problems mentioned above. Consider a few classic workplace examples. When a union negotiates an agreement for a group of people, there is a potential principal/agent situation if the union leaders do not act on behalf of the workers they purport to represent, but instead work for their own interests. Further, under what are called "right to work" laws, individuals have the option to not pay union dues, and there is an incentive to be a free rider, because they will typically benefit from negotiations and grievance handling services (since unions in the United States and many other countries still have a duty of fair representation).

When it comes to consortia the undercutting incentives show up early on, as a relatively small number of individuals carry a disproportionate amount of the work organizing the consortium. There are further disincentives in the home organization, where the rewards for engaging in a consortium may not be valued as highly as the work within the home organization. While these disincentives are a barrier to collective action, they don't have to be converted into incentives to drive action—it is typically enough to just reduce the disincentives. In Chapter 1 we introduced the Takeda pharmaceuticals case, where a growing number of scientists and managers within Takeda were joining public-private partnerships, but each was treated as a one-off membership. The result was variability in whether this work was supported or not. By creating the office of public-private partnerships, which we noted was home for approximately 100 partnerships at any time, some consistency was introduced across these many partnerships. What had been a barrier (inconsistent individual actions) became a driver (an office for public-private partnerships).

Power: The Iron Law of Oligarchy

Sociologist Robert Michels, in his 1911 book, *Political Parties*, identified one aspect of a collective action problem, which he termed "the iron law of oligarchy."[9] Michels studied political parties and trade unions, initially set up as democratic organizations, that eventually delegated leadership to a small group of individuals who would invariably evolve to exercise oligarchic control in the interest of sustaining the organization. The result is that organizational persistence eclipses the mission of the organization. This suggests that stakeholder alignment must be a continual accomplishment and that consortia may be time-bound with a given set of leaders, after which they will likely need to be reformed.

This dynamic can be seen in many long-serving consortia and consortia-like arrangements. For example, ICANN (the Internet Corporation for Assigned Names and Numbers) presents itself as a multistakeholder body, but does not fully operate as a consortium. The dynamics around its operation are complex and we only touch on one aspect here.

ICANN was founded in 1998 following a few years of debates about what it should be, how it should be scoped, what problem it was supposed to solve, and what it should be called. It was preceded by initiatives under what was then termed the Advanced Research Projects Agency Network (ARPANET), contracts through the National Science Foundation, and was initiated by a memorandum of understanding (MoU) from the US Department of Commerce. The government did not want to have the ongoing role of managing Internet names and address spaces. There was also a belief by several parties that there was significant money to be made by selling identifiers, so there was an element of a market for buying and selling domain names. Embedded in ICANN was an underlying debate around what should be subject to the market and what should be subject to regulation. A public-private partnership represented a middle ground.

While some aspects of the governance of the Internet are more consortia-like, such as the Internet Society (ISOC) and the Internet Engineering Task Force (IETF), ICANN incorporated as a nonprofit organization with a small group of leaders focused on appropriately carving out the middle ground between a market and regulation. The iron law of oligarchy was in play through a deeply embedded assumption that hierarchical authority in the hands of a relatively small number of people was needed to govern the assignment of names and numbers. Though these may be laudable intentions, the result has been a concentration of power in the hands of this small group of individuals and related companies. The result is that ICANN does not operate as a consortium where relevant stakeholders have full opportunities for voice or input. Mechanisms for conflict resolution when there are differences are not widely available.[10] As ICANN has expanded its scope over the years, there are not robust lateral mechanisms to provide checks and balance as can happen more readily with a consortium structure.

Closely related to the iron law of oligarchy is the potential for consortia to behave in territorial or monopolistic ways. The 1960 Organization of Arab Petroleum Exporting Countries (OPEC) and its successor entities are classic examples where the consortia structure is utilized to advance the self-interest of its members, leaving out of the discourse many other stakeholders. A challenge that motivates this book centers on an approach to the formation and sustainment of consortia that serve broader societal goals.

While the iron law of oligarchy constantly lurks as a barrier to collective action through a consortium, knowledge of this dynamic and dialogue about it can lead to commitments for leadership rotation, more inclusive forums, open membership, and other arrangements that mitigate the risk of what Michels would term an oligarchical elite. Once in place, these inclusive policies and procedures become drivers.

Power: Tokenism

Tokenism was advanced as a concept by Rosabeth Moss Kanter in her seminal 1977 book to describe women's experience as a minority group in the workplace.[11] Kanter observed that there was a tipping point after women represented more than 15% of the people in a given organization context (such as the leadership team) after which women's voices were not treated in stereotypical ways—as token representatives of their gender rather than as individuals with unique views that needed to be taken into account. At the same time, when representation of minorities increases above the 15% threshold, dominant groups are often threatened and this can give rise to backlash and discrimination, which Hubert Blalock termed in 1967 a theory of intrusiveness.[12]

Consortia have to wrestle both with stakeholder groups that are underrepresented and at risk of being treated as tokens and with groups that are appropriately represented and seen as intrusive. Through repeated interactions, such as coming to a consensus on decisions or working together on a committee, some of the power differences based on resources and social status may be reduced. Tokenism can be replaced by increased appreciation of alternative perspectives. Forms of power based on expertise, contributed time and other resources, and moral authority may be expanded. Not reducing some of these internal differences, at least to some degree, can undercut the work of a consortium.

Underlying tokenism are issues of power. People are treated as tokens in order to preserve the power of those treating them in this way. By including only token participation of underrepresented stakeholders, those in power can preserve their standing in the face of pressure to be inclusive. Social scientists have long held that power is not an absolute property, but rather something that is socially constructed. For example, Michel Foucault has argued that power is not a fixed property held by individuals, but rather is the product of complex networks of relationships.[13] In this formulation, power is constructed in order to exercise social control.[14]

Some forms of social control are challenged by the formation of consortia—they shift the complex networks that are in place. Central to our definition of a consortium are people accomplishing together what they cannot do separately. Often, what they cannot do separately is a result of entrenched forms of power that only allow token voice and engagement. In this regard, the very formation of a consortium is the product of diverse stakeholders combining different forms of power (a process of social construction) to change power relations in society. Of course, these same entrenched forms of power can undercut the work of a consortium.

Social Groupings: In-Group/Out-Group Bias

Social perspectives on human cognition emphasize how individuals do not think in a vacuum. The way we view the world and the way we think is heavily influenced by social factors in our experiences and our environments.[15] As individuals, we are socialized into social groups including families, nations, and peer groups, and these groups provide the schemas, language, and historically accepted ways of interpreting situations and acting in them. In short, group membership profoundly influences our human cognition.

Many have explored group identification in evolutionary terms.[16] Adopting group thinking is an efficient and relatively risk-free course of adaptive action. Humans have deeply entrenched survival biases toward group identification and loyalty and to treat outsiders with suspicion. This results in biases toward one's group, where perceptions of similarity are emphasized, and biases against those outside of one's group, where perceptions of differences are given prominence.

Natural and ubiquitous group biases stand in the way of collective action when groups have strong senses of identity and entrenched positions that contradict other groups' positions. In such situations, groups may demonize the other groups making it difficult to find common ground. Perhaps nowhere is this more apparent as a problem than in the political polarization evident in many Western societies. People identify with a political party and this results in an affective commitment to their group, including accentuation of the positives and unity of their group, with an associated affective bias against the other group, with an emphasis on differences.

The result of the in-group and out-group biases are issues of discrimination and disparate treatment of individuals and groups. These are collective action problems in which consortia are both part of the problem and part of the solution. Aspects of identity that include religion, race, class, gender, ethnicity, immigration status, disability, geography, and other classifications have a long history of serving as the basis for collective mistreatment and violence. In this context, consortia can be formed as part of a collective response to mitigate harm. In addition to directly mitigating harm, consortia also can be effective in leveling power differences among those involved, which is explored in more detail below and in Chapter 4. At the same time, groups that traffic in racism, antisemitism, homophobia, and other forms of discrimination and harm often use consortia structures to operate. Thus, as an institutional arrangement, consortia can serve to advance many types of collective interests—some highly admirable and some deeply problematic and even abhorrent.

Consortia not only can be both positive and negative (from various perspectives) in their aims and operations but also can encounter opposition that can be both constructive and obstructive. Indeed, individuals and groups whose interests are threatened by consortia can work specifically to undermine this form of collective action, as was illustrated in the Dodge City, Kansas, vignette at the beginning of this chapter.

While the many possible tensions between in-groups and out-groups are a barrier to collective action, embedded in the tensions are differences that can add value to a consortium. An appreciation of aspects of the out-group, such as its dedication to its values, can allow for the formation of what are termed "slender bridges." For example, decades ago there was a community dialogue in the Boston area between abortion rights groups and antiabortion groups. While they disagreed deeply on the issue of abortion, the multiday dialogue did surface mutual respect from each group for the other being dedicated to its views. On that slender bridge of mutual respect an agreement was reached to work together to prevent bombings in abortion clinics. The overall barrier between these two groups was still there, but it was lowered slightly and that was enough for the barrier to become a driver.[17]

Social Groupings: Knowledge Boundaries

In their classical work on innovative organizations, Lawrence and Lorsch[18] pointed out that different functions in an organization have different goals and processes for action, and as a result they have different orientations toward time, human interaction, and management in general. Because different functional groups do different things, they have different priorities and different assumptions about how to reach their goals. So it is difficult for them to work together because of these differences. We now know that these differences are not superficial, but are deeply embedded in the views that different functions, professions, and research communities have about what constitutes appropriate and defensible knowledge.[19] Integrating the knowledge of different communities is a challenge for any complex endeavor, and the solution is not trivial. Consortia dealing with complex issues need to draw on and value the different ways of knowing, and avoid overlooking or undervaluing others.

In the scholarly context, the spanning of knowledge boundaries can involve work that is cross-disciplinary, multidisciplinary, interdisciplinary, and even transdisciplinary (each of which is a distinct way of spanning across fields and disciplines). In the organizational context, cross-functional or multifunctional teams (involving, for example, finance, HR, marketing, operations, purchasing, and others) each bring distinctive forms of expertise. The challenge for consortia is that these and other types of knowledge boundaries are not typically discussed at the outset. Instead, they emerge as people discover they are using the same words or concepts in different ways or they are approaching problems with different underlying assumptions.

One activity that has proven impactful for consortia is what some of us have termed "assumption wrangling."[20] This involves surfacing deeply embedded assumptions in a given context—a group, an organization, or an ecosystem—and exploring what might be alternative guiding assumptions that might be more beneficial to all.

Combinations of Incentives, Power, and Social Groupings: Fissurization

In 2000, Robert D. Putnam documented in *Bowling Alone* how family, friends, and neighbors are increasingly disconnected in US society.[21] This had deep implications for maintaining a sense of community, Putnam notes, as well as for maintaining a shared sense of responsibility for the social order. Similar dynamics in employment are documented in a 2017 book, *The Fissured Workplace* by David Weil.[22] He describes the fragmentation of the traditional social contract at work between employers and employees. Weil notes that this fissurization provides power advantages to employers. The metaphor of fissurization comes from geology and has connotations of gaps that are hard to reconnect once they appear. In the context of employment relations, there was a time, in the 1970s and 1980s when there were many consortia arrangements that bridged labor, management, government, and others. This included the Work in America Institute (WIA), the American Quality and Productivity Center (AQPC), the Michigan Quality of Work Life Center (MQWLC), the Industrial Relations Research Association (IRRA), over 50 community Area Labor-Management Committees (ALMCs), and many others. Today, the successor to IRRA, the Labor and Employment Relations Association (LERA), remains, while most of the consortia in the earlier employment relations landscape have fragmented into separate groupings of employers, workers, and others who primarily just talk to others like themselves.

Consortia are formed, of course, to bridge across differences. At a time when the fragmentations are deepening and ossifying, this boundary spanning becomes more difficult. This is particularly the case since the fissurization serves some interests at the expense of others. In this sense, the combination of power advantages and deteriorating social groupings undercuts collective action.

Combinations of Incentives, Power, and Social Groupings: Dominant Worldviews

In today's world, there are deep divides marked by highly divergent worldviews. This is a particularly polarizing aspect of collective action. Worldviews are not the product of logical or rational choice, but rather are deeply embedded in our psyches and our societies, arising out of our lived experiences. This makes it difficult to bridge across worldviews based on logic or rational arguments. Indeed, there is a profound dilemma associated with discourse across worldviews. Calling attention to differences in worldviews tends to increase polarization. Failing to call attention to differences in worldviews becomes the proverbial elephant in the room. In a special issue of *Negotiation Journal* focused on bridging across worldviews, the special issue editor, Jeffrey Seul, points toward a way forward by first quoting Anaïs Nin, "We don't see things as they are, we see them as we are."[23] It is only by acknowledging basic human dignity, including appreciating differences in how we all see the world, that can begin to make progress. Seul further observes that all of our inherited theories and methods (including those in this book) have their roots in particular worldviews.

In contrast to the deep divides, another barrier to collective action involves what might be termed being superficial or performative—going through the motions of interaction, but not surfacing and addressing competing interests that are present but hidden. This can take the form of not moving forward until there is complete consensus, but also not directly discussing what is keeping a consensus from forming. For example, a turning point in the formation of the Minority Serving Cyberinfrastructure Consortium (MS-CC) happened when one of the participants, Urban Wiggins, then a professor of computer science at the University of Maryland Eastern Shore (now vice provost for decision science and visualization in the Office of Academic Affairs) observed that historically Black colleges and universities (HBCUs) had a long history of acting independently and even competitively with respect to each other. Until this was named as an issue, the discussion of potential collaboration was all very polite. Once named, the focus shifted toward a much more substantive direction around how best to address these deeply embedded aspects of the HBCU ecosystem culture. The barrier was in the process of becoming a driver.

An Example of Collective Action Dynamics within a Labor-Management Partnership

Labor-management partnerships have been documented for over a century in the United States, dating back to the 1910 Protocol of Peace championed by Louis Brandeis as an alternative to strikes and unsafe conditions in the garment manufacturing industry. This umbrella agreement operated as a form of consortium of unions and employers with arbitration as a mechanism to resolve disagreements. Brandeis championed this approach as a form of "industrial democracy" that would bring to the workplace the same democratic principles we valued in society. Although the Protocol did improve relations in the industry for approximately a half-dozen years, it was not able to survive divisions within the labor movement and among employers. In the many decades since then, there have been hundreds of notable labor-management partnerships but all have encountered undercutting tensions. These are illustrated here with the case of a current labor-management partnership that had to bridge multiple barriers to collective action.

On October 26, 2017, the labor and management leaders of the Labor-Management Partnership (LMP) at Kaiser Permanente met in what was termed a "reaffirmation session." At this point, the partnership had been in place for 21years and covered over 120,000 employees represented in 33 bargaining units affiliated with a range of national unions (AFSCME, IBT, OPEIU, SEIU, UFCW, UNITE HERE, USW, and others). The unions operated as the "Coalition" with a tradition of consensus decision-making on some issues, proportional voting on some issues (based on the size of the union local), and each union with one vote on other issues (regardless of the size of the local). The session was intended to support strategic dialogue on strengths and challenges, resulting in a reaffirmation of what was one of the world's leading labor-management partnerships operating in parallel with the collective bargaining relationship. What actually happened revealed a long simmering fault line among the unions in this partnership structure. It was a split within labor rather than a split between labor and management.

The reaffirmation session was preceded by individual and group interviews with a broad range of labor and management leaders, which surfaced a wide range of strengths and challenges. The interviews were conducted by outside consultants with a history of working with the parties, including Joel Cutcher-Gershenfeld, Charlie Huggins, Deborah Montesinos, and others.

Strengths highlighted in the interviews included:

- A robust network of over 3,500 unit-based teams driving continuous improvement in front-line operations.
- A range of regional and national labor-management forums for dialogue on training, new technology, and other matters of mutual interest.
- Labor peace for 20 years since the launch of the partnership in 1997.
- Industry leading wages and benefits.
- Growth of the Kaiser Permanente system.
- Continuous improvement in the quality of care.

Challenges highlighted in the interviews included:

- Meaningful engagement of the union in management strategic decision-making.

- Both labor and management being fully committed to each other's success.
- Lack of clarity and agreement on partnership expectations and accountability.
- Challenges around staffing and backfill in many parts of the operation.
- Addressing the expanding introduction of new technologies.

The top management leadership of Kaiser Permanente arrived ready to work on these issues with the top leadership of the unions in the coalition, with facilitation support from the individuals who had collected the presession data. But that is not what happened. Instead, there was a split between the largest union in the Coalition, which was joined by 12 of the other unions, together representing 85,000 of the employees, and a group of 21 unions representing 52,000 employees.

At issue was an internal dispute within the coalition that dated back to the 2015 negotiations. Dave Regan led the largest local union (SEIU-UHW), representing over 57,000 union members, and he objected to being outvoted by the other smaller unions on various issues. He called for a per capita voting model, while other unions did not want decision-making concentrated in one union. A few months before the October 2017 reaffirmation meeting, the issue had also been on the table in an August 2017 union delegates conference in Portland, Oregon. There was an attempt to resolve the governance disputes within the coalition, but it ultimately proved unsuccessful at resolving the disagreement.

Underlying the divide on decision-making within the Coalition of unions were a number of substantive issues, including a controversial ballot initiative in California backed by SEIU-UHW and opposed by Kaiser Permanente and a number of the unions, the degree to which there should be an adversarial or collaborative approach to collective bargaining, and other issues. This was all a core challenge to the internal alignment needed within labor in order to operate as a partnership with management.

Over the next few months partnership meetings were canceled while the unions attempted to work through the issues. By March of 2018, at the opening day of National Bargaining, with the issues still unresolved, a group of unions left the Coalition and formed the Alliance of

> Health Care Unions. This Alliance contained 21 locals, which have come to represent about 52,000 employees (local unions of AFSCME, UFCW, USW, IBT, KPNAA, IUOE, OFNHP [AFT], UNITE HERE, and ILWU). Regan and the 12 unions that were with him (SEIU and OPEIU locals) remained as the Coalition, representing about 85,000 employees.
>
> This split had direct implications for the collective bargaining relationship—management would now be bargaining separately with the Coalition unions and the Alliance unions. The split also divided the administration of the partnership activities, which were separate from collective bargaining. At the national level a 2018 collective bargaining agreement was negotiated with the Alliance establishing a new LMP Strategy Group, a new joint trust fund, and other initiatives. There remained an LMP Strategy Group and trust fund with the coalition, which was reaffirmed in a 2019 collective bargaining agreement. While things were divided at the strategic level, the parties did agree that the division would not be imposed on front-line operations where unit-based teams might include front-line workers affiliated with both the Alliance and Coalition unions.

The 2018 split into the Coalition and the Alliance illustrates the challenges around internal alignment within one part of the partnership and the resulting complexity when the structure changes. Collective action involving multiple parties depends on internal alignment within each.

Note that this case has echoes of the collective dynamics in the US Congress. The US Congress is supposed to have proportional representation in the House of Representatives and equal representation in the Senate. Each has its advantages and limitations when it comes to advancing collective interests. The Kaiser Permanente Partnership primarily had a structure like the US Senate, but the split resulted in one more like the US House of Representatives. It is interesting to consider whether the partnership would benefit from a model that more fully balanced both types of arrangements side by side.

Summing Up

Underneath the challenges associated with diverse stakeholders are barriers to collective action. It is human potential that motivates the formation and sustainment of consortia, as well as human limitations that account for why collective action is hard to initiate and sustain.

Consortia are essential because there are both common and competing interests among individuals and groups as stakeholders. Consortia are viable when the stakeholders can rise above self-interests and accomplish together what they can't accomplish separately. They are also essential because there are always self-interests and other complicated dynamics at play. Before there can be a consortia century, these dynamics need to be understood and addressed. As we have seen in this chapter, even acknowledging and beginning to lower the barriers facilitates their transition to the same forces becoming drivers.

Notes

1. This is the core insight in Kurt Lewin, *Field Theory in the Social Sciences* (New York: Harper & Brothers, 1951). In the book, Lewin described a force field of driving and restraining forces associated with social change. He observed that pushing harder on the drivers can engender resistance, while lowering the barriers enables the existing drivers to be operative.
2. See Mancur Olson, *The Logic of Collective Action: Public Goods and the Theory of Groups* (Cambridge, MA: Harvard University Press, 1965).
3. See Elinor Ostrom, *Governing the Commons: The Evolution of Institutions for Collective Action* (Cambridge: Cambridge University Press, 1990).
4. See Charlotte Hess and Elinor Ostrom, "Ideas, Artifacts, and Facilities: Information as a Common-Pool Resource," *Law and Contemporary Problems* 66 (Winter 2003): pp. 111–145, https://doi.org/10.2307/20059174; Brett M. Frischmann, Michael J. Madison, and Katherine J. Strandburg, *Governing the Knowledge Commons* (Oxford: Oxford University Press, 2014), https://doi.org/10.1093/acprof:oso/9780199972036.001.0001; and Yochai Benkler, "Commons and Growth: The Essential Role of Open Commons in Market Economies (Reviewing *Infrastructure: The Social Value of Shared Resources* by Brett M. Frischmann)," *University of Chicago Law Review* 80 (2013): pp. 1499–1555, https://chicagounbound.uchicago.edu/uclrev/vol80/iss3/12.
5. See Daniel Cole, "Learning from Lin: Lessons and Cautions from the Natural Commons for the Knowledge Commons," in *Governing Knowledge Commons*, edited by Brett Frischmann, Michael Madison, and Katherine Strandburg (Oxford: Oxford University Press, 2014), pp. 45–68.
6. For more on principal/agent theory, see John W. Pratt and Richard J. Zeckhauser, *Principals and Agents in the Structure of Business* (Cambridge, MA: Harvard Business School Press, 1985).
7. See Julia Adams, "Principals and Agents, Colonialists and Company Men: The Decay of Colonial Control in the Dutch East Indies," *American Sociological Review* 61, no. 1 (February 1996): pp. 12–28, https://doi.org/10.2307/2096404.
8. The phrase "show me the money" in the film *Jerry Maguire* centers on whether the agent (played by Tom Cruise) can be trusted to deliver results for the client (played by Cuba Gooding). Similarly, The Mamas & The Papas sing, "Broke, busted, disgusted; agents can't be trusted," in their 1967 song "Creeque Alley."
9. See Robert Michels, *Political Parties: A Sociological Study of the Oligarchical Tendencies of Modern Democracy* (Hearst's International Library Co., 1911, German, 1915, English).
10. This case vignette is drawn from the direct experience of a few members of our team. Another member of our team reports the same dynamic with Black Lives Matter, which emphasized collective leadership but initially lacked the mechanisms for the inevitable conflicts among the leaders that emerged.
11. See Rosabeth Moss Kanter, *Men and Women of the Corporation* (New York: Basic Books, 1977).
12. See Hubert Blalock, *Toward a Theory of Minority-Group Relations* (New York: John Wiley & Sons, 1967).
13. See, for example, Michel Foucault, *Power/Knowledge: Selected Interviews and Other Writings 1972–1977*, edited by Colin Gordon (New York: Pantheon Books, 1980). Here the focus is

on mental health, prisons, and sexuality, and population management, social protest, and other topics. Foucault argued that these complex networks of relationships between power, knowledge, and institutional formations serve as vehicles for normalization of human behavior, policy, and institutions. Foucault argued that the justifications for the exercise of power are, ultimately, shifting and arbitrary, as are processes of normalization of behaviors and institutions. He and others take a historical genealogical view of social institutions and human interactions that produce knowledge with effects of power and power used to justify systems of knowledge. In short, power is not just top-down or simply a product of political-scientific conceptions of the state. Power is not just repressive but also operates by a certain positivity that stimulates discourse; such production destabilizes as much as it stabilizes norms that everyday society takes for granted. Steven Lukes observes that domination only persists with compliance, so power is a product of these social interactions. See Steven Lukes, *Power: A Radical View*, 2nd ed. (New York: Palgrave, 2005).

14. For more on this issue, see Judith Butler's use of the social construction approach to point out that gender is not an innate characteristic but rather something that takes on different meanings in different societies based on repeated patterns of interaction, citable language, and bodily formation; social forces shape bodily repetition that creates gender, not the other way around (Judith Butler, *Bodies That Matter: On the Discursive Limits of "Sex"* [New York: Routledge, 1993]). Once there is a set of gender meanings, the meanings inform and reinforce various power relationships among men, women, and those who are gender variant. Again, the point is to focus on the interacting relationships that are behind what we call "gender."

15. Seminal books on this perspective include Albert Bandura's 1986 *Social Foundations of Thought and Action* (Hoboken, NJ: Prentice Hall), and Susan Fisk and Shelly Taylor's 1991 *Social Cognition* (Thousand Oaks, CA: Sage).

16. See, for example, Martie G. Haselton, Daniel Nettle, and Paul W. Andrews, "The Evolution of Cognitive Bias," in The Handbook of Evolutionary Psychology, edited by David M. Buss (New York: J. Wiley and Sons, 2015), pp. 724–746; and Coryy J. Clark, Brittany S. Liu, Bo M. Winegard, and Peter H. Ditto, "Tribalism Is Human Nature," *Current Directions in Psychological Science* 28, no. 6 (2019): pp. 587–592.

17. Retrieved from: https://whatisessential.org/impact-stories/abortion-dialogues-greater-boston.

18. Paul R. Lawrence and Jay W. Lorsch, *Organization and Environment–Managing Differentiation and Integration* (Boston: Harvard Business School Press, 1967).

19. See, for example, Richard J. Boland Jr. and Ram V. Tenkasi, "Perspective Making and Perspective Taking in Communities of Knowing," *Organization Science* 6, no. 4 (1965): pp. 350–372; and Deborah Dougherty, "Interpretive Barriers to Successful Product Innovation in Large Firms." *Organization Science* 3, no. 2 (1992): pp. 179–202.

20. See Joel Cutcher-Gershenfeld, "Assumption Wrangling: An Experiment in Culture Change," *Heller Magazine* (2018, Winter): pp. 34–37. Retrieved from: https://heller.brandeis.edu/news/items/releases/2018/winter-magazine-cutcher-gershenfeld.html.

21. See Robert Putnam, *Bowling Alone: The Collapse and Revival of American Community* (New York: Simon & Schuster, 2000).

22. See David Weil, The *Fissured Workplace: Why Work Became So Bad for So Many and What Can Be Done to Improve It* (Cambridge, MA: Harvard University Press, 2017).

23. See Jeffery R. Seul, "Introduction to Special Issue: Negotiating Across Worldviews," *Negotiation Journal* 38, no. 3 (2022): pp. 357–361, https://doi.org/10.1111/nejo.12409.

Chapter 4
Agile and Adaptive Consortia

The remarkable thing about consortia is that anyone can form one at any time, with no regulation or government oversight.[1] That doesn't mean that it is easy—there are considerable forces arrayed against collective action, as we saw in Chapter 3. It is just that there are few legal or administrative barriers. Of course, that may change later in the 21st century should broad-scale problems emerge with the arrangement. For now, most of the time, the legal or regulatory barriers to entry are low.

There are a wide range of consortia. Indeed, every other chapter in this book begins with an illustrative case example and others are included in the body of each chapter, representing a diversity of cases. We do not lead with a single case example in this chapter, because there is no single iconic type of consortia. The aim of this chapter is to provide an integrative theory and framework that spans the diversity of institutional arrangements.

Contrast with Hierarchical Control

Consortia are attractive because they sidestep the costs associated with governing by organizational fiat. Organizational fiat creates power hierarchies that limit membership to those who are willing to be contained with the hierarchy. The Biomarkers Consortium is a good example of not being constrained in this way: the US Federal Government cannot delegate its legislative authority. As a result, it can join the consortium as an independent member, but it can't be subject to oversight by others as would happen if it were subsumed into another hierarchy.

There's a narrowness to traditional, hierarchical organizations. Governing by fiat can narrow the influence of diverse voices because there is a clear order of control. When power and voice compete, power usually wins. By contrast, consortia are negotiated arrangements. This creates higher costs upfront for aligning and creating mutual governance. Yet once a charter is in place, the parties can operate independently and interdependently because they voluntarily consent to the arrangement.

Perhaps the biggest challenge to viable consortia is a shift in mindset. As indicated in Chapters 1 and 2, stakeholder alignment involves lateral thinking—a horizontal or middle-out mindset. At the core this means that there are multiple stakeholders with both common and competing interests. The diversity of stakeholders in a consortium can include the full spectrum of rights holders, such as Indigenous Peoples and others with legal or historical standing, parties with interests that are at stake but who have no formal standing, and even interested parties with less at stake. As a result, alignment of stakeholders takes negotiated dialogue among many parties on many issues or interests in order to achieve sufficient shared understanding and agreement for collective action.

Five Characteristics of Consortia

The lateral, agile mindset connects to the five characteristics of consortia (Table 4.1) that we introduced in Chapters 1 and 2. We return to these in this chapter in order to identify the underlying principles and theory associated with each one. This is not an exhaustive literature review, but rather an identification of illustrative and often iconic theories in each domain—designed to help in more fully understanding these characteristics.

Independence and Interdependence

The first characteristic of consortia identified in Chapter 1 is "independence and interdependence." In contrast with a unitary view of the world, which is a view from one party's perspective, this characteristic has its roots in the theory of pluralism and the scholarship of Sidney Webb and Beatrice Webb in the mid-1800s in England. This was in response to the growing embrace of the role of markets in a capitalist society. The benefits of capitalism as an engine of innovation were equally visible at the time with negative externalities in the form of child labor, industrial accidents, and environmental degradation.

Some contemporaries, such as Karl Marx and Fredrich Engels, saw these externalities and rejected the capitalist model, proposing various communal

Table 4.1 Key Characteristics of Consortia

Characteristics	Elaboration
Independence and Interdependence	Bringing together parties with separate identities is a defining feature of a consortium and a source of continued challenge.
Common and Competing Interests	Underlying the separate identities are a broad array of common and competing interests, all of which must be taken into account.
Dynamic and Continuous Processes	The parties, the interests, and the broader context are all changing, which drives dynamic and continuous processes.
Accomplishing together what can't be accomplished separately	Given the many challenges, parties would act separately if they could achieve the same or better results.
Achieving sufficient alignment for action	A full merger of identities and interests is not needed (and would be counterproductive), but enough alignment is needed for collective action.

alternatives. In contrast, the Webbs did not reject capitalism, but did call for a model that gave equal standing to parties other than the property or factory owners—unions and political parties in particular.[2] Their insight introduced a pluralistic view of capitalist society into the discourse. This was part of the founding of the field of industrial relations. In the early 1900s in the United States, Jane Addams helped to found the field of social work by expanding this pluralist view to include collective voice on the part of women, children, and the poor, with an interest in being treated with dignity and respect in society.[3]

Both the Webbs and Addams were very aware of power differences, so their pluralist view was not premised on all parties being seen as equal. Rather, they saw themselves as lifting up the voices of those who were not being fully heard and, in the process, leveling some of the differences. This is what consortia do—they give more parties standing to be in the conversation.

The implication for consortia is that there will be power differences (and different sources of power). There may even be parties with veto power, but the formation and sustainment of a consortium reflect independent parties recognizing their interdependence with others.[4] At a time of deep divides in society, those operating as a consortium are indicating some commitment to bridging across differences or at least not letting those differences get in the way of collective action.

This can be expressed as a principle: *Independence informs interdependence while interdependence tempers independence.*

Common and Competing Interests

Building on the assumption of independent yet also interdependent stakeholders is a closely related assumption of "common and competing interests." This aspect of consortia, which is sometimes termed a "mixed-motive" assumption, is foundational for the negotiation literature.

In 1933 Mary Parker Follett delivered the inaugural lecture at the launch of the School of Business at the London School of Economics.[5] It was remarkable for a woman to be selected for this honor at the time, but what she said was even more remarkable. She argued that too much of business was transacted based on dominance or compromise, which she noted either involved one side getting what it wanted or neither side getting what it wanted. Instead, she introduced a third option, which she termed "integration," where all parties understand each other sufficiently to develop options that neither had in mind but that made all better off. In introducing integration, Follett was not just focusing on common interests. As Follett observed, the engineer uses friction so that pulleys and gears can function and we can use friction in social relations to function effectively as well. She saw the friction of competing interests as just as important for integration as the common interests.

Three decades after Mary Parker Follett lifted up the concept of integration, Richard Walton and Robert McKersie gave the concept a central role in their 1965 book, *Behavioral Theory of Labor Negotiations*.[6] This book codified the mixed-motive assumption by observing that negotiations involve both integrative and distributive issues and the associated integrative and distributive processes, sometimes summed up as "expanding the pie" and "dividing the pie," or what David Lax and James Sebenius termed in 2006 "creating value" and "claiming value."[7] A common failure mode in negotiations is for parties to become invested in competing positions. Instead, those taking part in negotiations should focus on underlying interests of the parties (common and competing), of which there can be many. Taken together the combined interests can point to paths forward.[8]

The implication for consortia is that alignment is an interest-based negotiated process. Stakeholders in a consortium will not only be identifying and building on common interests but also navigating competing interests, which is crucial and often given insufficient attention. These competing interests are especially challenging when bridging across stakeholders whose lived experiences and power differentials give rise to distrust of the very collaborative architectures that could potentially help. As a result, processes for constructive conflict resolution will be as important as processes for creative innovation. This involves being aware of and surfacing many interests. Moreover, there will need to be continuing processes as the stakeholders and interests evolve.

The underlying principle here can be stated as: *Simultaneously advance common interests and address competing interests.*

Dynamic and Continuous Processes

Not only are the stakeholders independent and interdependent, with common and competing interests but also these elements change over time. As a result, consortia need to be dynamic, with continuous processes for agility, improvement, and, where appropriate, disbanding. There is a large and emerging literature centered on teams and organizations that are agile and adaptive in response to environmental changes and emergent learning. We extend these points to consortia.

The organizational literature celebrates how entrepreneurial firms and even more established organizations innovate with a "minimum viable product" that can be adapted based on initial customer feedback. In 2012, Steve Blank termed this a "lean start-up" approach. We adapted this approach in a 2021 article in the *Stanford Social Innovation Review*, introducing the idea of a "Minimum Viable Consortium" that can adapt with inputs from stakeholders. This draws on the work of sociotechnical theorists, who propose that social innovations should begin with the minimum viable structure, but no less![9]

In looking across a range of sample cases of consortia, including those featured in this book, we found that the "minimum" varied considerably.

In cases, such as the Biomarkers Consortium, where regulatory agencies were involved and antitrust laws were operable, the minimum involved a formal executive committee and four steering committees. In other cases, such as the Minority Serving Cyberinfrastructure Consortium (MS-CC), the minimum was initially just a leadership committee, which later evolved to include subcommittees and a memorandum of agreement with a fiscal agent (the nonprofit supplier of infrastructure services to universities and others, Internet2). This evolution was needed as grants came in to support the work of MS-CC and as the scope of its initiatives expanded.

In Chapter 1, we introduced Takeda, a leading pharmaceutical company, which has evolved from being a member of several public-private partnerships (PPPs, a form of consortium) in 2009 to membership in approximately 100 PPPs in 2023. There is a dynamic process by which these collaborations emerge and are maintained.[10]

> The PPP collaborations Takeda participated in vary in length but on average have a duration of 3–5 years, with each focusing on a specific complex, scientific challenge. In some instances, the PPP team at Takeda identifies opportunities and brings them to the awareness of relevant internal company scientists for consideration. In other instances, scientists in the company learn of PPP opportunities that may be of interest and bring them to the PPP team for advice and guidance. The portfolio of PPP memberships is always changing, with the longest participation being more than five years. Takeda is serving in a leadership capacity for PPPs that are focusing on some of Takeda's priority issues such as educating patients regarding sharing of their own data to improve their health outcomes. The Health Outcomes Observatory (H2O) is an example of a relatively recent PPP collaboration in which Takeda led the efforts to establish a consortium. This project was launched from Europe for strengthening patient voice in health care while maintaining full control of their data. Because the portfolio is dynamic and the PPPs themselves are project-driven, the entire partnership enterprise can be agile and adaptive in ways that far exceed what one company can do.
>
> Takeda's participation in PPPs has evolved over time to where it is today. A dedicated team provides global oversight of the PPP portfolio and ensures evolving strategic alignment while initiating more PPPs to address specific scientific challenges so that their scientists can accelerate and advance the development of innovative therapies to patients.

The implications for consortia can be stated as a principle: *begin with the minimum viable consortium.*

Accomplishing Together What Can't Be Accomplished Separately

Focusing on what can be accomplished together (that can't be accomplished separately) has roots in the literature on collaboration, partnership, and related approaches. As we noted in Chapter 1, Elinor Ostrom earned a Nobel Prize in Economics for her work documenting how PPPs could collaboratively manage a common pool of resources, such as water, more effectively than either markets or regulation. This literature has been extended to include institutional arrangements where knowledge is created and managed as a common resource and mediated through digital technologies; such scholarship is instructive for understanding knowledge-rich consortia in the digital age.

The principle of accomplishing together what can't be accomplished separately points to a key rule of thumb for what should or should not be on the agenda for a consortium. The sweet spot for agenda items and issues are those that necessarily require collective input across the consortium. Items and issues that can be accomplished by the market, regulation, or independent action by individual parties may be important, but they do not require a consortium.

The principle is: *Find the sweet spot—what the consortium can do that is valuable to stakeholders, and that other institutional arrangements are not doing.*[11]

Achieving Sufficient Alignment for Action

The concept of alignment is well developed in the management literature, with a focus on the internal alignment needed among operating units of an organization (divisions, regions, etc.), the alignment needed among support functions (finance, human resources, marketing, research and development, etc.), and the alignment needed between support functions and operating units. Robert Kaplan and David Norton's work on alignment highlights the necessary tension in these organizational matrices as reflected in a "balanced scorecard."[12] They observed that key performance indicators (KPIs) are necessarily in tension with each other, with the work of managers and leaders involving the achievement of appropriate balance.

The principle of balance, including competing interests, is extended across diverse stakeholders in consortia, although they do not have to fully combine in ways that cause them to abandon their differences. Indeed, it is precisely because of their differences that they can accomplish together what they can't do separately. The key is to achieve sufficient alignment for collective action, while also accepting differences as legitimate and separate.

One lesson from the negotiation literature is that interacting parties don't only negotiate with each other but also negotiate internally so that they can speak with one voice. This dynamic is also essential for consortia.

We express it as a principle: *Internal alignment is needed for lateral alignment.*

Checks and Balances on Unitary Power

In important ways, the US Constitution stands as an fundamental challenge to the unitarist model—rejecting rule by a single monarch and enacting instead a system of checks and balances among three arms of government—legislative, executive, and judicial. Private corporations are classically seen as exemplifying a unitarist model, but they are subject to checks and balances as well. Firms operate within legal and regulatory constraints, face competition, have internal governance structures, and may face countervailing forces from labor unions, community groups, and others. Even with the many checks and balances in public and private sectors, inequities, disparities, lost opportunities, and other consequences of incomplete checks and balances continue.

Consortia represent an additional set of possible checks and balances when they seek to accomplish together what they can't do separately. Only some consortia have charters that make such arrangements clear. Later in this chapter, we illustrate key points with the case of the Biomarkers Consortium, which brings together industry, government, academe, and patient advocacy organizations to support foundational research on biologic "markers" that are relevant to cancer, inflammation and immunity, metabolic disorders, and neuroscience (particularly Alzheimer's). The three founding organizations, Pharma, NIH, and FDA, have veto power on any project, representing a formal instantiation of the check-and-balance principle. In fact, this veto power is rarely exercised, which reflects a high degree of alignment around which projects to even explore.

An Agile and Adaptive Model

We introduce here a middle-out model for change. This contrasts with the top-down and bottom-up models that were signaled in Chapters 1 and 2 (which are more fully developed in Chapter 5). As is indicated in Figure 4.1, we have departed from drawing this as steps in a process or as a cycle. Instead, it is presented as two interacting strands or threads, with aligning and advancing happening concurrently in an intertwined way. This corresponds to the notion that alignment is a continuing accomplishment. Figure 4.1 offers a visual representation of the process and dynamics associated with forming and sustaining a multistakeholder consortium.

The elements are presented in an order, though it is not a strict ordering. Aligning does have a logic that goes from "mapping stakeholders and interests" to "aligning on a shared vision of success" based on the mapping. When there is sufficient alignment on the vision (what some term "true North"),

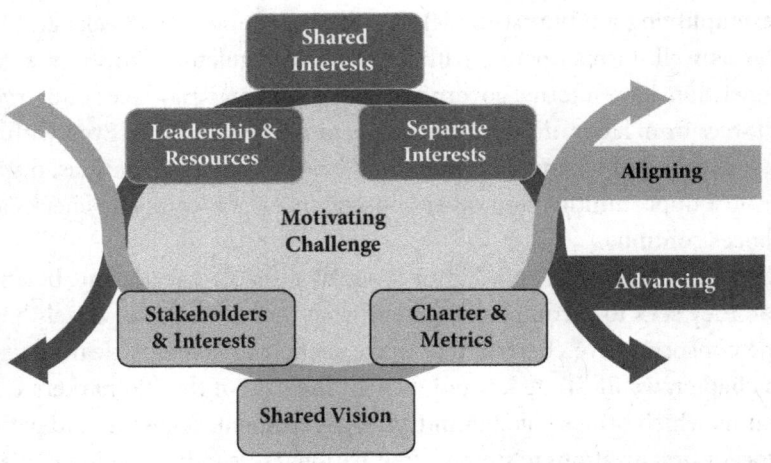

Figure 4.1 Stakeholder Alignment Model: Aligning and Advancing Stakeholders in a Consortium

it is possible to "build a charter" and, with all that in mind, "specify stakeholder value" in the form of distinct value propositions for each stakeholder on which delivery can now be promised.

Advancing also has a logic that goes from "ensuring resources and leadership" to "advance shared interests." Since this is a mixed-motive situation, all parties also need to "appreciate separate interests" and all need to "track progress and impacts," which involves both throughput measures and outcome measures.

These steps are presented as two interacting strands, with an intentional correspondence among items in parallel with each other on opposite sides.[13] There will likely be emergent leaders and potential resources identified when you map stakeholders and interests. Similarly, agreeing on a shared vision serves to guide the "advancing" of shared interests. The charter plays a key role in appreciating and addressing separate and even competing interests. Finally, it is against the stakeholder value propositions that progress and impacts can be tracked—a measure of success is the degree to which the value propositions are being met. Although these horizontal connections have a strong logic, it is not rigid—any of the elements can connect with others on the aligning side or on the advancing side.

The elements repeat to the left and right of the visualization. This indicates that the entire process corresponds to different phases in the life of a consortium, from launch to sustainment to dissolution. During sustainment there can be multiple phases as well, with changes in the mix of stakeholders and interests, changes in the true North vision, changes in the governing charter, and changes in the value propositions with successive rounds of alignment and realignment. Similarly, there will be changes in leadership and resources, changes in the shared interests advanced, and separate interests that need to be appreciated as well as changes in the way that progress and results are tracked.

Illustrating the Elements of the Model with the Biomarkers Consortium

The first element of the model involves specifying stakeholders and identifying interests. Specifying stakeholders is invariably an instructive process—certain stakeholders are quickly identified and then more and more emerge with dialogue. For example, when the Biomarkers

Consortium was being formed to carve out a precompetitive space to identify and qualify biomarkers that could inform drug development, the initial stakeholders in the founding conversation were large pharmaceutical firms (in the form of the Pharma trade association), smaller biotech firms (in form of the Bio trade association), the US Food and Drug Administration (FDA), the National Institutes of Health (NIH), some leading university researchers, and some leading patient advocacy organizations. The Foundation for NIH (FNIH) played a key convening role since it could accept funds to support projects, while the NIH could not do so. In each category, however, there were many entities not in the room but with an interest in what was being contemplated. In that sense, the representatives in each category had a considerable internal alignment challenge if they were to speak on behalf of all the stakeholders in that category. Moreover, the array of stakeholders is dynamic. For example, during the COVID-19 pandemic, many of the same stakeholders joined together in Accelerating COVID-19 Therapeutic Interventions and Vaccines (ACTIV).

Identifying interests is a highly generative process. Parties can quickly identify a number of interests that are "at stake" on a given issue or challenge. What then emerges is an ever-expanding and dynamic array of interests. With the Biomarkers Consortium, there was a high degree of alignment around the importance of sharing information among consortium members on the discovery and qualification of biomarkers, but many of the members had to be reminded that an open, precompetitive approach meant that nonmembers would also have access to the information. Further, as we have noted, the discovery and qualification of biomarkers is relatively easily defined as precompetitive for pharma, but some projects are in a competitive space for biotech firms. If these firms want to keep certain information as proprietary, they need to recuse themselves from the open science work done through the consortium. To date, there have been over 40 projects completed by the consortium, with a different mix of parties in each case.[14]

These distinctions are all about the complex mix of interests that are "at stake" for the consortium. Both specifying stakeholders and identifying interests are presented in more detail in Chapter 6—this overview is just designed to illustrate the first steps in the model.

The second set of elements of the model involves forging a shared vision, drafting a charter, and specifying stakeholder value propositions.[15] The emphasis in the shared vision is on "shared." It is not enough for a single leader to provide a compelling vision of what is possible. There is an interactive process by which the potential elements of a vision are discussed, adjusted, and further socialized until the emerging concept is broadly shared among the stakeholders. In this process it is often as important to articulate what is not shared in addition to what is shared. For the Biomarkers Consortium, this shared vision is expressed in the description, vision, and mission statements from its 2019 Membership Manual:

> The Biomarkers Consortium is a public-private biomedical research partnership managed by the Foundation for the National Institutes of Health (FNIH) that endeavors to discover, develop, and seek regulatory utilization (FDA Qualification) for drug development tools (e.g. biological markers or biomarkers) to support new drug development, preventive medicine, and medical diagnostics.
> *Vision*
> Improving health through meaningful measurements.
> *Mission*
> To create and lead cross-sector efforts that validate and qualify biomarkers and other drug development tools to accelerate better decision making for the development of new therapeutics and health technologies.
>
> The Biomarkers Consortium is helping facilitate, catalyze and support a new era of precision medicine, with more highly predictive drug development tools that have an impact during a patient's illness or lifespan. Its goal is to combine the forces of the public and private sectors to accelerate the development of biomarker-based technologies, medicines, and therapies for the prevention, early detection, diagnosis, and treatment of disease.

The shared vision may center on a mission statement, a success vision, or other unifying goal or objective. It must be broad enough to be inclusive of all relevant stakeholders, while being focused enough to give direction to the consortium activities.

Chartering is a process, not just the resulting document. Sometimes encompassing bylaws, terms of reference, principles, expectations, and other key information, the charter establishes the rules of the road for advancing common interests, navigating competing interests, and ensuring effective operations. Often the chartering process reveals additional interests that need discussion. For example, during the chartering process for the Biomarkers Consortium the industry members indicated the need to specify antitrust language. For the government stakeholders this was not part of their thinking, so they consulted with the General Counsel's Office in the Department of Commerce and learned that all meetings had to have a roster of attendees, a specified agenda, and a clear prohibition on discussions involving pricing or other potentially anticompetitive practices. Without such provisions, industry representatives faced the risk of violating antitrust policies. The chartering process revealed this interest on the part of certain stakeholders, not only helping to ensure appropriate processes and procedures but also educating government representatives on the boundary space within which a precompetitive consortium could operate. Further, this illustrates a mix of common and competing interests that had to be addressed for collaboration to go forward.

One interesting question that emerges during chartering is who has the legitimacy to draft a charter before a charter exists. Often, the organizations destined to be charter members can't formally join without seeing the charter, so the drafting must be done by individuals representing themselves rather than as organizational members and the charter has to be provisional until approved. In many ways, the ability to work together individually in the drafting is a formative process in the launch of a consortium—building trust among those involved. This is why we think of chartering as a process (a verb) not just a product (a noun).

New entrepreneurial enterprises are typically coached to identify their customer, specify the value proposition for the customer, and deliver on that value proposition—ideally what you do well that the customer wants, and that others are not doing. Sometimes, they may also be coached to think about the interests of other stakeholders such as employees, suppliers, regulators, and shareholders, but it is rarely developed as a full value proposition. For an entrepreneurial business, a value proposition is just a requirement to address in order to meet the needs of customers. This contrasts with consortia who need to think explicitly about multiple value propositions associated with the interests of key categories of stakeholders. Thus, for the Biomarkers Consortium the value proposition for industry centered on having the FDA in discussions about biomarkers well in advance of regulatory review so as to accelerate later reviews. For the FDA the value proposition was similar, but not identical—they wanted to avoid regulatory errors and ensure appropriate regulatory review processes with an early introduction to the science behind what was in development. For the FNIH, it was more about being in a convening role, while the NIH wanted to advance the frontiers of science with university researchers. The patient advocacy organizations wanted to see effective therapies reach patients. These value propositions were overlapping, but not identical. The challenge for the consortium is to address all the value propositions, which is a multidimensional optimization challenge. Therefore, we emphasize that beginning with the value propositions is a key first step in this process. Forging a shared vision, drafting a charter, and specifying stakeholder value propositions are presented in more detail in Chapter 7.

The third set of elements of the model involves ensuring resources and leadership, acting separately and collectively, and tracking progress and delivering results. The leadership of a consortium is different at founding than in later years. This was the case in the Biomarkers Consortium, where the early leadership was visionary around what was possible, while the next generation of leaders was more focused on establishing and sustaining effective operations.

> In addition to individual leaders, the FNIH has an important institutional leadership role to hold all parties accountable. David Wholley, who now serves as executive vice-president and chief strategy and business development officer for the FNIH and previously served as executive director of the Biomarkers Consortium, observes:
> This reflects the reality that members of the consortium all have their "day jobs" and so the FNIH is in the role of ensuring accountability when one party or another fails to deliver on a commitment. This could be a vendor delivering a required set of samples to a lab or a researcher performing a critical analysis, or some other commitment. Without persistent mechanisms for accountability a consortium risks drift in its mission and operations.[16]

The steady state project leadership provided by FNIH is illustrative of the "strong backbone" element of the collective impact model discussed in Chapter 1.

Members of consortia are both independent and interdependent. As a result, members act separately as well as jointly. In the case of the Biomarkers

Consortium, commercial members compete in the marketplace even as they collaborate on precompetitive research and discovery.

Tracking progress happens at many levels. In the Biomarkers Consortium, progress is measured around individual projects, of which there were over two dozen in the first decade and more since. Progress is also measured overall in the operations of four steering committees overseeing the various projects. Finally, progress is measured at the level of the consortium as a whole, as reflected in continued membership and engagement of the consortium members.

Acting separately and collectively, tracking progress, and delivering results are all presented in more detail in Chapter 8.

The model is presented as a continuing set of processes, because alignment, as we have noted, is a continuing accomplishment. This builds on the Deming continuous improvement Plan, Do, Check, Act (PDCA) cycle presented in Chapter 5, with the difference being that the continuous improvement is not within a given organization but across diverse stakeholders in a shared context, sector, or ecosystem.

Stakeholder alignment needs to be understood as a continuing accomplishment, since both the stakeholders and the interests change over time, as do leaders, resources, and even the vision. The Arctic Council presents a powerful example. When it was formed in 1996, there was a broad consensus among the Arctic States (Canada, Denmark, Finland, Norway, Iceland, Russia, Sweden, and the United States), Indigenous Peoples, and the inhabitants of the region around enhancing cooperation, coordination, and interaction on common Arctic issues. Currently, geopolitical tensions are intervening and Russia is seeking to pull China and India (an observer member) into a separate consortium. Maintaining alignment requires a deep understanding of the interests that make continued engagement in the consortium, and the interests that could pull it apart.

Structural Guidance

As has been shown in the previous section, the landscapes or ecosystems within which consortia operate can vary considerably. We focus here on two key features, which are the array of different types of stakeholders and the array of different types of issues that are "at stake." This can be thought of as a two-by-two space, as illustrated in Figure 4.2, with a range from few to many types of stakeholders on one dimension and few to many issues that are "at stake" on the other.

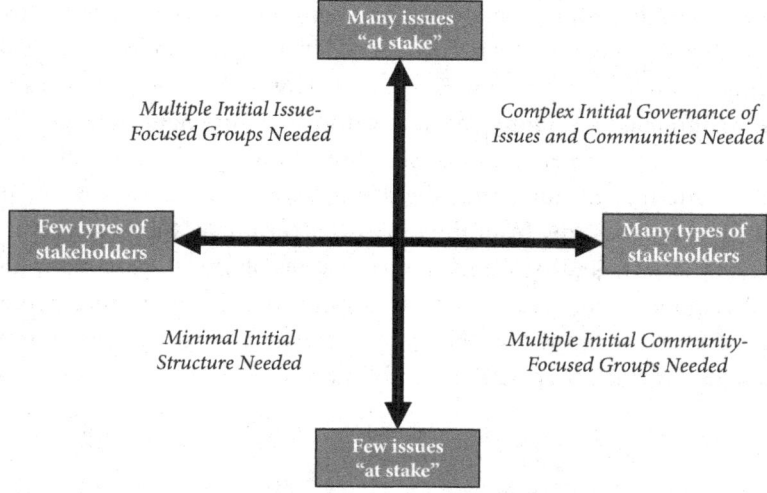

Figure 4.2 A Landscape of Stakeholders and Interests

As Figure 4.2 illustrates, some types of stakeholders and some issues "at stake" (bottom left quadrant) can be advanced with minimal initial structure—often just one steering committee. The MS-CC, which we use as an example in Part II of this book began in this quadrant with a single weekly meeting of whoever showed up at noon on Thursdays. At the outset the set of stakeholders was not overly complex—historically Black colleges and universities (HBCUs) and tribal colleges and universities (TCUs), each of which had administrative leaders, cyberinfrastructure professionals, faculty, students, and nearby communities. Similarly, the set of interests was not overly complex, including issues of cybersecurity, research data management, digital connectivity, and other matters. In time, a more formal structure has been instituted, with officers, a governing committee, and a membership committee, reflecting the addition of NSF funding for various "proof-of-concept" initiatives. In time, as the cyberinfrastructure becomes associated with an array of research and educational initiatives, MS-CC will move out of this quadrant to reflect an expanding array of stakeholder types and an expanding array of interests that are at stake.

When there are more issues (top left quadrant), then it is often the case that issue-focused subgroups are needed to hold forums for those with subject-matter expertise or strongly held views on a given issue. Our primary example in this chapter, the Biomarkers Consortium, is in this quadrant and has four separate steering committees, each of which oversees multiple projects that have dedicated subgroups of individuals. These steering committees reflect the Biomarkers Consortium priorities: cancer, inflammation and immunity, metabolic disorders, and neuroscience.

When there are many types of stakeholders with a focus on just a few issues (bottom right quadrant), the distinct communities of practice may need their own forums from the outset. For example, the Research Data Alliance (RDA) has a singular focus on research data, yet it spans many fields and disciplines. From the outset, its organizational architecture contemplated a diverse array of working groups, interest groups, and communities of practice,[17] which they outlined as follows:

> Working Groups (WG)
> WGs are short-term (18 months) and come together to develop and implement data infrastructure, which could be tools, policy, practices and products that are adopted and used by projects, organizations, and communities. Embedded within these groups are individuals who will use the infrastructure and help in making it broadly available to the public. Membership is open to the public, by creating an account on their website. Any RDA member can join or initiate a WG.
>
> Interest Groups (IG)
> IGs are open-ended in terms of longevity. They focus on solving a specific data sharing problem and identifying what kind of infrastructure needs to be built. These groups identify specific pieces of work and can start up a WG to tackle those projects. Any RDA member can join or initiate an IG.
>
> Communities of Practice (CoP)
> CoPs investigate, discuss, and provide knowledge and skills within a specific discipline and/or research domain. These groups are committed to directly or indirectly enabling data sharing, exchange, and/or interoperability by serving as THE coordination focal point for RDA in specific disciplines/research domains.[18]

Finally, when there are many types of stakeholders and many issues "at stake" (top right quadrant), a more complex structure with multiple forums focused on issues and communities is needed.

When the NSF launched the EarthCube initiative to better understand the Earth as a system, it quickly became apparent that there could not be a single cyberinfrastructure supporting the efforts. First, there were over two-dozen distinct fields and disciplines (from atmospheric modeling to coral reef systems, to critical zones, to deep sea floor dynamics, to experimental stratigraphy, to hydrology, to paleogeoscience, to sedimentary geology, to tectonics, and many others). Each one had unique data and system challenges, which led to an array of domain-specific workshops. Second, there were specific generational issues faced by early career geoscientists, which led to an early career workshop. Third, there were institutional and sustainability challenges faced by data repositories, which led to the formation of the Council of Data Facilities. Fourth, there were individual research grants, each with principal investigators (PIs), which led to PI workshops. Fifth, as tools and methods resulted from the research, it was necessary to ensure web availability and support for distribution and use of the tools. Finally, as an overall research initiative, there was a need to track, codify, and report on both the scientific merits and broader impacts of the work.

The role of a central office in helping to develop and sustain the EarthCube community was essential. The office served as the "glue" that brought cohesion to the initiative in a number of ways. Over its three incarnations, it helped define best practices, develop shared technical components, provide crucial engagement with early career researchers through travel grants and leadership opportunities, and promote and support important aspects of EarthCube's social fabric (such as standing committees, annual meetings, and visibility at domain-specific forums). Administering this as a single consortium was challenging, and required tailoring the office to the evolving needs of EarthCube. This included shifts in the support team including periods with more of a focus on facilitating roles, directing roles, and assessment roles.

The implications of the two-by-two framework in Figure 4.2 is that the structure and operation of a consortium builds on the array of stakeholders and the array of interests that are at stake. More structure is needed as the complexity increases or as the desired impact increases. Consider, for example, the journey of community health workers (CHWs) to professionalize their occupation:

Community health workers (CHWs) serve as liaisons between the community and social/health systems to facilitate access to care and to improve service quality. Many come from the communities they serve, often operating in multiple languages and addressing complex social determinants of health. Beginning in the 1960s, large-scale CHW programs were implemented globally to improve health conditions—primarily in the global South.[19] In the United States, federal policies in the mid-1960s promoted opportunities for CHWs to increase access to care for underserved communities. By the 1970s, CHWs organized themselves strategically by developing consortia across different states and aligning themselves with other professionals, researchers, community-based leaders, and policymakers.[20] One organizer described the initial impetus for getting organized to build mutual support for their work:

> The impetus was that a number of us across state-funded programs understood that CHWs weren't getting adequately supported, supervised, paid, all of those things, and that we needed to develop some department-wide policies. We said, "Are you an outreach worker, an outreach educator, a community health liaison? Come to this big room down here at the end of the hallway and let's talk about training and let's talk about supervision and let's talk about policy and let's talk about all of that stuff." This basically was the foundation of a [professional association] and we formed it out of the 75 CHWs [who] came to that meeting and out of that, a steering committee was formed.[21]

This led to a more formal organization as a section of the American Public Health Association (APHA). The section was initially called the New Professionals Special Primary Interest Group and later changed to the Community Health Worker section in 2009 based on an APHA policy resolution that recognized the contributions of CHWs in public health.[22] CHWs strategically aligned themselves with multiple stakeholders for their collective self-determination and control, first within states and later nationally by coming together through their own set of conferences (called the Unity conferences). A 2007 review of CHW training and certification in the United States analyzed 17 states that had "training and/or certification programs for 'lay health workers.'"[23] There is a projected 12% employment growth for CHWs from 2021–2031.[24]

Community health workers decided not to affiliate with labor unions because, as one CHW leader observed, unions were too constrictive and did not focus on the unique identity and role of CHWs in their communities:

> CHW's were, at the time feeling a need for there to be an organization that they could lead and have their voice at the forefront of, and joining a union would be too constrictive. It's come up over the years, but the idea really was to create an organization that would say to the world, "We're a profession." That is, we're not a tack on . . . we're all community health workers, we have a definition, that we fit, and then to be able to advocate for the workforce. That was the idea, to advocate for better support, supervision, pay, all of that stuff; people resisted the idea of unionizing at the time.[25]

Community health workers didn't want to form a union, and they did want a professional association that was highly inclusive. As one participant described, "CHWs include promotoras, peers, community health representatives, aunties, and dozens of other work and identity titles."[26]

From 2006 to 2009, CHWs started to build a national association for CHWs by convening representatives across 13 states to form the American Association of Community Health Workers (AACHW). Leaders focused their efforts on the self-determination of community health workers and adopted the Swahili word for self-determination, "Kujichagulia," to highlight the importance of having community health workers chart their own path as a workforce.[27] They developed a formal structure by electing a 15-member steering committee and organized sub-committees to build formal bylaws and policies. During this time, they also received funding from a foundation to support infrastructure development. However, this early attempt to form a national association disbanded, largely due to the voluntary nature of organizing.[28] Since then, CHWs created a new national association (in April 2019), the National Association for Community Health Workers (NACHW), which has been successful in establishing CHWs as a national profession.[29]

This case highlights the organizing work of CHWs, initially through a consortia arrangement, centered on their professional identity and the importance of self-determination. This organizing work led to state-level professional associations and now a national professional association. Importantly, this was an approach to professionalization that did not include operating as a union. It was also an inclusive approach that welcomed all workers.

There is a point when the array of stakeholders and array of interests exceeds what can be accomplished by a single consortium. This can lead to consortia of consortia and other innovative institutional arrangements that maintain agility while still enabling needed collective action. Alternatively, a consortium can make strategic choices to focus on fewer issues or a narrower mix of stakeholders, requiring less structure to be sustained.

Also relevant is the level of funding, with higher levels of funding needing more structure. Similarly, a broader geographic scope may require regional forums or other structural arrangements that are unnecessary when the scope is narrower. Note that the two-by-two framework is only the beginning of providing ways to map structural choices.

Summing Up

Globally and locally, we face challenges that exceed the scale and scope of any one organization. This calls for consortia—locally and globally—so that the skills, interests, and capabilities of multiple stakeholders can achieve collective impacts. The accelerating pace of technological change and the dynamic nature of the challenges add further urgency to the need for consortia.

Five principles have been introduced in this chapter, which are guideposts in the launch and sustainment of consortia:

- Independence and Interdependence
  - *Principle*: Independence informs interdependence while interdependence tempers independence.
- Common and Competing Interests
  - *Principle*: Simultaneously advance common interests and address competing interests.
- Dynamic and Continuous Processes
  - *Principle*: Begin with the minimum viable consortium
- Accomplishing together what can't be accomplished separately
  - *Principle*: Find the sweet spot—what the consortium can do, that is valuable to stakeholders, and that other institutional arrangements are not (and can't be) doing.
- Achieving sufficient alignment for action
  - *Principle*: Internal alignment is needed for lateral alignment.

Building on these five principles, a model for agile and adaptive consortia is presented as two interacting parallel processes that intertwine as they align and advance. Interests figure both in the aligning and the advancing—first to have situational awareness for the alligning and then to build on common interests and address compteting interests for the advancing.

Since there is variation in the number of stakeholder types and the array of interests that are at stake, the structure and operation of a consortium will vary accordingly—with more complexity requiring more structure, up to a point (after which agility is compromised). Ultimately this implies that we are heading into a period in which ecosystems or domains with many interacting consortia evolve in agile and adaptive ways. One major theme presented here is that consortia are better able to bring different stakeholder voices to the table than more hierarchical institutional arrangements. Maintaining a broad mix of stakeholder voices is crucial to sustaining these consortia.

Notes

1. As noted in Chapter 1, there are requirements in the European Union for the registration of associations, particularly those working on fundamental rights: nongovernmental organizations; trade unions; employers' organizations; relevant social and professional organizations; churches; religious, philosophical, and nonconfessional organizations; universities; and other qualified experts of European and international bodies and organizations. See "How to Register," European Union Agency for Fundamental Rights, accessed June 7, 2023, http://fra.europa.eu/en/cooperation/civil-society/how-to-register.
2. See David Farnham, "Beatrice and Sidney Webb and the Intellectual Origins of British Industrial Relations," *Employee Relations* 30, no. 5 (2008): pp. 534–553.
3. See Patricia M. Shields, Maurice Hamington, and Joseph Soeters, eds., *The Oxford Handbook of Jane Addams* (Oxford: Oxford University Press, 2022), https://doi.org/10.1093/oxfordhb/9780197544518.001.0001.
4. Independence and interdependence are examples of the complexity of human behavior from the collaboration perspective, but there are two additional orientations that can affect a person or group of persons: dependence and counterdependence. Dependence manifests itself in seeking the approval of others and deferring decisions and opinions to others. See Stephen R. Covey, *The 7 Habits of Highly Effective People: Restoring the Character Ethic* (New York: Free Press, 2004). Counterdependence is a flight from intimacy and shows itself as difficulty being close, needing to be right, self-centeredness, refusal to ask for help, and expecting perfection. See Barry K. Weinhold and Janae B. Weinhold, *Breaking Free of the Co-Dependency Trap* (Novato, CA: New World Library, 1989). In a consortium, either in its formative or mature stages, independence contributes to the creative tension of discovering differences and courses of action that can benefit the whole. Dependent behavior tends to sap group energy and fails to add to the discovery of options. Counterdependency creates problematic relationships and inhibits coalescing around decisions in the best interest of the whole.
5. See Henry C. Metcalf and L. Urwick, eds., *Dynamic Administration: The Collected Papers of Mary Parker Follett* (New York: Routledge, 2003), https://doi.org/10.4324/9780203486214.
6. See Richard Walton and Robert McKersie, *A Behavioral Theory of Labor Negotiations* (New York: McGraw Hill, 1965).

7. See David Lax and James Sebenius, *3-D Negotiation: Powerful Tools to Change the Game in Your Most Important Deals* (Boston: Harvard Business School Press, 2006).
8. This approach was popularized in *Getting to YES!* by Roger Fisher and William Ury (New York: Houghton Mifflin, 1981).
9. Joel Cutcher-Gershenfeld, interview with Eric Trist, 1981.
10. Again, we thank Akiko Otani and Ali Farid for their insights as we developed this vignette. Of course, the responsibility for the text is entirely ours as coauthors.
11. For more on the sweet spot for commercial organizations, see David J. Collis and Michael G. Rukstad, "Can You Say What Your Strategy Is?," Harvard Business School Case: HBS R0804E.
12. See Robert S. Kaplan and David Norton, *Alignment: Using the Balanced Scorecard to Create Corporate Synergies* (Boston: Harvard Business School Press, 2006).
13. We first attempted to draw the visualization as a double helix, with right and left side, joined by various bonds. Ultimately, the metaphor proved incomplete, but the notion that aligning and advancing are separate strands that happen in parallel and that are both needed to create something new still holds.
14. A summary of the projects with the associated partners is listed on the consortium website. See "Biomarkers Consortium: Programs," accessed June 8, 2023, https://fnih.org/our-programs/biomarkers-consortium/programs.
15. Retrieved from: https://fnih.org/wp-content/uploads/2023/05/Biomarkers-Consortium-Membership-Manual-May-2019.pdf.
16. Correspondence with David Wholley, July 14, 2023.
17. For a history of the first five years of RDA, see https://www.rd-alliance.org/sites/default/files/attachment/RDA%20RETROSPECTIVE%20FINAL%20-%20HDSR.pdf. For further information, see Francine Berman and Mercè Crosas, "The Research Data Alliance: Benefits and Challenges of Building a Community Organization." *Harvard Data Science Review* 2, no. 1 (2020), https://doi.org/10.1162/99608f92.5e126552.
18. For more information on the array of organizational architectures at the Research Data Alliance, see "RDA Groups," Research Data Alliance, accessed June 8, 2023, https://www.rd-alliance.org/groups.
19. D. Cepiku and F. Giordano, "Co-Production in Developing Countries: Insights from the Community Health Workers Experience," *Public Management Review* 16, no. 3 (2014): pp. 317–340, https://doi.org/10.1080/14719037.2013.822535.
20. This case draws on Yaminette Diaz-Linhart, "It May Not Be Rainbows and Sunshine Every Day, but I Know I Made a Difference: Voice as a Resource for Well-Being at Work," Doctoral Dissertation, Brandeis University, The Heller School for Social Policy and Management, 2022.
21. Ibid.
22. American Public Health Association, "Who We Are: APHA CHW Section History" (2021), https://www.apha.org/APHA-Communities/Member-Sections/Community-Health-Workers/Who-We-Are.
23. See B.A. Kash, M.L. May, and M. Tai-Seale, "Community Health Worker Training and Certification Programs in the United States: Findings from a National Survey," *Health Policy* 80, no. 1 (2007); pp. 32–42, https://doi.org/10.1016/j.healthpol.2006.02.010.
24. See US Bureau of Labor Statistics, "Occupational Outlook Handbook: Health Education Specialists and Community Health Workers," accessed January 27, 2022, https://www.bls.gov/ooh/community-and-social-service/health-educators.htm#tab-6.
25. Diaz-Linhart, "It May Not Be Rainbows."
26. Diaz-Linhart, "It May Not Be Rainbows."
27. Diaz-Linhart, "It May Not Be Rainbows."
28. See G.W. Wilkinson, A. Wennerstrom, N. Cottoms, K. Sutkowi, and C.H. Rush. "Uniting the Workforce: Building Capacity for a National Association of Community Health Workers," in *Promoting the Health of the Community: Community Health Workers Describing Their Roles, Competencies, and Practice*, edited by J.A.S. John, S.L. M.-Johnson, and W.D. Hernandez-Gordon, Doctoral Dissertation, Springer International Publishing, 2021, pp. 393–408.
29. See National Association of Community Health Workers, "Who We Are" (2022), https://nachw.org/about/.

PART II
ALIGNING STAKEHOLDERS

Chapter 5
Managing and Engaging (But Not Aligning) Stakeholders

> Liberia's deputy director general for the National Public Health Institute, Dr. Mosoka Fallahq, was facing a rising death toll during the 2014 Ebola outbreak. International stakeholders, such as the World Health Organization (WHO), along with local stakeholders, such as Liberia's national health service, each stepped forward to help, but each was acting independently. Moreover, the WHO and other global nongovernmental organizations too often discounted the knowledge and expertise of local healthcare professionals. The death toll continued to rise.
>
> Finally, in desperation, Dr. Fallahq commandeered a large arena, with separate tables set up for each of the different stakeholder entities. Co-located this way, they began to share information. One entity might be involved in clearing jungle roads that another needed for access to people in a remote location, and so on. As the coordination and collaboration increased, the death toll began to fall.[1]

This story illustrates how a diverse set of stakeholders can come together to deal with a complex problem. They needed to be managed and engaged in new ways. In this case, the effort was led by a central organization—the National Public Health Institute of Liberia, which both managed and engaged local and international stakeholders in a crisis, insisting that they talk to each other. Ultimately, some alignment was achieved, but this was not an ongoing consortium. It primarily illustrates stakeholder management and stakeholder engagement, which are distinct from stakeholder alignment. In this chapter, we focus on what stakeholder alignment is *not* in order to set the stage for what it *is*. Table 5.1 summarizes these three processes, stakeholder management and stakeholder engagement, outlined here, and stakeholder alignment, outlined in detail previously in Chapter 4 and in later chapters.

The Consortia Century. The Stakeholder Alignment Collaborative: Joel Cutcher-Gershenfeld et al., Oxford University Press. © Oxford University Press (2025). DOI: 10.1093/oso/9780197761649.003.0006

Table 5.1 Contrasting Stakeholder Management, Engagement, and Alignment

Stakeholder Management	Top-down (directive) initiatives led by one party, intended to mitigate risk.
Stakeholder Engagement	Top-down and bottom-up (directive and inclusive) initiatives led by one party, intended to enhance value.
Stakeholder Alignment	Lateral (facilitated) stakeholder interactions led by many parties to advance common interests and address competing interests.

Stakeholder management and stakeholder engagement are not new—they are the central focus of project management, public relations, government relations, and additional disciplines focused on how organizations manage and engage others in their external environment.[2] When the term "stakeholder management" is used, the focus is generally on managing stakeholders who are acting in ways that one party sees as threatening progress or in need of management oversight.[3] When the term "stakeholder engagement" is used, the focus is generally on inviting input by stakeholders who are seen by the inviting party as potentially contributing to progress and in need of inclusion to some degree.[4] Both approaches operate from the perspective of one group or organization looking out at an array of stakeholders—they are unitary approaches. Sometimes the term "actor mapping" is used to cover both stakeholder management and stakeholder engagement, still from the perspective of one party looking out at an array of stakeholders.

Both stakeholder engagement and stakeholder management are important, yet both are incomplete for addressing the challenges of the 21st century. Instead, we are advancing the concept of stakeholder alignment, a pluralist approach that takes the perspectives of many stakeholders. However, understanding the existing management and engagement approaches is important in order to contrast them with stakeholder alignment and because in some situations all three processes will happen at the same time.

Stakeholder Management

A vast array of publications, training seminars, and expert consultants focus on what is termed "stakeholder management." Stakeholder management theory has its roots in corporate governance research of the 1960s and 1970s, when management scholars realized that firms should expand beyond satisfying the narrow, financial self-interest of shareholders to also address employees, customers, suppliers, and society, among other stakeholders.[5] Stakeholder management approaches focus both on addressing ethical concerns of various stakeholders and on coordinating around the risks associated with conflicting interests—conflicts that must be managed. Essentially, stakeholder management maintains a view from one party's perspective looking out—a unitary approach. Business ethics scholar Julia Roloff characterizes this approach as being when a "corporation's managers apply stakeholder management for analyzing its environment, communicating with stakeholder groups and initiating collaboration, if desirable."[6]

We define stakeholder management as one party's systematic efforts to identify and influence or motivate others whose views and actions pose a risk for that party's initiatives and operations. This unitary approach to stakeholder management is perhaps most advanced in the world of project management. Opposition and even outrage over a project poses a risk to progress. A leading consultant on stakeholder management, Peter Sandman, motivates the approach with a formula: Risk = Hazard + Outrage.[7] In this context, the management of stakeholders depends on risk communication that addresses hazards and tempers outrage.

Effective practitioners of stakeholder management do generally see conflicting stakeholder interests as legitimate and worthy of management resources and constructive engagement. However, there is always an underlying agenda being advanced. A key method employed in stakeholder management involves the following steps:

1. Identification of key stakeholders
2. Classification of stakeholders along two dimensions: support and influence
3. Placement of stakeholders in a grid (see below) to envision the landscape
4. Setting targets for shifting the support of stakeholders (typically, moving opposition to neutral for some and moving neutral to high support for others)
5. Implementing action plans to shift the support as planned

Figure 5.1 shows a grid that can visually represent the landscape of stakeholders to be managed, in which "low" support is commonly defined as including opposition:

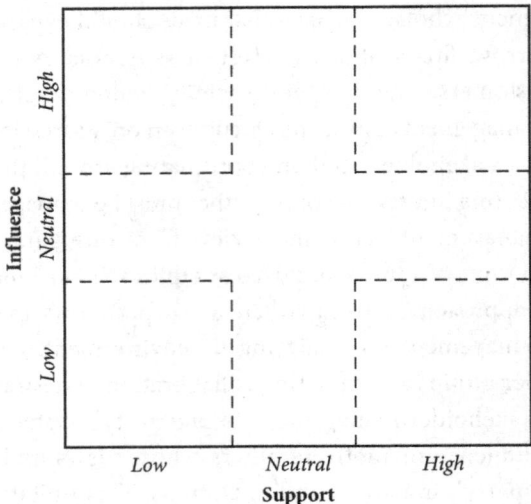

Figure 5.1 Sample stakeholder Management Grid with Support and Influence

The planning associated with the perceived change needed might involve rating each stakeholder in the current state on a five-point scale: 1 = strong opposition; 2 = moderate opposition; 3 = neutral; 4 = moderate support; and 5 = strong support. Then, a target state for each would be rated on the same scale. In setting the targets, the relative influence of the stakeholders (high, medium, and low) is taken into account. Thus, a highly influential stakeholder rated as a "1" might be targeted to shift to a "3" or a "4," while a less influential stakeholder also rated as a "1" might only be targeted to shift to a "2" or a "3."

Top-down models of change are typically employed for stakeholder management in order to make the desired change. These models typically involve fostering a sense of urgency, forming a winning coalition, and other instrumental moves. Note that "top-down" doesn't have to come just from top management in an organization. Any individual or group with sufficient authority and responsibility to initiate and lead change can apply a top-down approach, such as a middle manager or recognized advocate for a given issue. We refer to this as a unitary approach, since it is driven by the perspective of the party that is leading the change. The benchmark model in this respect is John Kotter's model for "leading change."[8] A visual representation of the Kotter model is shown in Figure 5.2.[9]

MANAGING AND ENGAGING STAKEHOLDERS   97

Figure 5.2 Kotter Model for Leading Change

At the top of the model, there is an acting party who is initiating the work, beginning with creating a sense of urgency. Note that the model was initially presented in 2012 as a single eight-step process and has now evolved to be presented as a cycle, which signals awareness that leading change is an ongoing process. In this model, the agenda of the acting party is presented as legitimate and even beneficial—worthy of being advanced or necessary to happen. The model doesn't anticipate what can be intensive debate and needed alignment around the merits of what is being advanced, just guidance for those leading change once the individual or group with authority have come to an agreement and now must manage and engage relevant stakeholders.

There is a large literature on what is termed "situational leadership,"[10] which highlights leader and follower situations requiring various combinations of delegating, supporting, coaching, and directing. Stakeholder management draws heavily on directive forms of leadership, with some coaching and supporting.

While stakeholder management approaches anticipate and seek to get ahead of potential opposition, there can be concurrent bottom-up change initiatives that crystallize in response—either in support or opposition. If bottom-up responses to stakeholder management are not contained, there is the risk of escalating conflict or a failed initiative. For example, the US Keystone XL Pipeline was a major infrastructure project in which the top-down change management plan was not sufficient to overcome partisan resistance and public opposition. Infrastructure projects are often at risk when the parties in power change, and the risk is heightened when there are vocal protests (consistent with "outrage" in Sandman's formula). A robust stakeholder management plan anticipates and finds effective ways to address these forms of resistance. Typically, the goal is not to turn opposition into support, but rather to neutralize outright resistance.

There will be times where a consortium is leading change in ways that will involve elements of stakeholder management and the associated models for change. Internal alignment within each party (discussed more fully in Chapter 4) will certainly depend on approaches such as the leading change model. While the classification of stakeholders based on influence and support, and the associated top-down methods, can be useful for consortia, caution is urged if they are implemented in a way that comes across as unitary rather than pluralistic. For example, the "guiding coalition" in the Kotter model will only have legitimacy in the consortia context if relevant stakeholders and their interests are represented. It can't just be seen as performative, superficial, or advancing one stakeholder's agenda at the expense of others. In this way, mapping the stakeholders and interests are essential elements in a change process that involves a consortium.

Stakeholder Engagement

Like stakeholder management, a vast array of publications, training seminars, and expert consultants focus on what is termed "stakeholder engagement." These approaches focus primarily on the importance and value of engaging diverse stakeholders—typically through discourse—to identify and pursue common interests.[11]

We define stakeholder engagement as one party's systematic efforts to identify and influence or control others whose views and actions could provide a potential benefit for that party's initiatives and operations. This approach to stakeholders is advanced in public policy arenas where public comment periods, town halls, community forums, focus groups, and other forms of engagement are leading practices. In organizations, stakeholder engagement is often treated as a proxy for corporate social responsibility and ethical management. Indeed, these forms of stakeholder engagement are often required by law. However, stakeholder engagement can also simply further an organization's self-interest and does not necessarily have moral or ethical implications.[12]

Effective practitioners of stakeholder engagement see outreach to stakeholders as likely to generate new insights and point to needed adjustments in what has been planned, but there is always an underlying agenda being advanced. The same five-step process outlined in stakeholder management and the associated grid can be employed for stakeholder engagement. Again, stakeholders in the current state would be rated on a five-point scale: 1 = strong opposition; 2 = moderate opposition; 3 = neutral; 4 = moderate support; and 5 = strong support. Then a target state for each would be rated on the same scale. In setting the targets, the relative influence of the stakeholders (high, medium, and low) is taken into account. Here the example might be that of a highly influential stakeholder rated as a "3" who might be targeted to shift to a "4" or a "5," while a less influential stakeholder also rated as a "3" might only be targeted to leave at "3" or shift to a "4."

Stakeholder engagement generally involves a mix of top-down and bottom-up change models. The top-down aspects relate, as noted above, to the importance of creating a sense of urgency, building a winning coalition, and other aspects of leading change. Central to stakeholder engagement is one party initiating the engagement because the voices of key stakeholders are valued. In healthcare, a leading example of this involves providing patient voice in research.

> Stakeholder engagement is a central element of the Patient Centered Outcomes Research Institute (PCORI), which is "an independent, nonprofit research organization that seeks to empower patients and others with actionable information about their health and healthcare choices."[13] In motivating the role of stakeholder engagement, PCORI states on its website:

> In PCORI-funded research, patients and other healthcare stakeholders are equitable partners—as opposed to research subjects—who leverage their lived experience and expertise to influence research to be more patient centered, relevant, and useful. Their early and continued involvement throughout a study can lead to greater use and uptake of research results by patients and stakeholders within the healthcare community.[14]

While PCORI acknowledges that some aspects of stakeholder engagement are unidirectional, they also note that the process can be bidirectional and collaborative:

> Engagement often occurs along a continuum ranging from stakeholder input, to consultation, to collaboration or shared leadership. Stakeholder input is primarily unidirectional, where partners share their perspectives or feedback on a particular topic in a singular forum. Collaboration or shared leadership reflects the bidirectional flow of information, decision-making authority, and leadership on a continued basis.[15]

PCORI also notes that there is also no one-size-fits-all approach to research engagement. The practices will vary across study goals and contextual factors. This includes PCORI projects that span a broader set of stakeholders including patients as well as patient families, clinical and residential treatment professionals, and organizational and government policymakers. Brandeis University professor Karen Donelan is a researcher working on a number of PCORI projects. She observes, "it's a very interesting process for some researchers. For example, we worked on a project on improving the quality of life of persons with disabilities and the project included co-principal investigators who each had significant physical disabilities. Historically, researchers were trained not to disclose our illnesses, family circumstances, and biases, but in PCORI research, lived experience is a qualification rather than a limitation."

When stakeholder engagement becomes bidirectional or even multidirectional, the process invariably moves beyond engagement and toward stakeholder alignment. At this point, shared decision-making and even shared leadership begins.

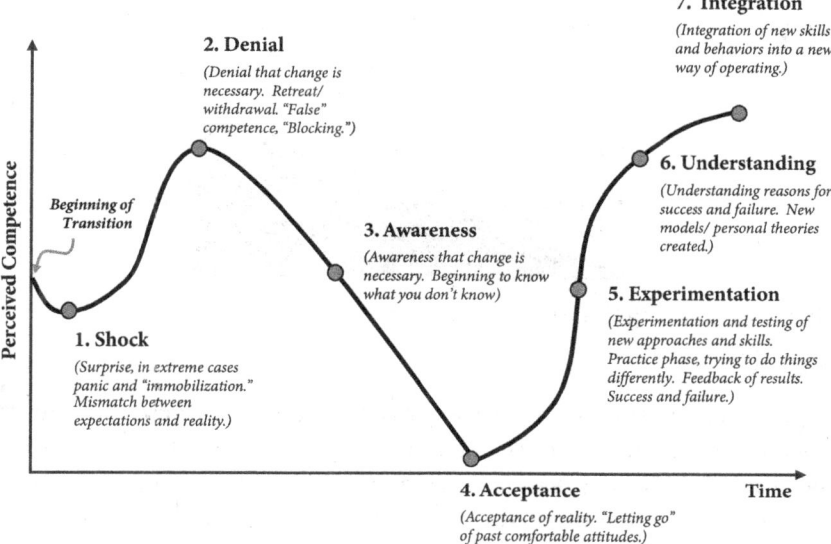

Figure 5.3 Model for the Impact of Change

For those seeking to engage stakeholders or even go further toward alignment, it is important to understand that the initial outreach is often new information. In this context, we note a key point from William Bridges and Susan Bridges, which is that parties need to let go of the old before they can accept what is new.[16] This approach is illustrated in Figure 5.3 showing a bottom-up change model on the impact of change, adapted from the work of Elisabeth Kübler-Ross.[17]

We term this as a bottom-up model since it reflects the views of those subject to change, rather than those leading change. The model signals that the parties impacted by change need to pass through stages of "shock," "denial," "awareness," and "acceptance" before they can be engaged in "experimentation," "understanding," and "integration."

Another bottom-up model comes from the literature and practice of continuous improvement. Here, Dr. Edwards Deming's classic model features four steps: Plan, Do, Check, Act (PDCA) as illustrated in Figure 5.4.

This model typically involves many distributed teams, with each following the PDCA steps as they make numerous incremental improvements.[18]

Further, the bottom-up aspect generally involves distributed communities who organize in response to the engagement invitation. The literature on

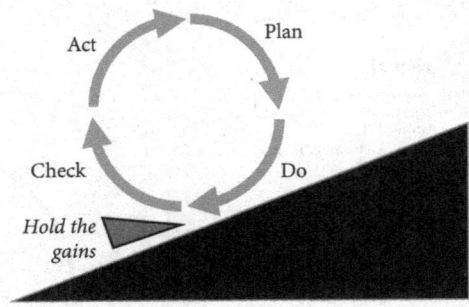

Figure 5.4 Deming Continuous Improvement Model

social movements is informative here as it points out that social movements emerge from social networks.[19] The advent of the Internet and associated social media is widely seen as a turning point in this context. We have seen the coevolution of #BlackLivesMatter and #MeToo, where the social networks have become instantiated in city chapters (in the case of #BlackLivesMatter) or formal initiatives (such as the Hollywood Commission addressing sexual harassment in the entertainment industry). Together, the social media–supported digital networks, combined with the formal instantiations, become social movements. The stakeholder engagement is both around joining with the hashtags and then joining further with the emerging institutional arrangements.

While consortia will often seek greater engagement from relevant stakeholders, caution is needed if the engagement is just a one-way communication approach. This approach risks the collective effort being seen as just another unitary actor, rather than as a pluralistic arrangement.

Combining Stakeholder Management and Stakeholder Engagement

Although stakeholder management and stakeholder engagement differ in their focus on competing versus common interests, they have one key element that is the same for both. This is the reality that both are driven by a single party seeking change. Both stakeholder management and stakeholder engagement operate from one stakeholder's perspective, looking out at others.

Stakeholder management and stakeholder engagement are often combined together, and this reflects the mix of common and competing interests that are invariably faced in efforts to influence key actors. Stakeholder management is oriented around potential risks from one party's perspective, while stakeholder engagement is oriented around potential benefits from one party's perspective. Together, they satisfy the need for an initiating party to address risks and benefits associated with a desired change.

Take, for example, President Biden's Day One Executive Order 13985, "On Advancing Racial Equity and Support for Underserved Communities through the Federal Government." This executive order called on federal agencies to conduct assessments to identify barriers to equity that underserved communities may face with respect to enrollment in and access to federal benefits and services. Agencies were expected to design action plans to mitigate specific barriers identified through this assessment and deliver equitable outcomes to communities. These plans involved both stakeholder management and stakeholder engagement.[20]

Presidential Executive Order 13985 is a first-of-its kind, "all of government" approach, which was designed to produce coordinated collective action across all federal agencies.[21] To accomplish this goal, the Office of Management and Budget, in close collaboration with the Domestic Policy Council, developed guidance for agencies, which included standing up and staffing agency equity teams, conducting equity assessments, and creating agency action plans. The guidance recommended that agency teams include members from data and evaluation officers, public-facing officials directly serving communities, and others spanning multiple functions in each agency. Later, Executive Order 14091, "Further Advancing Racial Equity and Support for Underserved Communities through the Federal Government," codified the differentiated expertise and roles agency equity teams should include and obligated these teams to report to senior agency officials.[22]

Change management models, such as the model for leading change in Figure 5.2, indicate that change is possible only when there is a sense of urgency. Both equity orders underscore the urgency at hand, stating: "a historic movement for justice has highlighted the unbearable costs of systemic racism." Once urgency is established, the key elements of change include: a clear change vision; a coalition of committed actors; opportunities for broad-based action; and short-term accomplishments. However, for change to develop traction, organizational cultures must also change, and the people in those cultures must consolidate new skills. All of this was on the agenda for the equity teams.

The agency equity teams involved multiple parties within each agency, but they did not have formal members outside of each agency. In that sense, they had to manage many of the dynamics faced by consortia, but they were not consortia, per se. While there was a shared vision guiding the work of each agency equity team, it was not the result of a consensus process. Executive orders have the status of law and that was the source of the guiding vision. In this case, President Biden's first executive order specified a definition of equity: "the consistent and systematic fair, just, and impartial treatment of all individuals, including individuals who belong to underserved communities." Both orders identified a blueprint, including equity assessments followed by equity action plans, including that all agencies address barriers to civil rights enforcement and barriers to equitable procurement and entering the federal marketplace. Clear definitions, identified methods, and goals created the conditions for effective stakeholder management and stakeholder engagement.

A report on the work of the equity teams, "Study to Identify Methods to Assess Equity: Report to the President," which was called for by Executive Order 13985, indicated that agency teams were expected to engage in dialogue processes and engagements with external stakeholders.[23] It was anticipated that in these processes, different stakeholder perspectives would be in tension. For example, even though the teams were obligated to promote common values—for example, of allocating resources fairly—different agency teams (or even different people on the same team) had different ideas about how to make policies and procedures more equitable. The agencies were encouraged to engage in data-driven approaches to create objective platforms for decision-making, but the equity teams still had to make choices and weigh trade-offs given a mandate to prioritize 3–5 actions for their agency action plans. This was an internal process involving both stakeholder management and stakeholder engagement.

As the report to the President under Executive Order 13985 indicated, "Equity-related concerns, however, are distinct from many other types of policy, because they can also implicate identity-based group membership. For example, when data analysis illuminates the possibility of more than one policy choice, the choice that is presumed to be "right" will be different for different people." For example, disparities identified by the Department of Agriculture involved historic challenges faced by small family farms owned by Black families. Addressing these disparities raised questions about disparities faced by small family farms owned by White families and others (which is addressed in more detail in Chapter 9). These types of issues meant that successful teams had to have the skills in managing tensions and conflicts. The report on the work of the equity teams noted that team members reported that these "difficult conversations" required flexible thinking. In some instances, this involved a willingness to reckon with history and a need for teams to develop new ways of working together.

One index of new capacities is that on April 14, 2022, more than 90 federal agencies made their agency equity plans public. Collectively these teams identified more than 300 concrete strategies and commitments to address the systemic barriers in our nation's policies and programs that hold too many underserved communities back from prosperity, dignity, and equality. Subsequent analyses of these action plans show that agency actions did in fact address multiple dimensions of equity (e.g., procedural, distributional, and structural), with each agency having one major action in each category.

In identifying and addressing equity issues, there were forms of stakeholder management and engagement that the equity teams could do—such as inviting public comments on the plans. They could not, however, set up ongoing consortia as standing advisory committees without following a formal and extensive process under the Federal Advisory Committee Act (FACA). The result was that the equity teams were remarkably consistent with each other across federal agencies, but the charter for the equity teams did not extend to a full process that mobilized the effort of various stakeholders to coordinate their efforts and collaborate. Essentially, while they effectively managed and engaged stakeholders, they could not fully align them for collective action.

Next, we describe the case of the Olympic Dam to illustrate the limitations of stakeholder management and engagement and reflect on how stakeholder alignment may have helped to avoid some of the pitfalls.[24]

Located in South Australia near the Roxby Downs Sheep Station, 550 km NNW of Adelaide, the Olympic Dam mine features extremely large deposits of iron ore, copper, gold, silver, and uranium oxide. It is the fourth-largest copper deposit in the world and the world's largest-known uranium deposit. Both an underground mine and a processing plant are on the site, which was acquired in 2005 by BHP Billiton, one of the world's largest mining companies. Converting from an underground mine to an open pit mine would vastly increase access to the natural resources, but doing so is highly controversial. This potential expansion of the Olympic Dam mine illustrates the combination of stakeholder management and stakeholder engagement as unitary approaches—driven from the perspective of one party seeking to manage risk and engage benefits.

Before expanding the mine, BHP Billiton needed approval of an environmental impact statement (EIS). Stakeholder management was employed to address potential opposition from antinuclear activists (opposed to the mining and transport of uranium), Aboriginal communities (living in the region for millennia before European settlers arrived in 1866 and concerned about a wide range of social and environmental impacts), environmentalists (concerned about the impacts the operation on the air, ground water, and ocean environments to the South), other states in Australia (through which the output of the mine would need to travel to reach ocean ports in the North), and others. Simultaneously, stakeholder engagement was employed with politicians interested in job creation and economic development, local residents (including Aboriginal communities) also interested in job creation and economic development, China and other nations interested in the potential output of the mine, and other parties.

As regards the scale of the operations, the March 2005 mine production rate was an annualized 9.1 million tons, making it one of Australia's larger mines at the time. In 2005, metal production was in excess of 220,000 tons of copper, 4,500 tons of uranium oxide, plus gold and silver. The copper and uranium oxide are exported through Port Adelaide, with China as a leading customer for the uranium oxide.[25]

As regards the social and environmental context, the area is remote and arid. There are aboriginal Dreamtime stories for the broader area and archaeological sites of significance, including sacred Aboriginal sites.

Most of the mine workers live in the nearby towns of Roxby Downs, which was built in 1987 to service the Olympic Dam, and Andamooka, which is smaller mining community. In 1920 the discovery of opals near Andamooka marked the beginning of mining in this area. Roxby Downs has approximately 4,000 residents and many amenities, such as swimming pools and other sporting facilities, a cinema, restaurants and cafes, and cultural facilities. In contrast, Andamooka has 528 residents and lacks such amenities. The Olympic Dam mine currently uses 35 million liters of Great Artesian Basin water each day in mining operations, making it the largest industrial user of underground water in the Southern Hemisphere.[26] The sizable use of artesian water threatens areas of high ecological significance in the region.

In May 2009, the company released a draft environmental impact statement (EIS) for public comment. The executive summary stated,

> BHP Billiton is seeking the approval of the Australian, South Australian and Northern Territory governments for a significant expansion of its existing mining and processing operation at Olympic Dam in northern South Australia.
>
> Should all necessary approvals be granted, BHP Billiton would commit to substantial capital investment at Olympic Dam and elsewhere, which would more than double direct employment at Olympic Dam, provide significant opportunities to third-party businesses, and increase considerably government and export revenues.
>
> The expansion is centred on the creation of a new open pit mine that would lift ore production six-fold and require expanded minerals processing facilities. Major support infrastructure would also be built, including a coastal desalination plant, a new power line and possibly a gas-fired power station, a rail line, an airport, port facilities, a village to accommodate workers, and more housing, retail, commercial and community facilities in the Roxby Downs township where much of Olympic Dam's operational workforce would continue to live.[27]

The stakeholder management process included the systematic identification of all relevant stakeholders, classifying each according to their influence and support. This was followed by meetings with state and local elected officials, state and federal environmental regulators, Aboriginal community leaders, environmental activists, media briefings, and the development of the proposed environmental impact statement. The stakeholder engagement process featured town hall meetings, public forums, investments in the Roxby Downs community infrastructure, and the establishment of funds to support the Aboriginal community in a variety of ways.

The two approaches came together in a remarkable way in the form of a single individual, Steven Green, and his family. Steven was an employee of BHP Billiton who moved with his family to this very remote area and lived with the local community for 10 years (until 2012). He provided leadership for the State and Federal environmental approvals of the Olympic Dam Expansion. He was open with all about his employer. His children went to the local school. When it came to the development of the EIS, his leadership reflected his learning on the ground. BHP Billiton adjusted its plans taking into account lessons learned by Steven during his long residency in the community. This led to a preliminary approval of the EIS in 2011.

Even with the combination of stakeholder management and stakeholder engagement, there was still strong resistance from environmental groups, antinuclear groups, some Aboriginal communities, and others, which substantially delayed the release of guidelines for assessing the EIS (a necessary additional step in the process). Further, the economics of the project continued to change based on the price of copper, new evidence of structural complexity in the deposits, and increased concern about nuclear energy following the Fukushima accident in Japan. In October 2020, BHP Billiton indicated it was no longer going to invest the $3.5 billion (AU) needed for the next round of expansion in the mine. Some observers saw this as a power move designed to motivate the negotiations needed to approve the EIS guidelines. Although BHP Billiton has indicated that the economics could change in a more favorable direction in the future, it insists that this is a true statement of the economics now. It continues to operate Olympic Dam today as a more limited underground mine.

This case illustrates the complex mix of stakeholders associated with the project management and government regulation of a large mining operation with the full array of associated stakeholder management and stakeholder engagement activities. These approaches even merged as a result of a representative of BHP Billiton living in the community with his family for a decade.

Missing, however, was the full process of stakeholder alignment, which is the focus of the balance of this book. Anticipating what is coming, here is a radical question: While there were smaller coalitions of subgroups, why not have a consortium of the whole? For each of the stakeholders that would involve giving up a measure of autonomy—perhaps more than they would be willing to do. After all, BHP Billiton owns the mine. Aboriginal communities have rights that extend back tens of thousands of years. Environmentalists insist that we think in terms of seven generations. Government leaders can't cede their administrative responsibilities. Yet, had there been sufficient alignment, a way might have been found to realize the full economic potential of the Olympic Dam mine, while also addressing the environmental, cultural, and other considerations. As such, this case illustrates the processes of both stakeholder management and stakeholder engagement as well as a boundary condition, beyond which stakeholder alignment and a consortium could be transformative but would be very hard to achieve.

Adding Stakeholder Alignment to Stakeholder Management and Engagement

Individual stakeholders are often independently engaged in stakeholder management and stakeholder engagement at the same time that efforts may be made laterally to achieve stakeholder alignment. This can be beneficial, benign, or challenging.

Many organizations leverage membership in consortia to identify partners for separate joint ventures and other collaborative activities. In this context, they are doing stakeholder engagement even as they are part of alignment processes, which is part of the value proposition associated with joining a consortium. We saw this in the Takeda case at the beginning of Chapter 1, where membership in public-private partnerships led to bilateral initiatives.

Because stakeholders are both independent and interdependent in a consortium, there will be examples of stakeholder engagement and stakeholder management that are unrelated to the consortium and happening in parallel to the collective efforts. These dynamics are generally benign. What is challenging is when one party is seeking to manage or engage stakeholders who are simultaneously in an alignment process. For example, members of the Minority Serving Cyberinfrastructure Consortium (MS-CC) work together to seek grants from the National Science Foundation and commercial firms. Individual campuses will also approach these stakeholders independently. MS-CC can't (and wouldn't want to) limit the efforts of its member organizations, but it is conceivable that the MS-CC could find itself in competition with its own members' efforts at stakeholder management and stakeholder engagement. This points to the need for avoiding surprises, while acknowledging the legitimacy of these parallel processes.

Summing Up

Managing and engaging stakeholders are two well-established approaches, both operating from the perspective of an initiating party. Stakeholder management is employed to anticipate and address potential resistance to change—often with the goal of neutralizing resistance (and not necessarily generating supporters). Stakeholder engagement is employed to include and learn from potential supporters of change—often with the goal of motivating neutral parties to become supporters. Both of these unitary approaches are important and each may be employed by consortia as initiating parties, but they are incomplete and counter to necessary pluralistic approaches when it comes to forming and sustaining consortia.

Notes

1. This vignette was shared by Dr. Fallahq with Joel Cutcher-Gershenfeld during a 2018 Global Challenges Foundation workshop in Stockholm, Sweden.
2. R. Edward Freeman, Jeffrey S. Harrison, Andrew C. Wicks, Bidhan Parmar, and Simone de Colle, *Stakeholder Theory: The State of the Art* (Cambridge: Cambridge University Press, 2010).
3. For example, Thomas A. Kochan and Saul A. Rubinstein, "Toward a Stakeholder Theory of the Firm: The Saturn Partnership," *Organization Science* 11, no. 4 (2000): pp. 367–386, http://www.jstor.org/stable/2640410; Axel v. Werder, "Corporate Governance and Stakeholder Opportunism," *Organization Science* 22, no. 5 (2011): pp. 1345–1358, http://www.jstor.org/stable/41303126.
4. For example, Michelle Greenwood, "Stakeholder Engagement: Beyond the Myth of Corporate Responsibility," *Journal of Business Ethics* 74 (2007): pp. 315–327, https://doi.org/10.1007/s10551-007-9509-y.
5. R. Edward Freeman and David L. Reed," Stockholders and Stakeholders: A New Perspective on Corporate Governance," *California Management Review* 25, no. 3 (Spring 1983): pp. 88–106, https://doi.org/10.2307/41165018.
6. See Julia Roloff, "Learning from Multi-Stakeholder Networks: Issue-Focussed Stakeholder Management," *Journal of Business Ethics* 82 (2008): pp. 233–250, https://doi.org/10.1007/s10551-007-9573-3.

7. See Peter Sandman, *Responding to Community Outrage: Strategies for Effective Risk Communication* (Fairfax, VA: American Industrial Hygiene Association, 1993); current resources at http://www.psandman.com.
8. See John Kotter, *Leading Change*, 1st rev. ed. (Boston: Harvard Business Review Press, 2012).
9. Source, https://www.kotterinc.com/methodology/8-steps/.
10. See Paul Hersey and Kenneth H. Blanchard, *Management of Organizational Behavior: Utilizing Human Resources*, 6th ed. (Hoboken NJ: Prentice-Hall, 1993).
11. Freeman et al., *Stakeholder Theory*. Also, for example, Thomas Kochan and Saul Rubinstein, "Toward a Stakeholder Theory of the Firm."
12. Greenwood, "Stakeholder Engagement."
13. For more on Patient-Centered Outcomes Research Institute (PCORI), see "About PCORI," accessed June 13, 2023, https://www.pcori.org/about/about-pcori. We thank Greg Martin and Karen Donelan for their insights as we developed this vignette. Of course, the responsibility for the text is entirely ours as coauthors.
14. See "The Value of Engagement," accessed June 13, 2023, https://www.pcori.org/engagement/value-engagement.
15. Ibid.
16. See William Bridges and Susan Bridges, *Transitions: Making Sense of Life's Changes*, 40th anniversary ed. (New York: Hachette Books).
17. This model was adapted from the Elizabeth Kübler-Ross model by the Ford Executive Development Center.
18. Originally published in 1982, see the MIT reprint, W. Edwards Deming, *Out of the Crisis* (Cambridge, MA: MIT Press, 2000). Adapted by Matthias Holweg in 2004 MIT presentation on "Latest Developments in Lean Thinking."
19. See, for example, Mario Diani and Doug McAdam, eds., *Social Movements and Networks: Relational Approaches to Collective Action, Comparative Politics* (Oxford: Oxford University Press, 2003).
20. This vignette draws on the extensive experience of coauthor Kimberlyn Leary and the more limited experience of Joel Cutcher-Gershenfeld with this initiative.
21. See: https://www.whitehouse.gov/briefing-room/presidential-actions/2021/01/20/executive-order-advancing-racial-equity-and-support-for-underserved-communities-through-the-federal-government/.
22. See: https://www.whitehouse.gov/briefing-room/presidential-actions/2023/02/16/executive-order-on-further-advancing-racial-equity-and-support-for-underserved-communities-through-the-federal-government/.
23. See: https://www.whitehouse.gov/wp-content/uploads/2021/08/OMB-Report-on-E013985-Implementation_508-Compliant-Secure-v1.1.pdf.
24. We thank Maurizio Floris for his insights, along with coauthor Joel Cutcher-Gershenfeld, as we developed this vignette. This vignette draws on a teaching case developed for the University of Sydney's John Grill Institute for Project Leadership. Of course, the responsibility for the text is entirely ours as coauthors.
25. See: https://en.wikipedia.org/wiki/Olympic_Dam_mine.
26. See John Pigram, ed. *Australia's Water Resources: From Use to Management* (Collingwood, Victoria: CSIRO Publishing, 2007), p. 112, https://doi.org/10.1071/9780643094116.
27. See:https://www.bhp.com/-/media/bhp/regulatory-information-media/copper/olympic-dam/0000/draft-eis-documents/drafteisexecutivesummary.pdf.

Chapter 6
Scoping

Specifying Stakeholders and Identifying Interests

In December 2003, the US Congress included in the Vision 100—Century of Aviation Reauthorization Act (H.R. 2115, Public Law 108-176) support for a study of aircraft noise and emissions. At the time, Congress was devoting considerable resources just to insulate homes near airports in order to settle lawsuits over aircraft noise. For example, in 2002, $125 million was allocated for this purpose in Los Angeles,[1] a 2001 National Academies study found that $408 million had been spent on sound insulation for residential and school buildings around Chicago's O'Hare International Airport,[2] and there were additional comparable investments around the country. Rather than addressing the root causes, the equivalent of band-aids were being put on the issue. Previously, there had been 35 studies on aspects of aircraft noise and emissions, but few tangible improvements. Expansion plans at 12 of the country's 50 busiest airports had been canceled or postponed indefinitely because of noise and emissions issues—impacting economic development. Military readiness was constrained by local limits on military airport base operations. The impact of aviation on climate had recently been evaluated and determined to be unique due to the role of directly depositing emissions at altitude.[3] Potential projects aimed at just noise, emissions, or economic development were stymied since progress on one issue was in tension with progress on others.

In order to identify how to proceed on these complex issues, a research team led by Ian Waitz, a professor in the Department of Aeronautics and Astronautics at MIT, identified 18 different types of stakeholders, including the Federal Aviation Administration (FAA), the National Aeronautics and Space Administration (NASA), the Department of Defense, and other federal agencies, along with aircraft manufacturers, airplane engine

The Consortia Century. The Stakeholder Alignment Collaborative: Joel Cutcher-Gershenfeld et al., Oxford University Press. © Oxford University Press (2025). DOI: 10.1093/oso/9780197761649.003.0007

manufacturers, commercial airlines, cities and towns near airports, environmental groups, and others. Interviews were conducted with representatives of these various groups to identify what interests were at stake for them with respect to aircraft noise and emissions. These included achieving absolute reductions in noise and emissions as well as increased coordination among federal agencies, developing robust metrics to track progress, and others. These key themes from the interviews were presented at a stakeholder meeting that drew 45 people from 31 organizations. After the meeting, a draft report was developed and circulated to all interviewees and attendees at the stakeholder meeting. Over 200 detailed comments were generated by 16 organizations, and a revised draft was generated in advance of a second stakeholder meeting.

The second stakeholder meeting drew 48 people from 32 organizations (the Environmental Protection Agency [EPA] was the additional organization in attendance). At that stakeholder meeting something unexpected happened. A multiparty form of what could be considered collective bargaining took place. Airplane engine manufacturers indicated that more fuel-efficient engines could be built if the airlines would buy them. Experiments with what was termed "steep descent" could be conducted to reduce noise near airports, but only if a number of key parties all worked together. The group reached preliminary agreements on these and other matters, and a consensus report, "Aviation and the Environment," was then sent to Congress.[4]

The first recommendation in the report was to establish a multistakeholder structure:

> A federal interagency group should be established for coordinating governmental action to reduce the negative impacts of aviation on local air quality, noise, and climate change. The group should have representation from the FAA, NASA, EPA, DoD, DOT, DOC, and DOI, and should be chaired by a representative from the FAA. The group should be formed within the Joint Planning and Development Office (JPDO). It should promote public-private partnerships with industry. This new interagency group should also be responsible for fostering a network of community forums to promote communication, idea exchange and joint action. These community forums should be given representation at the highest level in the interagency coordinating group.

> The resulting efforts were linked to an FAA project, the Next Generation Air Transportation System (NextGen), which has evolved to be recognized as "one of the most ambitious infrastructure projects in U.S. history." Its continuing focus is on aircraft noise and emissions as well as many other matters. It operates with the FAA as chair, under a charter with a multistakeholder advisory committee. Experiments and innovations in policy, technology, and practice are having tangible impacts that far exceed those achieved by only insulating homes near airports.[5]

As the aircraft noise and emissions case illustrates, collective impact begins with the specification of stakeholder types and the identification of the interests that are at stake. These two steps make it possible to see the landscape on which alignment will take place. Each step is simple as a concept but has many layers of complexity in practice. Together, these are the first steps in scoping the landscape for stakeholder alignment. Note that in this case, alignment was needed among federal agencies as well as with other stakeholders—a theme we will return to in Chapter 7. The initiative has now been institutionalized within the FAA rather than as a separate consortium—a theme we will return to in Chapter 8.

To further illustrate the processes of specifying stakeholders and identifying interests, we draw on the cases of the Minority Serving Cyberinfrastructure Consortium (MS-CC) and Takeda Pharmaceuticals in considerable detail. Of course, no one case is representative of all consortia, but for the purposes of this chapter and the next, providing this level of detail helps to envision how these steps might apply in other cases.

The MS-CC, introduced in the Prologue, originated with a group of historically Black colleges and universities (HBCUs), with later expansion to include tribal colleges and universities (TCUs), Hispanic serving institutions (HSIs), and other minority serving institutions (MSIs). We will discuss other cases where they become relevant for contrast or elaboration, but the primary focus of this chapter will be on the MS-CC.

During the scoping phase, there are predictable challenges, including:

- **Missing Stakeholders**: Parties with relevant interests who are not included because it is logistically complicated or there are substantive disagreements with the proposed focus of the consortium.

- **Superficial Engagement**: Engagement in a consortium that is superficially focused on only common interests, without fully taking into account competing interests and individual agency.
- **Insufficient Internal Alignment**: Insufficient internal alignment within consortia members that constrains lateral alignment across the consortium.

The tools and methods presented in this chapter are designed to address these challenges.

To position our discussion, note that the scoping discussed in this chapter is located within the designated area on our process map (Figure 6.1).

Specifying Stakeholders

In many domains, the stakeholder categories are well known. For example, in a commercial business, the typical list of stakeholders includes shareholders, customers, employees, and suppliers. Sometimes, communities, strategic partners, and regulators are added to the list. On closer inspection, even these well-established categories have subcategories. Employees as a category can be broken down further, for example, top management, middle

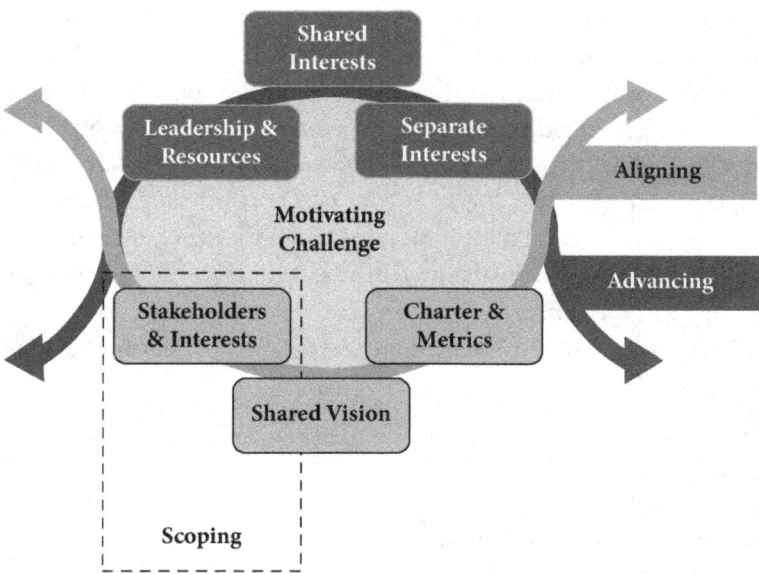

Figure 6.1 Stakeholder Alignment Model—Scoping the Landscape of Stakeholders and Interests

management, front-line supervisors, professional staff, front-line employees, and part-time/temporary employees. Similarly, suppliers are often broken down into first-, second-, and third-tier suppliers. Shareholders may have different classes of stock. Still, the high-level categories are fairly consistent across commercial enterprises.

When it comes to societal challenges, however, the identification of even the high-level categories requires fresh consideration. National, state, and local governments are often key stakeholders, as are various types of nongovernmental organizations. Further, there are often folks with relevant technical expertise, individuals who are in client or customer or user roles, commercial organizations, and many others. There are also challenging categories when it comes to inclusion, such as unborn generations or individuals on the wrong side of digital divides.

In the case of the MS-CC, the initial group of HBCUs came together in 2018 with support from the US National Science Foundation (NSF) to build out their research data, computing, and software capabilities, so they could expand the scale and scope of research by students and faculty on their campuses as well as citizens in their surrounding communities.[6]

Even the assumption that all HBCUs were stakeholders needed dialogue. Historically, HBCUs operate relatively independently from one another, so it was not guaranteed that all would want to be part of a consortium on cyberinfrastructure (CI). Indeed, the initial stakeholder survey that was conducted drew responses from only 24 of the 101 HBCUs in the United States. Two years later, a stakeholder survey that included HBCUs, TCUs, and HSIs drew responses from 44 of the 101 HBCUs, along with 32 of the 38 TCUs and 63 of the 539 HSIs. The use of the survey was impactful for individuals from these organizations as an initial signal that they saw themselves as stakeholders (at least enough to participate in the survey).

Within the overall ecosystem, there was an array of relevant stakeholders, including:

- Researchers/faculty
- Educators
- Students
- Cyberinfrastructure professionals
- Campus leaders
- Industry partners
- Foundations and funding agencies

Achieving sufficient stakeholder alignment for action requires understanding the views of these diverse stakeholders. Of course, each of these categories has many relevant subcategories. Students include undergraduate and graduate students. Both students and faculty are in diverse fields and disciplines. Campus leaders include presidents, provosts, chief information officers, vice presidents of research, head librarians, deans, department heads, and others. It is a considerable challenge to keep all these stakeholders in mind on a given issue. Some are well organized and can speak with a single voice, while others lack unity. Some groups don't realize where the points of alignment might be. Others think that all stakeholders see things as they do, when the reality is more complicated. This is where various forms of stakeholder maps are helpful, since they offer a visual representation and overview of the landscape.

Importantly, the mix of stakeholders and their composition (who is included in each category) changes over time. Specifying stakeholders is a continuing and sometimes challenging task. Social categorization is a deeply human process and, once organized, changing categories can be difficult. Further, many stakeholders may fit into more than one category—what are termed intersectional identities. Thus, it is helpful early on to view the specification of stakeholders as a dynamic process and to avoid thinking of stakeholders as fitting into only one category.

Invariably, there will be missing stakeholders. In some cases, there are logistic challenges in including additional perspectives. In other cases, there are stakeholders with various opposed interests. This poses a dilemma. If such stakeholders are included early on, the formations are far more complicated, but leaving them out builds resentment. So, even when key stakeholders are not included, finding ways to demonstrate that their interests were at least taken into account is important.

Beyond the challenge of keeping all the stakeholders in mind on a given issue, there is the challenge that many issues are "at stake" for these diverse stakeholders, which is our focus in the next section.

Identifying Interests

Issues at play for stakeholders are often framed as positions. A given stakeholder supports one issue, opposes another, and has mixed views on a third. A key lesson from effective negotiation involves shifting the focus from positions to underlying interests.[7] On a given issue, a party may have one position, but there are often many underlying interests that can be more productively addressed. For example, in an environmental consortium there may be a position that opposes a particular economic development plan. Underneath the opposition could be many interests, including mitigating the risk of pollution, protecting a Native American burial ground, ensuring community input into the plan, and other considerations. Knowing the interests at hand is key to constructive dialogue.

Stakeholder alignment is effectively advanced with this appreciation for interests and rights. Identifying the underlying interests that are "at stake" often requires dialogue with a diverse mix of stakeholder representatives. The aim is to identify interests that are relevant to collaboration—because they have the potential to be either drivers or barriers. In addition to interests, there may be legal rights that need to be specified. Then underlying interests relative to the rights also need to be discussed.

> In the case of MS-CC, some of the interests involved application of computing and data resources and expertise across various high-level topics, including:
> - Science and engineering
> - Workforce development
> - Social science and culture
> - Energy and environment
> - Health
> - Language education, arts, and digital humanities
>
> These applications will be familiar to most readers—they relate to domains that are common in higher education and the associated "interest" centers on cyberinfrastructure (CI) applications common to a given field or discipline.
>
> Additional interests involved CI technologies and practices, which included:
> - Cybersecurity
> - CI helping to attract, train, and retain faculty and students
> - CI helping to bringing in research funding
> - CI helping to build a stronger movement of minority-serving colleges and universities
> - Access to relevant CI training
> - Access to CI facilitators
> - Innovating in CI design and operation
> - A CI assessment tool

Readers not involved in research computing and data may be unfamiliar with these, but the key point is that there are multiple technical interests.

A third category of interests of MS-CC involved just how much collaboration would be supported, including:

- Collaboration between HBCUs and HSIs
- Collaboration between HBCUs and TCUs
- Active sharing in general among MSIs
- Collaboration between minority-serving and majority-serving (predominantly White) institutions
- Little or no sharing across campuses

While the specifics around different forms of collaboration are unique to this context, the broader issues of collaboration across stakeholders will be familiar to all readers. Notice that the interests go beyond superficial statements in support of collaboration and represent issues that are "at stake" at this point in the life of this consortium. Just as the mix of stakeholders changes over time, the mix of interests is also dynamic.

All of the above interests were discussed extensively in the formation of the MS-CC, while others are likely yet to emerge. The people involved with forming the MS-CC were highly motivated just seeing this much of the landscape.

In order to illustrate further how different interests combine in constructive ways, let's return to the case of Takeda, a leading pharmaceutical company. In 2009, they were a member of several public-private partnerships (PPPs), a form of consortium; by 2023, this has increased to approximately 100 PPPs. It is necessary to see the entire landscape of Takeda's relevant interests, including both common and competing interests, to fully understand its growing support for PPPs.[8] What follows is a partial analysis that illustrates the reciprocal relationships among the relevant interests, with Takeda represented in the category of "leading pharmaceutical companies":

Patients (and patient advocacy organizations)
- Getting better treatments faster
- Ensuring that treatments are affordable and accessible
- Ensuring patient data privacy and protection

Leading pharmaceutical companies
- Getting better treatments to patients faster
- Contributing to innovations at the frontiers of science
- Ensuring that regulators are knowledgeable on advances at the frontiers of science and are actively involved in formulating relevant policies and regulations
- Having a precompetitive space for innovation and an ability to opt out of projects in a competitive space
- Providing professional development opportunities for professional staff
- Ensuring that new treatments represent sustainable business models
- Solving complex scientific challenges
- Not violating antitrust regulations

Regulators' interests (United States, European Union, Japan, and others)
- Getting better treatments to patients faster
- Ensuring that new treatments provide value and are affordable, accessible, safe, and effective
- Learning about innovations at the frontiers of science from credible, neutral sources
- Not compromising regulatory independence

Leading biotech companies
- Getting better treatments to patients faster
- Having a precompetitive space for innovation and an ability to opt out of projects that are in a competitive space
- Forging constructive relationships with regulators, large pharmaceutical companies, academic researchers, and patient advocacy organizations
- Leveling the playing field with large pharmaceutical companies
- Ensuring the new treatments and other biomedical innovations (such as test equipment) represent sustainable business models
- Solving complex scientific challenges
- Not violating antitrust regulations

Academic researchers
- Getting better treatments to patients faster
- Advancing the leading edge of science
- Gain insights into the direction of industry and regulators
- Getting recognition for advances at the leading edge of science
- Forging constructive relationships with regulators, large pharmaceutical companies, biotech companies, and patient advocacy organizations
- Getting access to data

Healthcare providers
- Getting better treatments faster
- Advancing the leading edge of science
- Improving health outcomes
- Reducing healthcare provision costs
- Expanding healthcare services
- Providing better value in terms of improved care

The overarching interest driving PPPs is, of course, getting better treatments to patients faster. With that in mind, there are reciprocal combinations of interests enabled by the consortia structure that would not be possible if each party were acting alone. For example, academics can share information and pose questions with regulators in ways that are more acceptable compared to the same information or questions coming from companies. Patient advocacy organizations will have direct experience that academics need in order to best frame the research questions. Companies bring expertise, data, samples, and funding to the conversation that the academics don't have. So, there is a virtual combination of interests that wouldn't be possible if each party were acting separately.

Notice, however, that there are also tensions among the interests. Patients and regulators put great weight on the treatments being affordable, while companies' interest in sustainable business models can be in tension with affordability. The result will be a need for all stakeholders to align on giving greater weight to value in terms of accessibility and improved health outcomes than they might otherwise have done to appreciate the need for sustainability to a greater degree.

Companies value the ways in which a precompetitive space enables all to do together what they can't do separately, but will opt out of projects that impair their competitive interests. The result will be different combinations of companies on different projects. Academics will want embargo periods with data so that initial publications can be generated, but patient advocacy organizations will want open data soon to bring therapies and other advances to market sooner. Sustaining these consortia is therefore a dynamic process in which the full array of common and competing interests need to be taken into account. When it works well, stakeholders become more skilled in putting themselves in each other's shoes and finding ways to constructively address competing interests. For example, the concern that academics have about being "scooped" by others when making data open-access is balanced by the unique insights that come from relationships with patient advocacy organizations and other stakeholders.

Conducting Stakeholder Mapping Landscape Surveys

The landscape of stakeholders and interests can be thought of as a matrix with types of stakeholders on one axis and interests on the other. Similar to what we saw in Chapter 2, Figure 6.2 shows what the matrix would look like, in this case with four interests and three stakeholder categories (based on simplified actual MS-CC data):

	Interest 1: Undergraduate research opportunities related to computing and data skills	Interest 2: Funding to provide access to large-scale computing and data storage	Interest 3: Training for cyber-infrastructure professionals	Interest 4: Protections for sovereign tribal data
Stakeholder 1: HBCUs	+	0	+	0
Stakeholder 2: TCUs	+	0	+	+
Stakeholder 3: HSIs	+	0	0	0

Key:

Positive	Neutral	Negative
+	0	–

Figure 6.2 Illustrative Example of a Matrix of Stakeholders and Interests

SCOPING 123

In such a landscape analysis, the cells are filled in with the stakeholders' views on a given interest. These views may be on the importance of the interest, the difficulty in addressing the interest, or other aspects of the interest. The cells can be filled in based on assumptions (least useful) or focus groups and surveys (more useful).

> Consider the survey results on the interests identified above for the MS-CC. We will not review all the results, but rather highlight some lessons from the mapping of stakeholders and interests. beyond what is in Figure 6.2, building on data in this chapter's appendix.
>
> For example, among the application domains, it is not surprising that science and engineering applications were rated as important or very important by 88.1% of the respondents. When it came to other applications (social science and cultural research, energy and environmental research, health-related research, and language education, arts, and digital humanities), the cyberinfrastructure professionals gave the lowest importance ratings compared with other stakeholders. For leaders of MS-CC, this pointed to a potential bias among those providing technical support, which they then knew needed to be addressed.[9]
>
> Workforce development was also seen as a top priority, with 87.9% of the respondents indicating this was important or very important, but it was also seen as difficult or very difficult by 71.2% of the respondents. Respondents from TCUs saw this as the most difficult, with HBCUs next; HSIs also saw this as difficult, but not to the same degree as the others. This highlighted the structural barriers around workforce development, which are overlapping but distinct for TCUs and HBCUs.
>
> When it came to aspects of cyberinfrastructure, the top item for all stakeholders was cybersecurity, rated as important or very important by 96.2% of respondents. With this information, the first focus of the consortium became workshops on cybersecurity.
>
> Among aspects of cyberinfrastructure, the largest pain point was "leveraging research computing and data management capabilities at minority serving colleges and universities to recruit and retain faculty and students" (rated as important or very important by 94.5% of respondents and difficult or very difficult by 85.8% of respondents). This reflected the difficulty of leveraging research cyberinfrastructure investments in colleges and universities that are teaching-intensive and their importance to all stakeholders.[10]

Two questions seemed to be the most motivating for the consortium. First, we asked about the importance of minority-serving colleges and universities engaging in active sharing of research data management and computing resources and expertise, which was rated as important or very important by 81.3% respondents. Contrast this with each minority-serving college and university maintaining its own separate data management and computing resources and expertise, with little or no sharing across campuses, which was only rated as important or very important by 54% of respondents. While this was a strong vote for collaboration, it was not unanimous among all stakeholders, suggesting that there will still be some cultural challenges associated with collaboration.[11]

When those surveyed were asked to provide a phrase or metaphor to summarize their vision of success for data management and computing on their campuses, the responses were evocative and motivating for the consortium. Here are a few examples, in their own words (organized by the type of institution):

- A better aligned, cooperative, and forward-looking dynamic. (HBCU)
- No university stakeholder left behind. (HBCU)
- We're adequate today, but today is already yesterday. (TCU)
- We need a bigger, better data portal for our community. (TCU)
- Needed for sovereignty of Tribal needs and people. (TCU)
- Forward thinking. Seeing computing as it could be and not resigned to how it is. (HSI)
- Technology for upward mobility. (HSI)
- More diverse workforce-ready graduates. (Other MSI)

These stakeholder mapping processes provide essential information on the landscape within which consortia operate—pointing to "low-hanging fruit" as opportunities for early action and to challenging domains that will require increased time and resources to address. When stakeholders are basically all in agreement, time is saved by seeing this sooner rather than later.

Constructing Value Propositions

For commercial entrepreneurial businesses, it is expected that there be a core value proposition—what the business does that others are not doing and that customers want. In the case of a multistakeholder consortium, there are multiple stakeholders, each with a bundle of interests on which they have positive, negative, or neutral views. When combined together, the result is not one value proposition, but many—one (or more) for each stakeholder.

> Recall the six main stakeholder categories in the MS-CC mapping. With all of these data in front of the founders, they crafted six value propositions,[12] including this value proposition for **researchers and educators**:
>
>> Harnessing the power of data and computing resources to advance the frontiers of knowledge in ways that are aligned with the mission of HBCUs, TCUs, HSIs, and other minority serving colleges and universities—spanning science, engineering, social science, humanities, arts, and other domains.
>
> And this value proposition for **students**:
>
>> Students at HBCUs, TCUs, HSIs, and other minority serving colleges and universities addressing issues of importance to them with data and computing capabilities as well as preparing to be the next generation workforce—including future cyberinfrastructure professionals.
>
> Cyberinfrastructure professionals are central to the MS-CC, particularly those supporting research data and computing, yet most campuses did not have clear career paths for this work. So another focus is advancing **cyberinfrastructure professionals** on campuses:
>
>> Connecting cyberinfrastructure professionals across HBCU, TCU, HSI, and other minority serving colleges and universities so we can accomplish together what we can't do separately—including building capability, bringing in funding, establishing career paths, advancing knowledge, and pioneering new technologies.
>
> Campus leaders look at cyberinfrastructure through the lens of the college or university's mission. Other stakeholder categories also value the mission, but it rises up as central to the interests of **campus leaders**:
>
>> Making wise investments in the capabilities needed for a post-industrial, digital world—advancing the mission and impact of HBCUs, TCUs, HSIs, and other minority serving colleges and universities.

There are many commercial organizations that seek partnerships with HBCUs, TCUs, HSIs, and other MSIs, but the colleges and universities have found that the interest is superficial. When the interest is authentic, particularly around hiring the next-generation workforce and advancing the frontiers of technology, there is a viable value proposition for **industry leaders**:

> Enabling industry leaders to engage with HBCU, TCU, HSI, and other minority serving colleges and universities around new technologies, services, resources, and next-generation talent relevant to research and educational cyberinfrastructure.

Many **foundations and government funding agencies** have prioritized support for these colleges and universities, with a particular interest in impact:

> Enabling foundations and funding agencies to coordinate engagement with HBCU, TCU, HSI, and other minority serving colleges and universities around research priorities and community development relevant to research and educational cyberinfrastructure.

Finally, additional **strategic partners** also have distinct value propositions:

> Collaborating with organizations, institutions, professional societies, initiatives, and others with a demonstrated shared commitment to the MS-CC mission and values—working together to advance each institution and the MS-CC community.

These value propositions serve multiple purposes. First, they provide direction for the consortium in developing initiatives, programs, services, and other value-creating activities. Second, they provide a measuring stick against which to measure the value creating activities—that is, whether they are delivering on the various propositions. Third, they highlight trade-offs and balancing of the work—educating all stakeholders on what is "at stake" for others and fostering appreciation for the multiple concurrent priorities driving the consortium.

Complications with Stakeholders and Interests

The mapping of stakeholders and interests typically confirms views by most stakeholders, helps make stakeholders with very different views aware of where most stakeholders are at, and builds momentum for action. That was certainly the case with MS-CC, but it is not always the case.

In one of the consortia discussed in Chapter 3, we saw that a 2013 stakeholder map in Dodge City, Kansas, indicated wide support of a community initiative on bridging the digital divide. The initiative was led by a local political official, a leader from the local community college, and the librarian for the city. Opposition by a small group of citizens concerned about the implications for taxes or their cable bill undercut the effort.

An example of effective engagement happened in another early stakeholder mapping survey, which was conducted as part of the US NSF EarthCube initiative. This initiative centered on the open sharing of data, software, and other resources in the geosciences in order to better understand the Earth as a system. The challenges of global warming, severe weather, natural resource depletion, ecological degradation, and other issues within the Earth, on the Earth's surface, and in near space, motivated EarthCube.[13]

In the US NSF's EarthCube initiative, the immediate stakeholders were researchers, students, research staff, and cyberinfrastructure developers. In the first few years of the initiative, over 200 computer science and geoscience researchers attended a series of "charrettes," a term from design used to describe a short and intense group working sessions, to develop the supporting infrastructure. At this point, a number of relevant leaders conducted a stakeholder map of geoscientists in a wide range of fields and disciplines. This led to the discovery that computer science, information science, and other cyberinfrastructure professionals were out ahead of the geoscience researchers and students. There was support from some (but not all) of the researchers and students for the principles of data sharing and increased collaboration, with more support among students and early career researchers. One early career researcher reported the following comment from a senior faculty member: "I am going to my grave with my disk drive in my cold dead hand." Further, the map identified considerable variation across fields and disciplines, major gaps in knowledge and skills, and barriers when it came to the role of data sharing in professional recognition, rewards, and career advancement. The stakeholder map made it clear that the EarthCube initiative risked being a case of "build it but they don't come."[14]

In response to the stakeholder mapping data, NSF made a bold move. They pivoted from exclusively funding the development of tools and other infrastructure resources, adding support for 27 "end-user" workshops in a wide range of fields and disciplines (for example, atmospheric modeling, clouds and aerosols, coral reef systems, critical zones, early career geoscientists, geochronology, hydrology, paleogeoscience, petrology and geochemistry, and sedimentary geology). At each end-user workshop, data were presented from the stakeholder survey on where each group stood relative to other fields and disciplines, and what tools and methods would be useful for them to advance the field. After what could have been a major barrier had been addressed, progress could proceed on infrastructure investments that were better aligned with the interests of stakeholders (researchers, students, and cyberinfrastructure developers) across diverse fields and domains.

As the Kansas City and EarthCube examples illustrate, stakeholder alignment can (and often does) involve taking into account interests that are in tension with one another. Situational awareness of these points of misalignment and constructive ways of addressing them is crucial. In this way, stakeholder alignment can't be superficial—it must be substantive.

Summing Up

Forming a consortium without mapping the landscape of stakeholders and interests is, as noted in Chapter 1, like driving with a cloudy windshield and no GPS. As we have seen, however, there is no prescriptive formula for specifying stakeholders and identifying interests. Both are interactive processes in which the landscape is socially and iteratively constructed. Different consortia in the same domain will generate different maps of the relevant stakeholders and interests.

Once mapped, points of alignment and misalignment become more visible. The result is that people can perceive more quickly where they agree and where their interests diverge. It is only with this in mind that the various value propositions can be specified for different stakeholders. These value propositions will feature both common and competing interests, which means that a consortium must always be engaged in a dynamic balancing of the interests.

Appendix

MS-CC Priorities by Application Areas

Of six application areas for data and computing, here is the order of importance according to diverse stakeholders (on a scale from zero to 10, with 10 being "very important") and also difficulty (on a scale from zero to 10 with 0 being "very difficult"):

	Important/Very Important (7-10 on 10-point scale)	Difficult/Very Difficult (0-3 on 10-point scale)
Science and engineering	88.1%	68.6%
Workforce development	87.9%	71.2%
Social science and culture	83.8%	62.5%
Energy and environment	80.3%	69.3%
Health	78.5%	66.9%
Language education, arts, and digital humanities	78.0%	65.7%

MS-CC Priorities for Cyberinfrastructure

Of eight infrastructure issues associated with data and computing, in the order of importance (on a scale from 0 to 10, with 10 being "very important") and also difficulty (on a scale from 0 to 10 with 0 being "very difficult") is:

	Important/Very Important (7-10 on 10-point scale)	Difficult/Very Difficult (0-3 on 10-point scale)
Cybersecurity	96.2%	72.4%
CI helping to attract and retain faculty and students	94.5%	85.8%

continued

continued

	Important/Very Important (7-10 on 10-point scale)	Difficult/Very Difficult (0-3 on 10-point scale)
CI helping to bringing in research funding	94.3%	81.1%
CI helping to build a stronger movement of minority serving colleges and universities	92.9%	81.4%
Access to relevant CI training	89.5%	66.4%
Access to CI facilitators	88.4%	75.1%
Innovating in CI design and operation	87.8%	77.0%
A CI assessment tool	86.9%	72.8%

MS-CC Priorities for Collaboration

	Important/Very Important (7-10 on a 10-point scale)	Difficult/Very Difficult (0-3 on a 10-point scale)
Collaboration between HBCUs and HSIs	83.3%	78.9%
Active sharing in general among MSIs	81.3%	72.5%
Collaboration between minority serving and majority serving (predominantly White) institutions	78.9%	70.7%
Collaboration between HBCUs and TCUs	78.7%	78.2%
Little or no sharing across campuses	54%	75.1%

Notes

1. "$125-Million Insulation Plan for Airport Area," *LA Times*, April 16, 2002, pp. 1–56.
2. See National Academies of Sciences, Engineering, and Medicine, *For Greener Skies: Reducing Environmental Impacts of Aviation* (Washington, DC: National Academies Press, 2002): ch. 4, https://doi.org/10.17226/10353.
3. See Joyce E. Penner, David H. Lister, David J. Griggs, David J. Dokken, and Mack McFarland, eds., *Aviation in the Global Atmosphere*, Prepared in collaboration with the Scientific Assessment Panel to the Montreal Protocol on Substances that Deplete the Ozone Layer (Cambridge: Cambridge University Press, 1999), https://www.ipcc.ch/report/aviation-and-the-global-atmosphere-2/.
4. See: Ian Waitz, Jessica Townsend, Joel Cutcher-Gershenfeld, Edward Greitzer, ... Jack Kerrebrock. 2005. Report to Congress, Aviation and the Environment: A National Vision Statement, Goals and Recommended Actions, FAA/NASA, pp. 1-30.
5. We thank Ian Waitz for his insights as we developed this vignette, along with Joel Cutcher-Gershenfeld, who contributed to this initiative. Of course, the responsibility for the text is entirely all of ours as coauthors.
6. This case example draws on the experiences of coauthors who have contributed to MS-CC, including Pat Canavan, Bobby Clark, Joel Cutcher-Gershenfeld, Michael Haberman, and Barbara Mittleman.
7. As we noted in Chapter 4, the focus on underlying interests has its roots in Mary Parker Follett's 1933 lectures inaugurating management studies at the London School of Economics, where she introduced the concept of "integration" as an alternative to domination or compromise. This concept was codified in Richard Walton and Robert McKersie's 1965 *Behavioral Theory of Labor Negotiations* (New York: McGraw Hill), which, in turn, was foundational for Roger Fisher and William Ury's 1981 book *Getting to Yes!* (New York: Houghton Mifflin), which provided the specific recommendation of focusing on interests rather than positions.
8. We thank Akiko Otani and Ali Farid for their insights as we developed this vignette. Of course, the responsibility for the text is entirely ours as coauthors.
9. The chapter appendix has more complete data on priority applications.
10. The chapter appendix has more complete data on priority cyberinfrastructure issues.
11. The chapter appendix has more complete data on collaborations.
12. The following value propositions were recorded in session notes from the working sessions and are now featured in the MS-CC charter, which is available here: https://ms-cc.org/news/updated-ms-cc-charter/.
13. We thank Mike Daniels and the NSF for their insights as we developed this vignette, as well as drawing on the experiences of coauthors involved with EarthCube, including Karen Baker, Joel Cutcher-Gershenfeld, Michael Haberman, Christine Kirkpatrick, Chris Lenhardt, and Namchul Shin. Of course, the responsibility for the text is entirely ours as coauthors.
14. These developments were documented in a 2016 paper by the Stakeholder Alignment Collaborative, see Joel Cutcher-Gershenfeld et al., "Build It, but Will They Come? A Geoscience Cyberinfrastructure Baseline Analysis," *Data Science Journal* 15, no. 8 (2016): pp. 1–14, https://doi.org/10.5334/dsj-2016-008.

Chapter 7

Structuring

Forging a Shared Vision, Drafting a Charter, and Agreeing on Metrics

It is January 2014, and representatives from approximately 40 earth and space science data facilities are gathered at a hotel in Arlington, Virginia. The US National Science Foundation (NSF) supported the meeting in order to better identify the role of data facilities as part of EarthCube, a broad initiative to better understand the Earth as a system. The data sharing would be associated with pressing issues such as climate change, severe weather prediction, available water resources, and more. The first day of a three-day workshop provided little indication of the drama that would unfold on the second day.

The workshop began with discussions on the importance of open data, the interoperability of shared data sets, and the challenges facing data facilities. The second day begins with a "check in," during which there were questions about the mission and governance of the EarthCube initiative. In small groups, participants generated elements of a shared vision for success of the data facilities in connection to EarthCube.

At this point, one of the two facilitators of the session felt that the group was ready to move forward and charter a consortium of data facilities under the EarthCube umbrella. When this was suggested, however, the room erupted, and not in a good way. Some of the participants wanted to move forward and draft a charter for a council of data facilities, while others did not want to do so. The second facilitator called for a showing of interest—with people holding up five fingers if they wanted to proceed with the chartering, four if they were willing to do so, but with some reservations, and so on, down to a fist (no fingers) if they were opposed to moving forward in this way.

The Consortia Century. The Stakeholder Alignment Collaborative: Joel Cutcher-Gershenfeld et al., Oxford University Press. © Oxford University Press (2025). DOI: 10.1093/oso/9780197761649.003.0008

Approximately one-third of the participants held up four or five fingers—indicating support for moving forward with the chartering. Almost all of the remaining two-thirds of participants held up a fist or a single finger—indicating strong opposition to moving forward. This was a shock. There had been hints of discontent around concerns that researchers would be held responsible for outcomes with their data that they didn't fully control, for example. Still, the planners of the workshop had intended to establish some form of coalition or consortium among the data facilities as an outcome of the workshop.

Dialogue was clearly needed—the balance of the agenda was set aside. It quickly became clear that the NSF-funded data facilities were the ones wanting to charter a new council of data facilities, while those facilities funded through NASA, NOAA, and other government agencies were opposed. These other data facilities were not attending the session with the goal of collaborating, but rather to keep an eye on the developments. Simply put, they were there to make sure there were no threats to their funding. With further dialogue, everyone came to appreciate that the data facilities with NASA, NOAA, and other funding sources already had forums in which they can act collectively, while NSF-funded data facilities did not.

Although approximately two-thirds of the participants do not want to launch any new collective efforts, these participants agreed to suspend their opposition and let the NSF-funded data facilities explore what a charter might look like if an entity were to be formed. During this time, the others focused on topics of importance to them, such as data citation and data management.

Interestingly, as the opposition group discussed the issues of data citation and data management, periodic mention was made of tasks that could be undertaken by a council of data facilities if one existed. Meanwhile, the group working on a potential charter set out to make it as lightweight as possible so as to not interfere with the time and effort already going into existing forums. When the subgroup reports were made on the third day, there was full support for the idea of a Council of Data Facilities.

Before the group adjourned, however, a key question arose. Although the participants came from some of the world's leading geoscience data

> facilities, none came with an explicit mandate from their home organization to form a Council of Data Facilities. As such, most indicated that they could become charter members as individuals, but they would have to go back to their home organizations and establish an internal decision-making process to consider whether to join the newly forming council as organizations.[1]

The formation of the Council of Data Facilities in the geosciences illustrates a dramatic moment in which interests became visible in unexpected ways. It also illustrates how taking these interests into account made it possible to reach sufficient alignment to launch a consortium that was well matched to the needs of the stakeholders.

During this structuring phase, there are a few predictable challenges:

- **Vision Is Not Shared:** The vision for the consortium is formulated by just a few stakeholders and is not widely shared, adapted, and embraced.
- **Incomplete Measures:** Not instituting process and outcomes measures early on, as well as measuring only what is easy to observe.
- **Mission Creep:** An expanding mission that focuses consortia in ways that are not sustainable.

The process of reaching sufficient stakeholder alignment to launch a consortium does not begin with a shared vision—that is something that has to be constructed. Both the "vision" part and the "shared" part take work. Once there is enough of a shared vision, it is possible to construct a charter to guide efforts in the direction of that vision. These two elements of the stakeholder alignment process provide much-needed direction and guidance for consortia.

There is no one template or "ideal type" for a vision statement or charter. What follow are thought starters for the visioning and chartering processes.

Structuring is shown in the lower half of our process map (Figure 7.1).

Examples from the Minority Serving Cyberinfrastructure Consortium (MS-CC) are included as further illustration, as in Chapter 6.[2] This level of detail provided for one case allows specifics to be seen and adapted for other contexts, creating the dilemma that due to limited space details of other cases could not be covered in such depth. For clarity, we signal how some other cases vary in key places.

In the case of MS-CC, the shared vision statement has four sentences and the charter spans five pages. In some cases, the shared vision may be 1–2

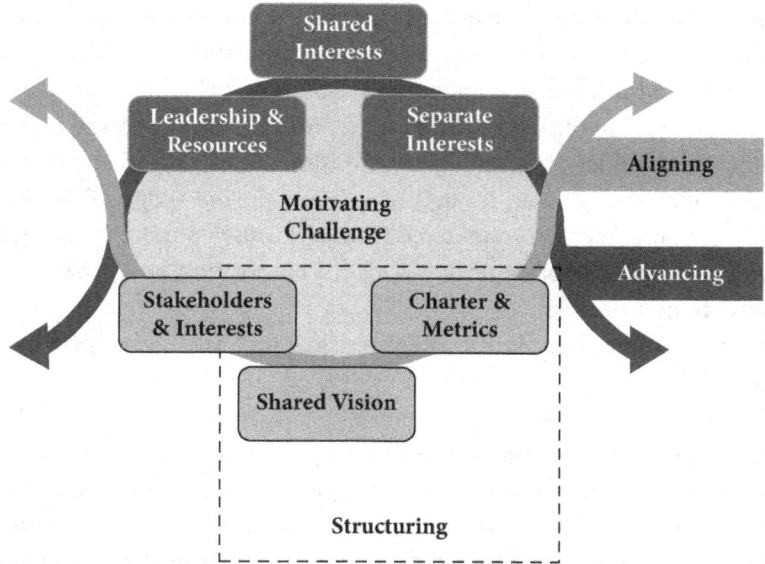

Figure 7.1 Stakeholder Alignment Model—Structuring a Shared Vision, Charter, and Metrics

sentences and the charter may be a paragraph or a page, with the amount of direction and structure that is spelled out being matched to the application situation. It is our experience that examples are important, even if others depart from the model in various ways.

Where appropriate, underlying principles associated with visioning and chartering are noted below. Both these processes are associated with getting diverse stakeholders sufficiently aligned for collective action. We draw on principles of governance, creativity, operations, and conflict resolution.

Constructing a Shared Vision

The process of constructing a shared vision typically begins with an initial group of leaders who are motivated by a collective challenge. Sometimes with facilitation, a brainstorming process is used to generate potential elements of a shared vision. At this point no confirmation or commitment is expected, just identification of what this group sees as possible. A small group then takes the elements and produces a draft vision statement, usually approximately 3–5 sentences, though a more concise vision may be sufficient.

Ideally, the draft vision statement is then shared with a diverse mix of stakeholders for their feedback. This is an opportunity to widen the circle of support for a consortium in two ways—both bringing in people who are "back home" in the organizations after initial involvement and bringing in other stakeholder representatives. Adjustments will invariably be made as additional voices enter, though usually within the scope of the initial thinking. Sometimes, of course, the feedback causes a more fundamental reconsideration of whether or not to form a consortium or of what kind of a consortium is needed.

As an example, here is the shared vision that was developed by the MS-CC:[3]

> We envision a transformational partnership to promote advanced cyberinfrastructure (CI) capabilities on HBCU, TCU, HSIs, and MSI campuses. We are advancing collaboration across campuses around data, research computing, teaching, curriculum development, professional development, and capacity-building. We will learn and grow as a consortium, lifting up all participating institutions by advancing cyberinfrastructure for research and education across diverse fields, disciplines, and communities in ways that reflect the unique voices, cultural identities, and interests of our communities. We will engage as full contributors to the global research and education community.

The statement is concise and compelling. It has helped to bring in many higher education institutions and other parties who were not part of the initial discussion.

The original draft of the charter didn't include the language reflecting "the unique voices, cultural identities, and interests of our communities." This was added following the use of the MS-CC vision and charter in training that a few of us provided as part of an equity initiative with US federal agencies under a January 20, 2020, executive order by US President Biden. Presenting the vision statement in that context suggested the potential value of adding this language, which was brought back to the MS-CC leadership and quickly embraced.

Constructing the vision statement did not begin with wordsmithing. Instead, it began with a broad-ranging discussion. There is a Native American expression that, "the problem is like a pumpkin—first you walk around the pumpkin and see it from all sides before you cut into it." That is what happened with the initial discussions. To illustrate the point, we present parts of the discussion here, taken from the session notes, to illustrate the range of topics from which a concise vision statement was distilled. This builds on a core aspect of creativity, which involves ideating around the concept before codifying the direction to be taken.

The initial brainstorming that led up to this statement had a number of elements, beginning with the idea of "open connections among minority serving institutions (MSIs)" that included these thoughts:

- Everyone open (not afraid) to start conversations with anyone else
- Recognition that everyone will have gaps and no one would be embarrassed by where they were—beginning with the heart-to-heart conversation

As a part of this discussion, one participant observed, "I am from a [developing] country and I see things here that are less advanced." This prompted a discussion about a baseline across institutions, with comments such as:

- There should be a baseline infrastructure common across all MSIs
- There is a need to establish a standard for a common baseline
- There could be an approach to the NSF for support to establish the baseline

Another participant noted that "Beyond the baseline, there should also be a vision." This pointed to the following discussion of a vision, as well as ways to make it a shared vision:

- This is not just cyber research, but research in all the fields and domains where we each have expertise
- Appreciate the diversity among HBCUs
- Bring in some of the young faculty to inform what we are doing
- All institutions have researchers and we are seeking to maximize their potential

This prompted further dialogue on the different types of stakeholders who would need to share in the vision, including:

- The interests of young and untenured faculty need to be taken into account
- The interests of a tenured faculty member might center on giving back to the community
- The interests of IT are distinct as well

Beyond these and other stakeholders, it was noted that cyberinfrastructure can be a catalyst for something more with students and faculty, including comments such as:

- Advancing the frontiers of research
- Attracting and retaining faculty
- Documenting on each campus where research expertise is
- Innovating in educational offerings

A number of themes from the brainstorming made it into the final vision statements, which called for a transformational partnership spanning research and education in ways that would lift up all institutions to have broad impacts in society. Other parts of the brainstorming pointed to what would become the charter for MS-CC.

Note that a shared vision can be more than just text. In Chapter 3, we presented the case of Kaiser Permanente and the range of unions with which it has partnership relations. While that example illustrated tensions within a consortium structure, the same example appears here because its shared vision was expressed in a visualization shown in Figure 7.2—what they term their value compass.[4]

Since Kaiser Permanente is a healthcare delivery system and an HMO membership organization, its vision centers both the patients and members. "Best quality" and "best service" are expected aspirations, but adding "most affordable" and "best place to work" signals the desire for social impact by reducing costs and valuing its workforce. A shared vision expressed as an image may be more accessible and memorable.

The report to Congress on aviation and the environment presented at the beginning of Chapter 6 had both a vision statement and supporting visualization. The statement of a national vision for aviation and the environment was as follows:[5]

In 2025, significant health and welfare impacts of aviation community noise and local air quality emissions will be reduced in absolute

Figure 7.2 Visualization of a Shared Vision by Kaiser Permanente

terms, notwithstanding the anticipated growth in aviation. Uncertainties regarding both the contribution of aviation to climate change, and the impacts of aviation particulate matter and hazardous air pollutants, will be reduced to levels that enable appropriate action. Through broad inclusion and sustained commitment among all stakeholders, the US aerospace enterprise will be the global leader in researching, developing and implementing technological, operational and policy initiatives that jointly address mobility and environmental needs.

Together these words and the image in Figure 7.3 succinctly convey the collaborative work advanced by the Next Generation Air Transportation System initiative, which now operates within the Federal Aviation Administration with a multistakeholder advisory structure.

Toward a Consortium Charter

A charter instantiates the vision in operational ways. Because consortia are dynamic, charters are living documents. The Protein Data Bank has operated for more than 50 years, with three major shifts in its charter, as we will see toward the end of this chapter. These shifts illustrate the likelihood that governance will need to evolve to match the work of the consortia.

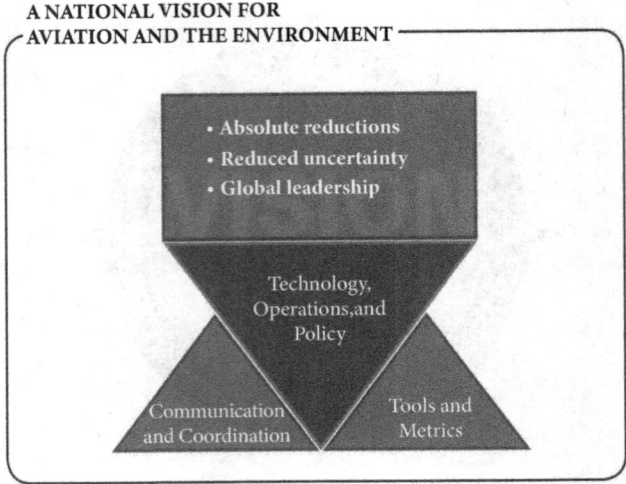

Figure 7.3 Visualization of Collaborative Work by Aviation and the Environment

In the case of MS-CC, some of the initial brainstorming signaled what needed to be addressed in a charter. This began with questions around funding, including supporting grants and the issue of continuity across multiple grants and opportunities:

- How will this be different?
- How do we differentiate ourselves?
- How to sustain things beyond a launch grant?
- How to ensure that each grant builds on past ones?
- Once a grant is complete you are in a different place than you were when you began—this means that the structure will evolve
- The baseline will evolve

Some participants noted that there are multiple relevant types of grants, including those that support community building, those that support collaborative research, and those that support computing equipment and network infrastructure. As one participant noted, "It is not just about getting grants—they are just the vehicle to get where we need to go." This surfaced the theme of "broadening participation" in the area of cyberinfrastructure. The effort was likened to national research centers, but with an orientation to minority serving institutions (MSIs).

With the ideas of a national center in mind, the conversation focused on operational elements, including:

- Begin with charter members—approximately 30 members initially
- Set up entry for additional members
- Anticipate shared services—expertise, documentation, etc.
- Charter members begin the process of collaborating to get to the baseline
- Driven by shared commitment to each other
- [Embrace this] as an inflection point
- [Work with] predominantly White institutions (PWIs) that are actively assisting HBCUs and MSIs in grant solicitations in positive and constructive ways
- Tribal colleges—[nearly] 40 with presidents and IT being supported by the NSF, some in very remote locations

With this in mind, we will present each of the elements of the MS-CC charter in detail to enable adaptation to other settings.

Charter Elements: Preamble and Shared Vision

Although there is no required structure for a consortium charter, we have found it helpful to begin with a preamble stating that it is a living document, followed by a shared vision statement, a statement of purpose, and a listing of value propositions for the relevant stakeholders. In the case of MS-CC, here is the preamble that was drafted:

> This charter serves to codify the structure and operation of the Minority Serving Cyberinfrastructure Consortium (MS-CC) to advance the use of cyberinfrastructure for education and research, identify services to be provided to faculty, students and institutions, as well as professional development on member campuses and other locations as may serve the varied interests of the membership so we can accomplish more together than we could do independently. It is a living document that can be updated by the Consortium Leadership Board and approved by its members.

The preamble indicates that it is a living document and also conveys the spirit of the consortium—accomplishing together what can't be done separately. This is the first thing seen by anyone who reads the charter; therefore it must set an appropriate tone.

The preamble is followed by the shared vision statement (quoted earlier in this chapter). For this to continue to be a shared vision, prospective members and contributors are invited by the word "shared" to consider joining.

Charter Element: Statement of Purpose

A statement of purpose goes beyond the vision and spells out the intended scale and scope of the association's purposeful activities. As an example, here is the MS-CC statement of purpose, which has five main elements:

Increasing Access to CI Resources: MS-CC explores and develops effective strategies and leading practices that campuses may use to engage their students, faculty, and staff to access and become more effective users of advanced research and educational cyberinfrastructure (CI) at local and broader levels, leveraging state, regional, national, and international resources.

Enhancing Interactions and Effectiveness among Researchers and CI Professionals: MS-CC is further dedicated to extending and enhancing the reach and impact of campus and national research computing infrastructures to institutions with minority serving missions to promote research conducted at the campus level and through multi-institutional collaborations.

Enabling Innovation in New and Diverse Teaching and Learning Environments: MS-CC is dedicated to enabling innovation in teaching and learning environments, particularly where advanced cyberinfrastructure enhances the effectiveness, impact, and reach of those environments.

Professional and Career Development: MS-CC is dedicated to providing and sharing in career development activities, curricula, and training for professional CI staff and faculty, researchers, and students. This includes supporting campus research computing and data efforts through enhancing interactions among both professional CI staff and researchers to better utilize, share, and prepare a workforce for the future using advanced computing resources.

Community Alignment and Development: MS-CC appreciates the unique cultures and missions of HBCUs, TCUs, HSIs, other MSIs, and other institutions, while simultaneously lifting up the shared values and interests across MS-CC. This involves full engagement with dialogue and ongoing alignment for decision-making and action. We are guided by the principle from the disability movement of "nothing about us, without us" reflecting the commitment to self-determination by MS-CC and its member institutions.

These statements build on the brainstorming presented earlier in this chapter and other dialogue during the exploratory meeting. This goes beyond the vision statement to emphasize additional themes, such as career development for cyberinfrastructure professionals. Of course, not all consortia will have five different elements when listing their purpose, but having more than one purpose will better reflect the diversity of stakeholder types.

Charter Elements: Guiding Values and Stakeholder Value Propositions

When the US Declaration of Independence was drafted, it included "truths held to be self-evident," beginning with "all men are created equal." Of course, at the time, this was not self-evident where there were monarchies or enslaved people. Further, focusing just on men was limiting in ways that would today be unacceptable in many societies. Chartering documents often state underlying values, even if they are widely understood and shared among the founders. This is an assertion for others who may not share these values and it sends an important signal to future members and contributors. As well, a statement of guiding values provides a touchstone when there are potential violations or challenges around these values.

As an example, here are the guiding values as set forth by the founders of MS-CC:

Inclusion: Dignity, respect, diversity, equity, and trust are advanced based on productive engagement and the principle of equitable voice.
Innovation: Advancing the frontiers of research computing and data with creativity, learning, dialogue, and action, which are advanced through

mentoring, coaching, collaboration, and the principle of being "hard on the problem, not each other."

Stakeholder Value: Voice, governance, independence, interdependence, safety, risk, and reward are advanced based on the principle of "we can accomplish more together than we could do independently."

Openness: Operating in an open and inclusive way, with effective, clear, honest, and accountable communication to the greatest extent possible across MC-CC.

In Chapter 6, we presented the MS-CC stakeholder value propositions. Spelling these out was an important part of the initial mapping of the landscape for the consortium. Once spelled out, it was helpful for the MS-CC to include them in the charter to signal appreciation for what is "at stake" for the various stakeholders. As we noted in Chapter 6, having multiple value propositions stands in contrast to a commercial entrepreneurial organization, which typically has a single value proposition—what it does well that others don't do. For a consortium, the mix of stakeholders indicates more than one value proposition is in play.

Charter Elements: Governance

Beyond the initial elements of a preamble, shared vision, statement of purpose, guiding values, and stakeholder value propositions, the charter spells out the structures involved in the governance of a consortium.

In the case of MS-CC, the decision was made to form a Consortium Leadership Council (CLC). A few years later, this was further formalized as the Consortium Leadership Board (CLB) to act more like a board of directors. Here is the language on the CLB that was added to the charter:

> The governing body of the MS-CC is the Consortium Leadership Board (CLB), which provides oversight on policy and strategic direction for MS-CC. CLB membership includes HBCUs, TCUs, HSIs, and other minority serving colleges, and university representatives. Membership is staggered and renewable for three-year terms. The CLB has no less than five and no more than nineteen representatives. CLB includes at least 50% CI professionals from the voting membership category who can speak on behalf

of their campuses for CI issues. The CLB should also include representation from faculty on campuses (including people with multiple roles) and representatives from the non-voting membership category (no more than 20%).

Members of the CLB are approved by the Membership and Nominating Committee. Potential CLB members must present a letter of participation (as defined by the Membership and Nominating Committee) signed by their respective institution's President.

The CLB elects a Chair, Vice-Chair, and Secretary from within the CLB. The Chair and Vice-Chair positions alternate between a faculty and CI professional. The Chair presides over meetings of the CLB (and the Vice-Chair in the absence of the Chair). The Secretary ensures that meeting minutes are correct and documented and that the agenda is approved.

The CLB meets every other month (during the last week) or as needed.

While to shift from a CLC to a CLB reflects an increased level of responsibility and formalization, there is an open question around the degree to which this will be in tension with the aim of being agile and adaptive.

The charter indicates the purpose of this body, as well as the size, composition, leadership, and operations. These same elements are spelled out for committees and other working groups, which are as follows for MS-CC:

> The CLB shall approve the creation of standing working groups, ad hoc working groups, and other bodies as appropriate. Each of these groups will be a subset of the full committees. The CLB or Committee Chair shall designate the chair or co-chairs of each standing working group, ad hoc working group, or other body. Members of working groups will be selected from among the CLB, MS-CC membership, or external parties. All committees, working groups and other bodies will maintain minutes of their meetings or provide reports to the CLB on their work. The CLB can convene external advisory groups as needed. At least one board member will serve on each committee, but CLB members are not required to be on working groups.

Consortia governance structures often have some form of membership committee, since questions invariably arise around who can and can't be a member and around different membership categories. For the MS-CC, the charter includes the following on the Membership and Nominating Committee (MNC):

> The Membership and Nominating Committee is responsible for identifying and onboarding new MS-CC members, oversight of the CLB nominations, and CLB Officer nominations. The MNC is comprised of at least one member of the CLB. It can have no less than three members and no more than seven members. It can include representatives as needed from the MS-CC membership. The committee will establish application procedures and standards. This committee will serve as a liaison when hiring takes place in service of MS-CC through Internet2.

In the early phases of a consortium, program and priority decisions are in the hands of the leadership team. In time, however, the array of services and activities may require its own supporting committee. In the case of the MS-CC, here is what is included in the charter on their Program and Priorities Committee (PPC):

> The Program and Priorities Committee is responsible for providing guidance to the CLB and MS-CC staff on priorities and programs for the MS-CC. The PPC will serve for the time being as the committee that will provide steering of activities for current NSF funded activities, and as needed with other funding sources/projects where applicable. The PPC is composed of at least one member of the CLB. It can have no less than three members and no more than seven members. It can include representatives as needed from the MS-CC membership. The PPC can establish Working Groups, in coordination with the CLB, for specific MS-CC programs and initiatives as appropriate.

Many consortia are formed before formal incorporation as a for-profit or nonprofit organization. Since funding may be needed for consortium operations, there is often a search to identify an appropriate fiscal agent to hold and administer the funds. In some cases, this is a relatively simple pass-through arrangement (with appropriate record keeping and government reporting by the fiscal agent). In these cases, the direct support to the fiscal agent from the consortium may be modest. In other cases, considerable staff time may be provided by the fiscal agent to the consortium with proportionally greater levels of funding. In any case, it is common for a consortium to have a treasurer or a secretary and treasurer once money is involved. With higher levels of funding, a supporting committee is also constituted. The MS-CC charter describes the Finance and Development Committee (FDC):

> The Finance and Development Committee is responsible for identifying and pursuing future funding opportunities, developing financial strategies for MS-CC, and presenting a proposed budget and financial reports at regular CLB meetings (in collaboration with the MS-CC fiscal agent, Internet2, for funds held by Internet2, and with other entities if funds are held elsewhere). The CLB must approve the budget. All expenditures shall be within the budget unless approved by the CLB. Any major change in the budget must be approved by the CLB. The Finance and Development Committee is comprised of at least two members of the CLB, including the CLB Chair or Vice-Chair, and can have no less than three and no more than seven members. It can include representatives as needed from the MS-CC membership. Working Groups may be established to pursue development opportunities.

The issue of funding for a consortium goes beyond the language presented here and additional language in the charter on the fiscal year that will be used. It includes questions of dues or other member contributions as well as fee-for-service activities and support from foundations or other sources of grants. We return to this issue in Chapter 8 as part of a discussion of sustaining consortia.

In addition to committees, consortia may have general members who also meet periodically. In the case of the MS-CC, here is the charter language on the Membership Meeting:

> The full MS-CC membership shall meet at least once per year in a "Membership Annual Meeting" for the purpose of reviewing activities and progress, sharing information and current practices, enabling collaborations and mechanisms for undertaking new activities, amending this charter, and other community activities.

The MS-CC specified that members of the CLB serve on the various committees. These individuals serve as "linking pins" connecting the committees back to the CLB and the CLB to the committees. Although not spelled out in the MS-CC charter, linking-pin roles connecting various committees to each other may also be relevant. All of these linking pins serve in what are termed "boundary spanning" roles. As we noted in Chapter 3, boundary spanners invariably face a dilemma of honoring their home entity while also learning and engaging in the additional entity. They can't forget where they came from, nor can they speak only from the perspective of the home entity. Ultimately, when a boundary-spanning role is enacted well, it involves two-way learning for all entities, prompted by the unique perspective of the boundary spanner.

Charter Elements: Decision-Making and Revisions to the Charter

Beyond spelling out the consortium structure (leadership, committees, etc.), a charter also provides guidance on consortium operations. This typically begins with agreements on how decisions will be made—whether by consensus, voting, or other means. In the case of MS-CC, here is how decision-making is described in the charter:

> The MS-CC strives to make timely, effective decisions in the best interest of MS-CC. We are accountable for resolving complex issues as constructively and quickly as possible, documenting our decisions and letting impacted parties know about our decisions. We strive for consensus. If we do not have consensus we take decisions by simple majority vote of the MS-CC.

With a preamble specifying that the charter is a living document, procedures need to be spelled out on how to change the charter. In the case of MS-CC this leads to the following language in the charter on revisions:

> The MS-CC Secretary holds this charter and records revisions by the MS-CC membership. This charter can be revised by members of MS-CC—by consensus or, failing that, by a 2/3 majority of MS-CC members. Each member institution has one vote.

Charter Elements: Membership

In addition to having a membership committee, a charter should provide guidance for the committee on membership decisions. As we saw toward the end of Chapter 3, some consortia have just one or a few types of stakeholders and, as a result, have limited membership categories. Others have a broader span and proportionally more categories of membership types. "In-groups" and "out-groups" have been with us since before recorded history, with all the benefits and complications that come with the deeply human tendency. In the case of MS-CC, here is how it is spelled out:

> The Consortium has the following membership categories:
>
> - Minority Serving Institutional Members (voting members)
> - Affiliate Institutional/Not-for-Profit Members
> - Affiliate Industry Members
> - Affiliate Strategic Partners
> - Affiliate Individual Members
>
> An additional designation of "Founding Member" may include individuals in any of the above categories.

Most charters do not include the category of a founding member, which is an opportunity lost. Being a founding member is a point of pride for many individuals and a basis for contributions of funding, time, and other resources over the years. In another part of the charter for MS-CC, the founding member role is spelled out as follows:

> At the inception period of the MS-CC, for the initial five-year period following the MS-CC launch (ending in December 2024), "Founding Members" will be memorialized as having had early and foundational roles and commitments to the work of the MS-CC. The Founding Members are listed in an appendix to this Charter. Founding members will have roles, rights and responsibilities of all MS-CC members. Individuals, affiliates and corporations can be founding members in their respective roles.

Beyond membership categories, there is typically an application process for membership. Here is how MC-CC spells out the membership application process in their charter:

> Prospective members may apply for membership in the Consortium by indicating their commitment to this charter. Applications are submitted to the Membership and Nominating Committee and brought to the CLB, with

endorsement by a simple majority of CLB members. A standard application form per membership category will be developed by the Membership and Nominating Committee.

Based on membership categories and tiered levels within the categories, the CLC will establish membership reasonable dues levels and fees that correspond to services and value propositions.

Charter Elements: Core Members

Consortia typically have a core set of stakeholder categories that are the primary focus of their operation. In the case of MS-CC, this is spelled out as follows:

Institutional membership in the MS-CC is open to any organization that is either a public or private minority serving academic institution (or component thereof), or a national or regional non-profit institution or organization that involves or supports minority education and research computing. Minority serving organizations specified by the U.S. Department of Education include:

- Historically Black Colleges and Universities (HBCUs) (§322 of the HEA, 20 U.S.C. §1061)
- Tribal Colleges and Universities (TCUs) (§316 of the HEA, 20 U.S.C. §1059c)
- Hispanic Serving Institutions (HSIs) (§502 of the HEA, 20 U.S.C. §1101a)
- Alaska Native–serving institutions or Native Hawaiian–serving institutions (§317(b) of the HEA, 20 U.S.C. §1059d(b))
- Predominantly Black Institutions (§§318(b) and 371(c)(9) of the HEA; 20 U.S.C. §§ 1059e(b) and 1067q(c)(9))
- Asian American and Native American Pacific Islander–serving institutions (§§ 320(b) and 371(c)(2) of the HEA, 20 U.S.C. §§1059g(b) and 1067q(c)(2)
- Native American–serving nontribal institutions (§§319(b) and 371(c)(8) of the HEA; 20 U.S.C. §§ 1059f(b) and 1067q(c)(8).

MS-CC is a prism and change agent that will help advance strategies and programs that directly engage and support diversity and inclusion in the 21st century digital STEM workforce by advancing the important research and education work of HBCUs, TCUs, Hispanic Serving Institutions (HSIs) and other MSIs.

A minority-serving institutional member shall be entitled to vote on all matters submitted to a vote of MS-CC members and shall be eligible for election as a Voting Member of the CLC (with one vote per institutional member). It is the responsibility of each institutional member to designate the individual who votes on behalf of the institution, but broad involvement of many people from a member institution is encouraged.

The core members of MS-CC include federally designated categories for these institutions. It will not always be the case that there are preexisting legal categories for membership types. Where there is not a pre-existing legal category, some additional specification may be needed.

Charter Elements: Affiliate Members

In addition to the core members, consortia often have additional categories of affiliates whose membership status also needs to be spelled out. For MS-CC this is outlined in the charter as follows:

> Affiliate members entail several categories and include institutions and organizations that are aligned and committed to the mission of the MS-CC. Affiliate members may participate fully in MS-CC dialogue, but should issues come to a vote, affiliates will only serve in a non-voting ex-officio role so as to ensure the full voice of minority serving institutions.
>
> Affiliate members may be in a position to financially support the MS-CC as a whole and/or MS-CC projects. In this instance, the flow of resources and money will be contractually defined and the oversight and decision-making of the expenditure of those monies will be also defined within the contract.
>
> **Affiliate Institutional/Not-for-Profit Members:**
> Institutions and not-for-profit organizations aligned and committed to the mission of MS-CC are eligible to join in this category of membership (non-voting). This category could include, for example, foundations, academic organizations and entities such as institutions who are not in the Minority

Serving Institutional membership category, professional societies, research institutes, and non-profit organizations committed to advancing the work of MS-CC.

Affiliate Industry Members:
Companies in support of the MS-CC mission, vision and goals may join the MS-CC as industry members (non-voting).

Affiliate Strategic Members:
Strategic partners in support of the MS-CC mission, vision and goals may join the MS-CC as strategic members (non-voting).

Affiliate Individual Members:
Independent, non-affiliated individuals in support of the MS-CC mission, vision and goals may join the MS-CC as individual members (non-voting).

Note the potential for both individual and institutional members. This is particularly important where there are contributing individuals who may not be in a position to participate in a formal way on behalf of their home institution. For example, the home institution may be a government agency or other organization for which the mission of the consortium is outside the scope of their mission and charter. Equally, the mission of the consortium may be within scope, but the decision-making process has not yet been set in motion or completed.

Charter Elements: Removal of Members

One of the most difficult moments in the life of a consortium is when a member is no longer in good standing and faces involuntary removal. Here is how this is addressed in the MS-CC charter:

Members are expected to make good faith efforts to meet their membership commitments and to participate actively in the MS-CC. In addition, if any member has concerns about another member's participation in MS-CC activities, they can contact the CLB Chair and/or Vice Chair, who will appoint a committee to investigate. Constructive efforts by the Chair and Vice Chair and/or the committee will be made to resolve any identified issues through discussion with the Member. However, if discussions with the Member do not adequately resolve issues identified during the review process, the CLB Chair will recommend to the CLB that the Member be removed. Removal is by a majority vote of the CLB.

Charter Elements: Conflict Resolution

In governance it is important that decisions be not just fair and appropriate on the substance but also experienced as procedurally fair. Too often, however, charters fail to include language on conflict resolution procedures. There is often an overarching sense of good will at the founding of a consortium, so conversations about conflict seem unnecessary. Recall, however, our key assumption of common and competing interests, which strongly suggests that conflict is inevitable. Here is how MS-CC addresses conflict resolution in its charter:

> **Complaints:** Perceived violations of this charter or other issues associated with the MS-CC should be entered on an issue tracking record maintained by the CLB. Constructive dialogue is then encouraged—being hard on the problem, not each other. Issues that are confidential or sensitive can be registered directly with the arbitrators indicated below or other organizations or agencies as appropriate.
>
> **Mediation:** Individuals or groups involved in a disagreement or complaint may request that any other individual in the MS-CC serves as a peer mediator. Individuals can turn down the request (no need to specify the reason). If an individual agrees to serve as a mediator, they will facilitate a three-step process: 1) Each party states what it understands to be the problem or the issue, with time for clarifying questions; 2) All parties identify relevant options—these are just options, no one is agreeing to anything; and 3) All parties explore whether one or more options can serve as a resolution.
>
> **Arbitration:** One or more individuals who are highly trusted by all members should be identified so that they can serve as arbitrators of disputes that can't be resolved through constructive dialogue or mediation.

Metrics: Agreeing on KPIs

When it comes to what commercial firms term key performance indicators (KPIs), there are both throughput measures (how many people have been trained, for example) and outcome measures (what are people now doing with the training). As well, some of these measures are leading indicators (knowing where we are headed) and some are lagging indicators (knowing where we have been). The idea of a balanced scorecard within an organization reflects the inevitable reality that all KPIs can't be optimized at once—so a balancing process is needed. The same is true for consortia, only here the balancing is relative to the interest of the different stakeholders rather than different parts of the same organization.

For MS-CC, the specification of KPIs initially centered on throughput measures—numbers of participants attending workshops and related events, for example. In time, however, with increased levels of funding, there was a need to spell out a full set of KPIs, as shown in Table 7.1.

As noted, some of these KPIs are throughput measures—such as the number of people participating in training or workshops, the number of stakeholder maps conducted, and the number of MS-CC members, and others are outcome measures—such as new forums established, new research projects, and pedagogical innovations enabled by cyberinfrastructure. Most are lagging indicators—such as placements of students, faculty, and staff or budget spending. More complex relationships among the KPIs are possible. For example, research innovations may translate into pedagogical innovations or vice-versa. In time, stakeholders in a consortium come to understand what they can and can't do together based on what they learn from the KPIs. Of course, the KPIs themselves will evolve as the operation of the consortium evolves.

The Evolution of Charters: The Protein Data Bank

The Protein Data Bank (PDB) is governed through a consortium, which began with an informal structure and evolved under a series of charters. The evolution was driven by the increase in scale of the PDB and by changes in the underlying science, which increasingly relied on this shared community resource.[6] Aspects of the case are presented here, and additional developments around sustaining this resource are presented in Chapter 8.[7]

Table 7.1 MS-CC Key Performance Indicators

Cyberinfrastructure KPIs

- CI networking initiatives (by campus and across campuses)
- CI data initiatives (by campus and focus, and across campuses)
- CI high performance computing initiatives (by campus and across campuses)
- Other CI initiatives

Workforce KPIs

- Number of people participating in training and workshops (by topic)
- New CI professionals supporting MS-CC campuses
- Students, faculty, and staff associated with MS-CC hired into industry (by company and location)
- Students, faculty, and staff associated with MS-CC hired into government (by agency and location)
- Students, faculty, and staff associated with MS-CC hired by other universities and other organizations (by location)

Research KPIs

- New science and engineering research projects enabled by cyberinfrastructure capabilities
- New social science and economics research projects enabled by cyberinfrastructure capabilities
- New arts and humanities research projects enabled by cyberinfrastructure capabilities
- Other research projects enabled by cyberinfrastructure capabilities

Education KPIs

- Pedagogical innovations enabled by cyberinfrastructure in the sciences and engineering
- Pedagogical innovations enabled by cyberinfrastructure in the social sciences and economics
- Pedagogical innovations enabled by cyberinfrastructure in the arts and humanities
- Other pedagogical innovations projects enabled by cyberinfrastructure capabilities

Stakeholder Alignment KPIs

- Campus stakeholder maps conducted
- New campus research computing and data advisory forums established
- New research computing and data communities of practice established

MS-CC Membership, Staffing, and Financial KPIs

- MS-CC membership (by category)
- Internet2/grant-funded staff supporting MS-CC
- Budget projections and actual spending for MS-CC

In 1957, the first three-dimensional structure of a protein myoglobin was determined using the methods of x-ray crystallography; shortly thereafter the structure of hemoglobin was announced. This work marked a major milestone in biology for which Kendrew and Perutz won Nobel Prizes in 1962. As more structures were determined, scientists keen to analyze the structures in terms of their architecture and function required access to the three-dimensional coordinates. There were in-person meetings and snail mail exchanges to discuss how best to create an archive for protein structures. These grassroots efforts resulted in the creation of the PDB in 1971 as a collaboration between Brookhaven National Laboratory (BNL) and the Cambridge Crystallographic Data Centre (CCDC). Multiple stakeholders were essential to this collaboration, including scientists and staff establishing data standards, those contributing to the Data Bank, those using the data, and others. At this point, it was not a formal consortium, just a partnership between BNL and CCDC.

The terms for how the data would be collected by both centers, processed at BNL, and distributed were agreed on by both parties. The first iteration of the PDB consisted of seven protein structures. In time, distribution centers with mirrors of the data were created worldwide with individual agreements between these centers and BNL. By this point, PDB was an informal consortium among the many distribution centers.

By 1998, when there were about 9,000 structures in the PDB, a more formal consortium called the Research Collaboratory for Structural Bioinformatics (RCSB) was established. This consisted of groups from Rutgers University, San Diego Supercomputer Center, and the National Institute of Standards and Technology (NIST). RCSB responded to a Request for Proposals from the NSF that resulted in RCSB becoming the new managers of the PDB. The responsibilities for each member of RCSB were clearly laid out and a Scientific Advisory Committee (SAC) was formed to provide advice from the community. Although this was a more formal structure, there was no formal charter.

At the same time, new data centers were independently created in Europe and Japan. In the interest of creating a single global archive, the heads of the three centers created the Worldwide Protein Data Bank (wwPDB) in 2003. For the first time a formal charter was drawn up that defined the rationale for the creation of the wwPDB, the definition of membership and terms, guidelines for responsibilities of each member including file format definitions, the creation of a single archive keeper, and operation details including the SAC.

While every site was bound by strict curation and validation standards, so that the files distributed by any site would be identical, each site could have its own website with potentially competing services for visualization, search, outreach, and education. The initial term of the agreement was 10 years and the agreement was signed by the heads of each site and institutional representatives. In 2006, the charter was amended to add a new member—BioMedResBank (BMRB). In 2013 the renewal charter that was created was very similar to the first charter except that implementation details such as file formats were moved to an appendix.

The addition of the EMDB data resource in 2021 and the emergence of new structural biology methods and repositories necessitated the creation of a new charter that allowed for different types of members. The roles and responsibilities of Core, Associated, and Federated members are described in a fair amount of detail. In addition, wwPDB Core Archives and Federated Resources are also defined. The Appendix to this charter spells out many implementation details. Because the field is growing so rapidly it is likely that the next charter will be written in fewer than 10 years.

Today more than 50 years after the PDB first began with 7 protein structures, the PDB now contains more than 200,000 entries. The user base is large and diverse. Every day more than 60 million highly curated, coordinate files are downloaded from the wwPDB member sites. The power of having well-curated data in machine readable format made it possible for DeepMind to use artificial intelligence to meet one of the grand challenges of biology—the prediction of protein structure from its amino acid sequence.

The half-century journey of the PDB illustrates increasing scale combined with increasing formalization. Agreement on common standards for data input has been a key to success, as has been flexibility to encompass emerging data types as the science and technology have evolved. Along this journey, the PDB went from a two-party partnership (with no charter) to an informal multiparty consortium (with an initial charter) to a global collaborative (with an expanded and adjusted charter).

Summing Up

Constructing a shared vision involves both a visioning process and a process by which the visioning becomes shared. Invariably, not all stakeholders are present to begin the visioning, and even the vision itself is not in everyone's mind in the same way. As a result, there is process of brainstorming potential elements of a vision, a process of codifying these elements in a draft statement, and a process of socializing the draft statement with a representative set of stakeholders (with adjustments based on the feedback) so that it can be codified as a shared vision. In time, edits and adjustments to the vision are likely, which is a sign of an agile and adaptive consortium.

Drafting a charter is a key step toward formalizing the structure and operations of a consortium. Charters can be relatively simple, one-page statements or more extensive documents. With greater numbers of stakeholder types, greater scope of issues, and the arrival of funding, more detail is invariably needed.

KPIs represent a crucial source of feedback for any organization. In the case of a consortium, they help diverse stakeholders to better understand what a consortium is (and is not) able to accomplish together that the parties can't do separately.

Notes

1. For more on EarthCube, see https://www.earthcube.org/. Also, see our analysis of the dynamics that followed this session in Stakeholder Alignment Collaboration, Karen Baker, Nick Berente, Dorothy Carter, Joel Cutcher-Gershenfeld, Leslie DeChurch, Courtney Flint, Gabriel Gershenfeld, Michael Haberman, Christine Kirkpatrick, John L. King, Eric Knight, Barbara Lawrence, Spenser Lewis, Chris Lenhardt, Pablo Lopez, Matt Mayernik, Charles Mcelroy, Barbara Mittleman, Victor Nichol, Mark Nolan, Namchul Shin, Cheryl Thompson, Susan Winter, and Ilya Zaslavsky, "Build It, but Will They Come? A Geoscience Cyberinfrastructure Baseline Analysis," *Data Science Journal* 15 (2016): pp. 1–14.
2. For more on MS-CC, see https://www.ms-cc.org/. This case example draws on the experiences of coauthors who have contributed to MS-CC, including Pat Canavan, Bobby Clark, Joel Cutcher-Gershenfeld, Michael Haberman, and Barbara Mittleman. Of course, the responsibility for the text is entirely all of ours as coauthors.
3. For the current version of the full charter, including the vision statement and other elements introduced below, see: https://docs.google.com/document/d/1SeD58X4CRsIXS4pAoZrdalYwt7GnC-WIoCufXGxn0fY/edit?tab=t.0.

4. For more on the value compass, see https://www.lmpartnership.org/focus-areas/value-compass.
5. See Ian Waitz, Jessica Townsend, Joel Cutcher-Gershenfeld, Edward Greitzer, and Jack Kerrebrock, "Report to Congress, Aviation and the Environment: A National Vision Statement, Goals and Recommended Actions," FAA/NASA (2005), pp. 1–30.
6. See Helen M. Berman, "Creating a Community Resource for Protein Science," *Protein Science* 21 (2012): pp. 1587–1596, https://doi.org/10.1002/pro.2154.
7. This case vignette draws on the experience of coauthor Helen Berman, who is a cofounder of the Protein Data Bank.

Chapter 8
Sustaining
Delivering Results, Adjusting, and Adapting

In 2002, an assembly of digital fabrication equipment in the Vigyan Ashram in Maharashtra, India, led to the idea of a fab lab. A fab lab combines digital fabrication equipment (such as a laser cutter, 3D printer, 3D scanner, milling machine, circuit board assembly, and more) with a focus on fostering design thinking, building digital literacy, and enabling people in each community to make what they need. The fab lab idea was enabled by a National Science Foundation (NSF) grant to MIT's Center for Bits and Atoms, led by Neil Gershenfeld. Under this grant, Neil was assembling a broad cross-section of digital fabrication machinery all in one space at MIT. Bill Mitchell, former dean of MIT's School of Architecture and Planning, advised Neil to meet with Mel King, a colleague at MIT's Department of Urban Studies and Planning and a community leader in Boston. Mel had already set up a neighborhood technology center in the South End of Boston, helping kids to increase digital literacies, including how to repair and program computers. Together, Mel and Neil expanded what the Vigyan Ashram had been doing and launched the first complete prototype for a fab lab—open to the community in the South End of Boston.

The idea of a community-based fab lab was infectious. Soon the number of fab labs in the world began to double approximately every 18 months—an exponential rate of change. Today there are over 2,500 fab labs in the world as well as a comparable number of maker spaces. While the maker spaces are largely independent entities, the fab labs began with a consortia-like structure for sharing digital designs and learning materials.

Three forms of formalization now sustain the world's fab labs. First, the Fab Foundation was established in 2009 in response to the growing requests for guidance in launching a fab lab and community programming. Led by Sherry Lassiter, the Fab Foundation formalized what had been informal support provided by the MIT's Center for Bits and Atoms. Second, the Fab Academy was also established in 2009 to codify online learning about digital fabrication. It began with a fast paced, hands-on curriculum of weekly rapid-prototyping projects. It has since evolved into what is called the "Academany" with curriculum on bio-fab for learning synthetic biology technologies, a Fabricademy for innovation in design and wearable technology in the textile and fashion industries, a "Fab All-In" curriculum on community inclusion, and other curricula. Third, the Fab Cities initiative was founded in 2014, led by the Institute for Advanced Architecture of Catalonia (IAAC), with the mission to establish a 40-year roadmap that would enable Barcelona to break its dependence on supply chains and instead have self-sufficient productive capability. Today, over 40 cities have joined Barcelona on this journey. Formalizing initiatives have emerged throughout the ecosystem centered on the fabrication of prosthetic devices (Enable), self-sufficient disaster response (Field Ready), supply chain transformation (World Economic Forum), sustainable materials (Materiom), and others.

In each case, the sustaining activities build on assemblies of motivated stakeholders taking informal activities and formalizing things with a mix of institutional arrangements that have features of an organization, a consortium, and a social movement.[1]

Sustaining a consortium (and other associated arrangements) doesn't mean that it all persists forever. A consortium should only persist as long as the parties are accomplishing together what they can't do separately. In the process, they are advancing shared interests, appreciating separate interests, and ensuring needed leadership and resources. Then, when the work is sufficiently complete, the consortium may disband, fade away, or transform.

During this sustaining phase there are a number of predictable challenges, including:

- **Problematic Leadership Dynamics**: Leadership turnover and leadership mismatches as the needs of consortia evolve;
- **Insufficient Resources**: Resource variability, particularly when it comes to sustaining a consortium; and

- **Failed Dissolution**: Failure to dissolve or restructure consortia when the mission is sufficiently complete.

In some consortia considered in this book, such as the Protein Data Bank (PDB), its persistence includes a celebration of its 50th anniversary and a continuing impact, such as providing the structural data critical for the development of the messenger RNA vaccines for COVID-19. In other cases, such as we will see with the National Data Service (NDS), it disbanded long before realizing its envisioned impact.

Like the shark, which must always be moving forward to stay alive, consortia must always be advancing. While Chapters 6 and 7 focused on the journey to sufficient alignment for action, this chapter is focused on the parallel and continuing process of advancement.

Advancing

We repeat the visualization from Chapter 4 with the sustaining elements highlighted in Figure 8.1.

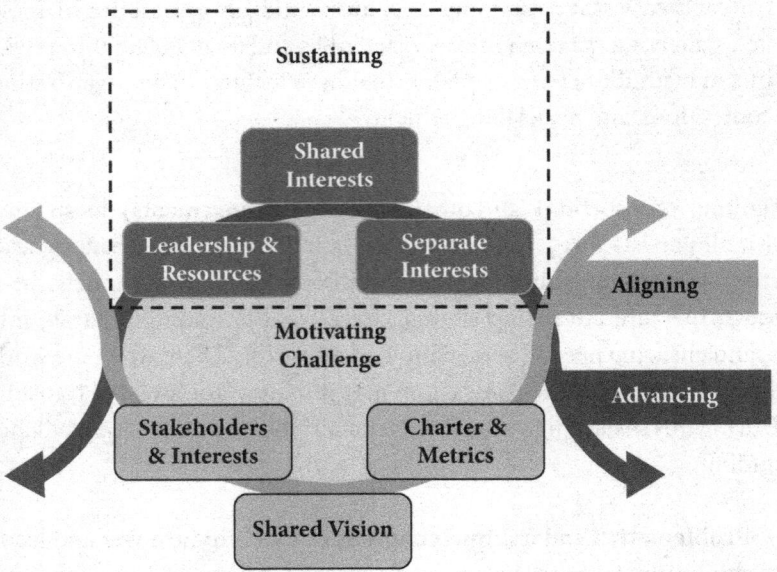

Figure 8.1 Stakeholder Alignment Model—Delivering Results, Adjusting, and Adapting

To illustrate the sustaining elements, we continue from Chapters 6 and 7 in drawing on the experiences of the Minority Serving Cyberinfrastructure Consortium (MS-CC) during its first five years of operation and add examples from the Biomarkers Consortium, the National Data Service, and other cases.

Leadership

Even as we all celebrate great leaders, we are mindful that transformational change in the world is invariably the product of distributed leadership rather than just the work of any one individual. Indeed, consortia serve as a counterpoint to the "great man" or "great woman" model of leadership. Consortia bring together leaders from many different groups and organizations and then foster emergent leaders to further advance the mission.

Learning to lead laterally is different from top-down or bottom-up leadership within a given hierarchy. Leadership within a hierarchy involves the interplay of authority and responsibility, both of which derive from the hierarchical structure. Influence is important, but always understood to be in the context of authority and responsibility. By contrast, lateral leadership begins with influence. Authority and responsibility are limited, particularly at the outset. Until staff are involved, no one is the "boss" of anyone else. There may be respect for the positional authority that people have in their home organizations, but that has more to do with influence in the consortium in the early stages. For example, in the formation of the Biomarkers Consortium, Garry Neil was respected for his positional role as a corporate vice president at J&J Pharmaceuticals, which enabled him to have sufficient influence to convene others. At the same time, representatives from other pharmaceutical firms, National Institutes of Health (NIH), the Food and Drug Administration (FDA), and other consortium members each retained their own independent sources of power and influence.

When it comes to sustaining a consortium, there are three underlying leadership principles at play. The first is "internal alignment for lateral alignment." That is, individuals involved in the formation and sustainment of a consortium each need to have sufficient internal alignment or autonomy in their home group or organization in order to be part of collective action. As we noted in Chapter 6, there is invariably a complicated dynamic during formation in which individuals have to declare how far they can go with the consortium on their own authority as compared to when they need a formal mandate from their own organization. When it comes to sustaining the consortium, this process shifts into a continuing dynamic with each consortium member achieving sufficient internal alignment for continued connection to the consortium. We use the word "sufficient," since there will rarely be total or equivalent enthusiasm within each associated group or organization. This requires consortium members to be transparent with their internal dynamics (something not normally revealed when relations are competitive), so that collective activities can go forward.

In the case of the National Data Service (NDS), there was not sufficient internal alignment at NSF, a key stakeholder, around using the name "the National Data Service." The concept was borrowed from the National Data Service in Australia, but the NSF viewed any initiative being designated as "the" national body as requiring far more prework and a more extensive track record of accomplishment before the consortium could claim this title. Without that internal alignment, including within this one key stakeholder organization, the overall efforts of the consortium were constrained.

The second principle relevant to lateral leadership is "boundary spanning," which was highlighted in Chapter 1. All leaders of a consortium face a dilemma. On one hand, they cannot forget where they came from, and, on the other, they are helping to create something new. In this respect, they are spanning the boundary between their home group or organization and the consortium. Invariably, there will be pulls and tugs in both directions and boundary spanners have a twofold educational task. First, they must educate the home group or organization around what is new (the internal alignment mentioned above) and then educate the consortium about just how far and how fast their work can go without creating complications back in the home group or organization.

> When the concept of boundary spanning was introduced to members of the Campus Research Computing Consortium (CaRCC) it was instantly embraced. The members of this organization of research computing and data professionals understood that the consortium would be advancing initiatives relevant to their individual campuses and other professional communities, including other consortia in which they were

already participating. The group instantly appreciated that they had to simultaneously attend to separate and collective interests.

The mix of common and competing interests is evident in the development of capability assessment tools, job postings for the profession, and basic questions of time and effort. Each institution wants to advance research data and computing capability, while bringing in the best talent and maximizing the work of its staff. While all universities benefit from common hiring language, there is still the reality that one campus may be taking talent from another by using this shared language. Using common tools for campus-level capability assessments allows for useful comparisons, but also requires each campus to openly share aspects of their internal assessment outcomes to be meaningful. Campuses must weigh complex interests in having their staff belong to the CaRCC. Engagement with CaRCC aligns with the universities' broader mission in society and benefits the collective interest of the consortium as a whole, but their participation also takes away from time that could be used to address parochial campus priorities. At stake are issues of hiring, transparency, and allocation of time and effort.[2]

Acknowledging a boundary spanner role can help consortium members identify opportunities for shared progress and assist them in making a case back at their home organizations about the benefits of a collective effort versus operating separately.

The third principle relevant to lateral leadership is "dynamic institutionalization." The term "institutionalization" has connotations of stability and even ossification, but what is often institutionalized in a consortium is something dynamic. For example, the consortium may formalize membership categories, but these will evolve as the relevant mix of stakeholders changes. Similarly, the establishment of a mechanism to select or elect leaders is a key form of institutionalization in a consortium, but this mechanism may evolve over time. Relevant leaders at the formation of a consortium are typically visionary individuals who see what is possible. In time, a different type of leader is needed who is able to deliver results on various programs and initiatives that have been launched. Anticipating this dynamic, a charter may provide for term limits, rotation, or other mechanisms for leadership changes. Invariably this cycles back to a need to reinvigorate the vision. If the selection or election process can support this dynamic, then it can be institutionalized in that way. If, however, the process over time only produces one type of leader (either visionary or operational), then the process itself will need adjustment.

> In the case of the MS-CC, many of the initial founders were chief information officers (CIOs) in historically Black colleges and universities (HBCUs) and tribal colleges and universities (TCUs). For the TCUs, institutionalization was enabled by the existence of the American Indian Higher Education Consortium (AIHEC), which regularly convened the presidents and other leaders of TCUs. MS-CC was enabled by this institutional connection to AIHEC. By contrast, there was no comparable organization for HBCUs. As a result, organizing happened in an indirect way. In 2022, the US White House was convening activities around "HBCU week," an annual set of events honoring the role of HBCUs in society and MS-CC signaled an ability to contribute. The signals were sent through multiple channels, including connections of some HBCUs with leaders in Congress such as South Carolina Congressman Jim Clyburn, as well as policy leaders associated with MS-CC's fiscal agent, Internet2. When this was accepted, many of the CIOs in MS-CC then reached out to their respective university presidents to bring them together for a reception centered on research and educational computing and data. Informal internal conversations along these lines were ongoing at many of the campuses, but the institutional legitimacy of a White House event advanced the effort in important ways

Resources

Consortia often begin with limited resources, drawing on volunteers who are deeply committed to the overarching aim. In some cases, such as the Biomarkers Consortium, these volunteers all had formal support from their home organizations (pharmaceutical firms, biotech companies, government agencies, patient advocacy organizations, and universities) to dedicate time to the consortium. In other cases, such as MS-CC, the initial organization involved discretionary time on the part of those involved, with formal support from their home organizations coming later as the time commitment expanded from periodic meetings to being an ongoing enterprise.

With funding and the requirements of associated infrastructure, for example, staff, budgets, and so forth, there is a need for increased formalization. In the case of the Biomarkers Consortium, that was reflected in the chartering of four steering committees in different therapeutic areas (cancer, inflammation and immunity, metabolic disorders, and neuroscience), as well as an Executive Committee. Moreover, the Foundation for NIH (FNIH) was identified as the organizational home and fiscal agent for the Biomarkers Consortium.[3] Since many consortia begin informally, they are not established as private corporations or nonprofit organizations, so the need for a fiscal agent arises as soon as money is involved. In contrast to the chartering of the consortium (addressed in Chapter 6), the fiscal agent will start with its own charter and associated structure. In the case of the Biomarkers Consortium, FNIH brought its full committee infrastructure, which included the following (each with its own charter):

- Advancement and Development Committee
- Communications Committee
- Compensation Committee
- Finance and Audit Committee
- Governance Committee
- Investment Subcommittee
- Portfolio Oversight Committee

This infrastructure was essential, since the four therapeutic steering committees and the executive committee were launching multiple projects each year, with associated funding, staffing, and oversight needs. The charters for each of these FNIH committees follow a common structure, which is as follows:

- Purpose
- Membership
- Meetings
- Minutes
- Responsibilities

For example, here is the charter for the FNIH Governance Committee,[4] which may be instructive for any organization setting up a governance committee:

FNIH Finance and Audit Committee Charter
1. **Purpose:** The Finance and Audit Committee ("Committee") is established by the Board ("Board") of the Foundation for the National Institutes of Health ("FNIH") to support the Board in fulfilling its oversight responsibilities relating to the FNIH's financial reporting, investment, and budgeting processes as well as the adequacy of internal controls and the performance of the independent auditors.
2. **Members:** The Finance and Audit Committee shall consist of at least three voting, independent members of the Board of Directors. A majority of the Committee's voting membership shall constitute a quorum to conduct business. The Chair of the Board and the President and Executive Director shall serve as ex officio members.
3. **Meetings:** The Finance and Audit Committee shall meet at those times and places as determined by the Chair of the Committee, and normally not less than twice per year. It shall meet with the President and Executive Director, and any other Officers or employees the Committee deems appropriate, to discuss and review matters contemplated by this Charter. Reasonable notice of meetings shall be given to all Committee members or may be waived in the same manner as required for meetings of the Board. Meetings of the Committee may be held by means of conference telephone or other communications equipment that allow all persons participating in the meeting to hear and speak to each other. In carrying out its role, the Committee may form subcommittees or retain outside consultants so long as it is within a budget approved by the Board for that purpose.
4. **Minutes:** The Finance and Audit Committee shall maintain minutes of its meetings and regularly report to the Board on its findings, recommendations, actions, and any other matters the Committee deems appropriate or the Board requests.
5. **Responsibilities:** The Finance and Audit Committee shall from time to time unless another interval is stated:
   - Each year review the proposed annual budget and recommend its approval to the Board.
   - Review intra-year financial performance against approved budgets; Re-forecast budgets.

- Each year recommend to the Board the appointment and/or termination of the independent auditors and independent tax advisor.
- Each year review with management and the independent auditors the FNIH's audited annual financial statements and management letter and recommend the approval of the financial statements to the Board.
- Each year review any disagreements among management and the independent auditors in connection with the annual audit and any restrictions on the scope of work or access to required information in the FNIH Finance and Audit Committee Charter.
- Review and discuss with management and the independent auditors the adequacy of the FNIH's financial reporting processes, policies, and internal controls.
- Recommend to the Board changes to management's signature authority concerning contractual agreements, checks, wire transfers, and banking and investment accounts.
- Review management's cash management plans and strategies.
- Review changes to the FNIH's banking structure.
- Ensure proper oversight of the FNIH's investments, including the setting of the investment policy statement, review of the strategic asset allocation, and the appointment and termination of investment managers.
- Review potential material financial obligations or encumbrances outside the normal course of business including security interests, asset pledges, and leases.
- Oversee management's administration of the employee defined contribution benefit plan.
- Ensure there are adequate ethical standards, conflicts of interest, whistleblower, and document retention policies in place.
- Review any legal matter that could have a significant impact on the FNIH's financial statements.
- Perform such other duties as are necessary or appropriate to further the Committee's purposes, or as the Board may from time to time assign to it.

The charter continues to include an approval date: in this version it reads, "Approved by the Board of Directors on May 23, 2019." This implicitly signals that it is a living document that can be further revised and approved. Some charters include a procedure for making revisions to help define this process.

Shared Interests

Alignment around a shared vision sets the stage for progress advancing shared interests. Consortia advance shared interests in ways as varied as the array of consortia themselves. Just considering the consortia we have highlighted in this book, these include:

- Workshops
- Shared staff
- Data repositories
- Culture change initiatives
- Basic science research
- Precompetitive applied research
- Educational innovation

In the case of MS-CC, a series of stakeholder "pulse" surveys have been used to identify shared interests to focus on in workshops and other consortium initiatives. The first of these "pulse" surveys, conducted in 2022, provided a ranking of potential programming topics as shown in Table 8.1 (with the "score" based on assigning 7 points to a number 1 ranking, 6 to a number 2 ranking, and so on for all seven options).

As a result, the MS-CC prioritized cybersecurity (the top ranked choice in Table 8.1) for a series of 2022 workshops on HBCU and TCU campuses.

Separate Interests

Often overlooked in the writing on collaboration are the concurrent competing interests. When we published an article on agile consortia in the *Stanford Social Innovation Review*, it prompted an online comment from Douglas Bitonti Stewart, executive director of Detroit's Max M. and Marjorie S. Fisher Foundation, which lifted up the focus on competing as well as common interests:[5]

Table 8.1 Example Pulse Survey Ranking Potential Programming Topics for MS-CC

Topic	Rank	Score
Cybersecurity (campus assessment, improving risk profile, and shared services)	1	1,227
Funding for advancing campus cyberinfrastructure	2	1,147
Cyberinfrastructure tools and methods (including best practices, technology road maps, self-assessment, and new technology/solutions)	3	1,100
Career and workforce development (research data professionals and cyberinfrastructure engineers)	4	888
Research acceleration (fostering research on topics of priority to students, faculty, staff, and the local community)	5	881
Collaboration opportunities with other institutions and organizations on research data, computing, and cyberinfrastructure	6	773
Science DMZs (a research environment that is secure, scalable, and structured for data transfer, use, instrumentation, and computing)	7	623

I am so grateful for this article—and in particular for one sentence that drew something out that is always there, but rarely discussed: ". . . that stakeholders have both common and competing interests . . . ."

As someone who has spent half my career raising money and relationships/partners—and the other half serving a family foundation in Detroit, I rarely hear or discuss competing interests when in collaborations. Perhaps it is the Midwest mentality, perhaps it is our general conflict avoidant culture in the funding community, or a simple but critical oversight—when we collaborate as funders and do not recognize the competing interests of our partners who seek our funding, we are missing a huge part of the picture.

Perhaps even as important as [this,] we should recognize and make plain that funders often compete for attribution versus simply focusing on contributing toward social or environmental justice. This competition between communication shops, the wrestling that comes with who is at the podium, is not invisible to our partners in the field and even our neighbors who live closest to the issues we are working on together.

So, my gratitude to the many authors of this article and the work it represents. I will pledge to make visible this important dynamic in two collaboratives we are involved in this week!

Acknowledging competing interests increases the ability to foster constructive dialogue rather than having them surface in unexpected and unconstructive ways.

For example, the MS-CC operates in partnership with Internet2 as its fiscal agent. This has enabled MS-CC to receive two grants totaling over $18 million in funding from the NSF that are the primary focus of its activities. Separately, individual campuses are pursuing support from the US Department of Energy (DOE), the National Telecommunications and Information Administration (NTIA), and other sources to bridge what are termed "digital divides" in Internet access. These are not at present an overall initiative of the consortium, but independent activities of consortium members. It is important for MS-CC members to be unrestrained in pursuing these and other separate initiatives at the same time that they work together on research and educational computing activities on their campuses.

Adjusting

Continuous improvement is at the heart of successful consortia, which involves agility as the mix of stakeholders, interests, and broader contextual forces change. A key step in setting the stage for agility, as we have noted in Chapter 1, is to begin with the minimum viable consortium (no more and no less).

Feedback is central to agile adjustments. This can take the form of periodic stakeholder mapping surveys that document continuing and changing points of alignment and misalignment. For example, the MS-CC members were always aware of digital divides in their home communities but saw community Internet access as outside the scope of their campus focus. When the COVID-19 pandemic forced many classes to shift to virtual delivery, the Internet resources of the surrounding communities moved to mission critical. Within MS-CC, this initially took the form of pursuing DOE grants for Internet access on individual campuses. As it became clear that this was a shared interest, the focus shifted from separate activities by the MS-CC members to shared dialogue on strategies and responses, as well as exploration of common supporting infrastructure (such as the capability to do community stakeholder maps on digital divide matters).

Making agile adjustments runs up against a number of contending forces, such as the "iron law of oligarchy" introduced in Chapter 3. The iron law results in a focus on sustaining leadership and the consortia itself, which can generate resistance to change. While there is always a risk of "iron law" dynamics, the risk can be mitigated with understandings included in the charter that the consortium is intended to be agile and adaptive (beginning with a preamble that states that it is a living document and extending to include flexibility in membership categories, leadership transitions, and consortium structure).

The case of the Protein Data Bank (PDB), a science infrastructure consortium founded in 1957 and introduced in Chapter 7, involved adjustments driven in part by the expanding needs of science as outlined here:[6]

> In the early days, the molecular structures in the PDB were relatively small and exclusively determined using a single method (x-ray crystallography). As time went on and the technology for data collection and analysis improved, it became possible to determine the structures of large and complex molecules. New structure determination methods such as nuclear magnetic resonance (NMR) spectroscopy and three-dimensional electron microscopy (3DEM) began to emerge and the PDB created the infrastructure to manage these data. Now the PDB contains more than 200,000 structures ranging from very small single domains to large macromolecular machines.
>
> Ten years after its creation, it became clear to the PDB leadership that the data were so important to the public good that depositing data needed to be mandatory. Again, a committee was formed by the International Union of Crystallography (IUCr) to come up with a set of guidelines for archiving. The committee strongly recommended that depositing data into the PDB become a requirement for publication. This is now the standard for all structural biology publications.
>
> A new consortium called the Research Collaboratory for Structural Bioinformatics (RCSB) was awarded a grant to manage the PDB in 1998. To ensure that there would be a single global archive, RCSB teamed up with partners in Europe and Asia to form the wwPDB. To ensure that the data were well curated, the wwPDB created validation task forces that consisted of experts in each of the methods represented in the PDB. The recommendations made by the task forces were reviewed by the wwPDB partners and implemented into the data processing pipeline.

> Users in the early days were mostly depositors of the data, now most are scientists who study topics such as protein function, protein design, and most recently protein structure prediction. The importance of the PDB to drug discovery cannot be overstated. During the AIDS epidemic the structures of the machinery of HIV were crucial to the development of drugs that have made it possible to live with the disease. During the COVID epidemic, and in agreement with the depositors, the PDB made the data of COVID-related proteins available prior to publication which was key to the development of the vaccines.

It is a synergy of science, technology, and community that allowed the PDB to become the vital resource it is today.

Disbanding

In the life of most consortia, there comes a time when there has been sufficient progress or substantial barriers arise that call into question the continued existence of the consortium. In some cases, the disbanding results from losing its original purpose, which is what happened with the Iridium global satellite initiative.[7]

> The Iridium global satellite communication story is a perennial case study in business schools of a large commercial failure. But inside the Iridium story is a commercial consortium story—one of the first global commercial consortia bringing together sovereign wealth funds, telecommunications giants, satellite launch partners, and private investors.
>
> Motorola engineers advanced the concept in 1987, suggesting that it would be possible to link low earth orbit (LEO) wireless communication satellites to ground stations on Earth, thus providing ubiquitous connectivity from any point on earth to any other. Motorola performed the initial R&D, funded the expansion of the concept, and soon learned that the level of investment would be too large for one company. In the early 1990s, Iridium Inc. was formed and a few investors took shares in the new company, which was still tightly bound to Motorola. The challenges continued to grow: applying for patents, securing approval from national and global telecommunications regulators, designing the system, building satellites, and finding launch partners. The demands outstripped the resources available.

> In July 1993, Iridium Inc. invited additional investors and the equity was transferred to a newly formed company, Iridium LLC. Motorola received a $3.37 billion contract from Iridium LLC to build and launch the system and $2.5 billion to maintain it. These new investors were from Brazil, Japan, China, Russia, Thailand, Italy, France, Saudi Arabia, Venezuela, South Korea, Taiwan, Indonesia, Australia, the United States, and other countries—operating with both consortia-like features and organizational features. Board meetings were held around the world with simultaneous translators in tow. The charter and governance framework sought consensus in decisions and defaulted to majority vote when required. No company, country, or partner had more sway than the others.
>
> Even though the technology was ultimately successful, the initiative was eclipsed by the rapid expansion of cellular telephony. The satellite system had global connectivity not offered by cell phones, but it had limited reach inside buildings, the phones were bulky, and the service was expensive. In August 1999, Iridium LLC disbanded, just one year after going live, with the assets subject to a bankruptcy filing.

The Iridium story shows that not all consortia structures are sufficiently agile to persist. In this case, the delays associated with the chosen technology made the initiative vulnerable to an alternative technology. Although the multiparty structure disbanded, Iridium Satellite Inc. emerged from the bankruptcy and is now a highly successful satellite communication company listed on NASDAQ and focusing on communication services in areas not reached by cell phones.

Another case of disbanding involved the National Data Service (NDS), discussed earlier in this chapter. A number of promising projects had been initiated, but there was not sufficient support to continue to operate as a free-standing consortium. A home was found for key projects at GO FAIR US, a multistakeholder consortium with a related mission and the original home institutions of NDS, the San Diego Supercomputing Center (SDSC), and the National Center for Supercomputing Applications (NCSA).We will never know what the benefits might have been if NDS stayed together as a whole, but the case illustrates that consortia need to periodically ask whether continued operation is in the best interest of the associated stakeholders.

Disbanding runs up against one of the key forces identified in Chapter 3, which is the iron law of oligarchy. Strategies should be integrated from the start to mitigate the risk of a small group of people becoming entrenched in their leadership roles and maintaining a consortium beyond the point at which it is adding value for the stakeholders. A charter can anticipate disbanding and signal what the indicators are to raise this issue. Similarly, projects can require buy-in to be launched, which sets a natural constraint when there isn't support. Regular stakeholder maps can signal whether alignment is increasing or deteriorating.

Transforming

Instead of disbanding, consortia may transform their mission, structure, and operations into something that is sustainable.

For example, a group of advanced regional research networking infrastructure initiatives, operating as "The Quilt," began with Internet2 as their fiscal agent. As their work advanced, they incorporated as a nonprofit organization and spun off from Internet2. Even though all parties knew this was the likely next step in the evolution of this initiative, there were still challenges in navigating the change since there were aspects of networking that both the Quilt and Internet2 saw as part of their mission. This made for a difficult transformation.

The case of the US Long-Term Ecological Research (LTER) program, with its set of study sites, provides an example of a data management consortium transforming in a highly collaborative way. Here the transformation included beginning at sites developing shared data practices and local data systems and then creating a centralized information system sheltered within the LTER research community. Finally, while still working with LTER, the centralized information system was scaled and structured as the Network Office, an independent program supporting a data management office as a national data infrastructure for multiple communities.[8]

> The LTER network currently consists of 27 geographically distributed sites, each studying a different biome. An information management committee formed as a "community of practice," made up of members from each site within the LTER network.[9] Meetings of the committee began in the early 1980s for sharing experiences and coordinating data activities.
>
> In time, a Network Information System was envisioned and evolved in partnership with data and software specialists at the Network Office.

A charter was created in 2010 by the information managers to more formally support the group's governance as a consortium sheltered within the LTER network.

In 2016, some members of the committee and staff from the LTER Network Office partnered on a successful proposal to expand the LTER network information system as an approach to supporting collective data management at a larger scale. The proposal titled "Environmental Data Initiative—Streamlining Data Curation to Accelerate Scientific Inquiry" (EDI) resulted in an NSF award that transformed data infrastructure developed for the LTER community into a national data management office.[10] The new office and information systems together represent a contemporary data infrastructure for research individuals, groups, and communities in the environmental sciences. The LTER committee continues as the leadership of a consortium for LTER data managers while submitting ecological data to the larger-scale EDI system rather than to an LTER-specific information system. In this way, there was a transformation from an informal community-of-practice to an LTER consortium with a standing committee and finally to associates working with a national data office.

Summing Up

Aligning stakeholders (the focus of Chapters 5 and 6) enables and advances collective impact, which is the focus of this chapter. Advancing begins with leadership and resources, each of which are dynamic throughout the life of a consortium.

Common interests motivate the shared vision and are the focus of much of the literature on collaboration. Less attention is given to separate, competing interests, though we argue here that both common and competing interests are in play and each needs attention.

Invariably, adjustments are needed over time, which places a premium on mechanisms for feedback. Both stakeholders and interests change and the consortium itself may be moving toward increased formalization. In time, however, the consortium may become less formal or even disband—once its work is complete or it encounters barriers that can't be overcome. At the same time, there are powerful institutional forces that may push for continued operations even after the work is complete—so sustaining a consortium requires flexibility and what may be difficult decisions about disbanding or transforming.

Ultimately, consortia in the 21st century may well have massive impact, but they are less likely to become household names in the same way as multinational organizations became in the 20th century. This is the result of consortia featuring smaller, more agile structures that increase their ability to act dynamically.

Notes

1. We thank Neil Gershenfeld and Sherry Lassiter for their insights as we developed this vignette, also drawing on the experiences of Joel Cutcher-Gershenfeld with this initiative. Of course, the responsibility for the text is entirely all of ours as coauthors.
2. We thank Dana Brunson, Patrick Schimtz, and Scott Yokel for their insights as we developed this vignette, also drawing on the experiences of coauthors Nick Berente, Joel Cuthcer-Gershenfeld, Michael Haberman, and Lauren Michaels with this initiative. Of course, the responsibility for the text is entirely all of ours as coauthors.
3. For more on the Biomarkers Consortium, see https://fnih.org/our-programs/biomarkers-consortium/. This analysis draws on the extensive experience of coauthor Barbara Mittleman with the Biomarkers Consortium, as well as the additional experience of Joel Cutcher-Gershenfeld with this consortium.
4. The 2019 charter can be found here: https://fnih.org/wp-content/uploads/2023/05/Finance-and-Audit-Committee-Charter-190523.pdf.
5. Quote included with permission by Douglas Bitonti Stewart, retrieved from https://ssir.org/articles/entry/when_launching_a_collaboration_keep_it_agile#.
6. This case vignette draws on the experience of coauthor Helen Berman, who is a cofounder of the Protein Data Bank.
7. This case vignette draws on the experience of coauthor Pat Canavan, who was at the time serving as an executive leader at Motorola with responsibilities that included Iridium.
8. This case draws on the experience of coauthor Karen S. Baker, who had a data leadership role in LTER and has published studies on LTER data practices. We appreciate the review by Mark Servilla of this vignette. Of course, the responsibility for the text is entirely ours. Also, see Robert B. Waide and Sharon E. Kingsland, eds., *The Challenges and Accomplishments of Long-Term Ecological Research: New Perspectives on the Past, Present, and Future of Ecological Science* (New York: Springer, 2021), https://doi.org/10.1007/978-3-030-66933-1.
9. See Helena Karasti, Karen S. Baker, and Eija Halkola, "Enriching the Notion of Data Curation in e-Science: Data Managing and Information Infrastructure in the Long Term Ecological Research (LTER) Network," *Computer Supported Cooperative Work* 15, no. 4 (2006): pp. 321–358, https://doi.org/10.1007/s10606-9023-2; Karen Baker and Florence Millerand, Infrastructuring Ecology: Challenges in Achieving Data Sharing, in *Collaboration in the New Life Sciences*, edited by J. N. Parker, N. Vermeulen, and B. Penders (Burlington, VT: Ashgate, 2010): pp. 111–138, https://doi.org/10.4324/9781315572628; William K. Michener, John Porter, Mark Servilla, and Kristin Vanderbilt, "Long Term Ecological Research and Information Management," *Ecological Informatics* 6, no. 1 (2011): pp. 13–24, https://doi.org/10.1016/j.ecoinf.2010.11.005.
10. See Corinna Gries, Paul C. Hanson, Margaret O'Brien, Mark Servilla, Kristin Vanderbilt, and Robert Waide, "The Environmental Data Initiative: Connecting the Past to the Future through Data Reuse," *Ecology and Evolution* 13, no.1 (2023): pp. 1–14, https://doi.org/10.1002/ece3.9592.

PART III
LOOKING FORWARD

Chapter 9
Storm Clouds on the Horizon

US President Biden's day one Executive Order 13985, "On Advancing Racial Equity and Support for Underserved Communities through the Federal Government," required federal agencies to form equity teams, conduct equity assessments, and create agency action plans to mitigate barriers underserved communities may face with respect to enrollment in and access to federal benefits and services. This was introduced in Chapter 5 as an example of stakeholder management and stakeholder engagement, although there were also alignment processes involving the equity teams within and across federal agencies. Some aspects of the coordination of the equity initiatives operated as consortia-like arrangements within and across federal agencies. We return to the executive order on equity here because of the way it surfaced deep divides that had to be bridged.[1]

The focus of the equity order included mitigating barriers faced by underserved communities when dealing with the federal government, which required specifying what was meant by "underserved." The executive order defined this term as referring to "populations sharing a particular characteristic, as well as geographic communities, that have been systematically denied a full opportunity to participate in aspects of economic, social, and civic life." This required agencies to recognize sameness and differences within the same population. Mitigation would be required not only for particular classes of persons but also for communities where systematic government actions resulted in truncated opportunity.

The American Rescue Plan Act, for example, included provisions to address long-standing (and long-documented) disparities faced by Black farmers. The Act allocated funds to support debt relief and access to credit, technical assistance, and land acquisition. However, in April 2021, a group of White farmers filed a lawsuit challenging the constitutionality of the debt relief program, arguing that it discriminated against them based on race. The lawsuit sought to halt the distribution of relief funds to Black farmers. This was a direct challenge to the equity team in the US Department of Agriculture and created turbulence across the equity teams in all agencies. They were aligned around advancing the requirements of the executive order and now that was thrown into question by a deep divide in society.

With the passage of the Inflation Reduction Act of 2022, new legislation was introduced in place of the initial relief program. This served to address the issues raised in the lawsuit. The legislation created two new funds (Assistance for Distressed Borrowers[2] and the Discrimination Financial Assistance Program[3]) which made more than $5B available for farmers, ranchers, and others who experienced discrimination in the context of certain USDA programs prior to 2021. While these new vehicles no longer prioritized Black and other farmers of color, they aimed to advance equity through "targeted universalism."[4] This is where a universal policy is broadly inclusive, such as addressing the needs of any farmers who faced discrimination or disparate treatment. The aim of reaching those facing the deepest disparities is accomplished without excluding those who are also experiencing difficulties that federal relief or other programs are designed to address.[5]

The challenges of the 21st century are driving the increased formation of consortia, which will emerge as a defining institutional arrangement of the era. Other institutional arrangements, such as multinational corporations, nonprofit organizations, regulatory agencies, universities, and countless others will not disappear. It is just that multistakeholder consortia, with sufficient alignment, will play increasingly prominent roles bridging across existing organizations and institutions. There will also be considerable tensions and dilemmas. Our goal in this chapter is to anticipate the headwinds or storm clouds on the horizon that consortia will face in the coming decades.

Many of the dynamics that consortia are presently encountering have already been documented in this book. We review the challenges here, briefly, and then look ahead to the storm clouds that go beyond these challenges. Challenges are currently both operational and strategic. In Chapter 6, we highlighted the challenges relevant during the scoping phase:

- **Missing Stakeholders:** Parties with relevant interests who are not included because it is logistically complicated or there are substantive disagreements with the proposed focus of the consortium.
- **Superficial Engagement:** Engagement in a consortium that is superficially focused on only common interests, without fully taking into account competing interests and individual agency.
- **Insufficient Internal Alignment:** Insufficient internal alignment within consortia members that constrains lateral alignment across the consortium.

Additional predictable challenges highlighted in Chapter 7 include:

- **Vision Is Not Shared:** The vision for the consortium is formulated by just a few stakeholders and is not widely shared, adapted, and embraced.
- **Incomplete Measures:** Not instituting process and outcomes measures early on as well as only measuring what is easy to observe.
- **Mission Creep:** An expanding mission that focuses consortia in ways that are not sustainable.

In Chapter 8, we highlighted these further predictable challenges:

- **Problematic Leadership Dynamics:** Leadership turnover and leadership mismatches as the needs of consortia evolve.
- **Insufficient Resources:** Resource variability, particularly when it comes to sustaining a consortium.
- **Failed Dissolution:** Failure to dissolve or restructure consortia when the mission is sufficiently complete.

These challenges are predictable and consequential and they will continue to face consortia going forward. But looking ahead, other concerns emerge. To address them, we return to the long-standing barriers to collective action signaled in Chapter 3 and provide ideas about how these barriers might play out in the 21st century.

The tools and methods documented in Chapters 6, 7, and 8 are designed to address some of these dynamics, but looking ahead, more tools, methods, and mindsets will be needed to address broad future trends, dilemmas, and tensions that are already emerging and likely will continue to develop. These are summarized in Table 9.1, which is organized around the same broad categories as in Chapter 3.

Addressing these challenges will not be easy for consortia. However, doing so will not only reduce barriers but also create additional drivers.[6]

Over time, many of the barriers may be met, but new ones will emerge—so the challenges covered in this chapter are illustrative, not exhaustive. Indeed, it is risky to assume that any set of established theories will, even when applied skillfully, suffice to produce successful consortia. A useful theory, policy, and practice foundation is offered here, but we see the need for considerably more development of this foundation and the associated guidance. Think of this chapter as a series of thought starters, with an invitation for others to build on these ideas.

Accelerating Rates of Change

Consortia thrive in unstable environments. Many of the longest-running examples of consortia in this book are in areas of instability: biotech, big data, computing, social service gaps, and others. In these contexts, consortia

Table 9.1 Storm Clouds on the Horizon

Storm Clouds	Implications for Consortia
Incentives • *Accelerating Rates of Change*	Accelerating rates of change associated with digital technologies that call for agile and adaptive social systems.
Power Dynamics • *Entrenched Interests*	Deeply entrenched interests that call for creative ways to carve out spaces for shared interests and soften hard edges.
Social Groupings • *Deep Divides*	Social divides, intensified by various types of digital divides, undercut pluralistic norms advanced by consortia.
Combinations of Incentives, Power, and Social Groupingss • *Legitimacy Crisis* • *Future Generations, Nature as a Stakeholder, and Complex Identities*	Institutions, including consortia, face core challenges to their legitimacy. Sharing power with those not present and those with complex identities. Challenging simple stakeholder categories, existing incentives, and fostering creative new structures and process.

can be more agile and adaptive than long-standing organizational and institutional arrangements (commercial organizations, regulatory government agencies, international nongovernmental organizations, etc.). Yet, consortia will still struggle in the coming years and decades with accelerating rates of change. They are both a product of this change and are impacted by the shifting dynamics.

The importance of accelerating rates of change with digital technologies was signaled in 1965 by Gordon Moore with what is now termed Moore's Law. In his delightfully titled article, "Cramming More Components onto Integrated Circuits," Moore extrapolated from five data points over a half-dozen years, documenting an exponential increase in the capability of integrated circuits and related microelectronics—with a doubling of capability every 18 months.[7] Both the prediction and the response at the time are relevant to this discussion of consortia in the 21st century. Moore predicted that this rate of change for integrated circuits would "lead to such wonders as home computers—or at least terminals connected to a central computer—automatic controls for automobiles, and personal portable communications equipment. The electronic wristwatch needs only a display to be feasible today." At the time, Moore's article, which also wrestled with many technical constraints such as heat, yields, and reliability, was widely criticized. One negative reviewer tried to identify the most absurd implication of this analysis, stating that Moore's Law would have us believing that someday microelectronics would be in the door knobs of hotel rooms. Of course, that is exactly what has happened. Indeed, such automation makes it possible to centrally lock and unlock all doors in a building. More generally, the capability of integrated circuits has been doubling every 18 months on a fairly consistent basis for six decades.[8] We may be approaching the physical limits of what is possible with an integrated circuit, but quantum computing holds promise for continuing accelerating rates of change in computing capabilities.[9]

There are other technologies that are also advancing with accelerating rates of change, such as artificial intelligence and machine learning, biomedical devices, social media, and many others. While there are dystopian views of technology displacing people and disrupting society ("racing against the machine"), there is also the potential for people to "race with the machine."[10] For multistakeholder consortia, these advances have far-reaching implications. All technologies coevolve with social systems, and many existing organizational and institutional arrangements are, at best, capable of linear rates of change. In this respect, consortia hold promise as agile and adaptive social systems that might match this rate of change (a theme advanced in Chapter 10), but actually coevolving with accelerating digital technologies is hard to do. These technologies will invariably involve shifting power dynamics among stakeholders, changing channels for communication and emerging capabilities, all of which represent a dynamic context for consortia (and other organizational and institutional arrangements). At the same time, as we saw in Chapter 4, there are examples such as the Research Data Alliance (RDA), which is structured around modular elements that allow for this flexibility: short-term working groups (WGs), long-term interest groups (IGs), and domain-specific communities of practice (CoP).

At their core, digital technologies are modular and consortia also have the potential to operate in modular ways. For example, many consortia are organized around project-based work, with different combinations of stakeholders coming together to match the demands of a given project, and then disbanding that combination of stakeholders when the work is complete. This is very different from established facilities, divisions, functions, and other long-standing aspects of many organizations. Language in a charter can support modularity, such as we saw in Chapter 4 with the RDA, where there was an array of different types of groups and initiatives—some with more structure and a longer time horizon (e.g., communities of practice and interest groups) and some with less structure and a shorter time horizon (e.g., working groups).

Most consortia feature some form of overarching steering committee or other governance arrangement that oversees the full range of consortium activities. Keeping these overarching bodies agile and adaptive is challenging. Membership changes may not happen as quickly as the context requires. This points back to the leadership as it is set up in the charter—it should anticipate periodic pivots with appropriate changes in leadership. There is a dilemma around the importance of stability and the importance of flexibility. The charter should signal both aims. Ironically, a robust alignment of stakeholders makes it easier to accommodate leadership changes, while high degrees of misalignment likely require stability (provided leadership is seen as having good will toward all parties).

While accelerating rates of change pose many challenges for consortia, those that develop agile and adaptive structures will be more likely to have sustained impacts—with barriers that can become drivers if well managed.

Entrenched Interests

As their numbers grow, consortia will increasingly gain the notice of commercial organizations, government agencies, nongovernmental organizations, and others. These groups will, in turn, seek to limit the scope of consortia or undercut their very existence; the iron law of oligarchy is very much alive and well in the 21st century.

Many of the consortia featured in this book were initiated by leaders in these various types of established organizations and institutions. In this respect, they are helping these entities to accomplish together what they can't do separately. But what if there are entrenched interests that see consortia as a threat?

> Consider the case of ride-share drivers, such as Uber and Lyft drivers.[11] Although independent (and often in competition for business), they share a mutual interest in higher wages and better working conditions. In the early days of the "gig economy," these workers began to form consortia to share information and strategies, coordinate their demands, and raise the visibility of their labor concerns. Yet once these consortia began to grow, many drivers noticed a steady uptick in the number of "pro-company" voices in their consortia. Later, media reports would indicate that rideshare companies retained lobbying and consulting firms to counter workers' online presence.

Entrenched interests show up at multiple stages of the life cycle of a consortium. We have observed examples in which, right before a new consortium is ready to launch, small numbers of powerful stakeholders prevent the formation of consortia or shift the agenda in various ways. During regular operations, consortia do reduce the salience of power differences among stakeholders, but those differences still show up in various ways. When it comes to the potential dissolution of a consortium, entrenched interests can insist on continuing the operation longer than might be appropriate or bring it to a close prematurely.

Looking ahead, policies, practices, and procedures will be needed to manage the relationships among consortia as well as the relationships between consortia and various types of organizations (for-profit and nonprofit) and other institutional actors. In the Biomarkers Consortium, a number of the large pharmaceutical organizations in the group found that they were members of so many consortia that they had to create an internal forum to track and manage these many interdependent relationships. Boundary-spanning individuals are essential in this work, which points to the need for consortia to have individuals and groups among their members and leaders who can serve effectively both in their home setting and in consortia.

Furthermore, mechanisms for conflict resolution at the boundaries of consortia will be increasingly important. This could be the boundaries between consortia and competitive markets; the boundaries between consortia and regulatory processes; the boundaries between consortia and nonprofit/nongovernmental organizations; and other boundaries.

There are multiple ways in which entrenched interests can undercut the work of consortia. When there are bridges between the consortia and the various organizational and institutional homes of these interests, the work of a consortia does become more challenging but the potential impact is also greater—again, the barrier can become a driver, but not easily.

Deep Divides

The study of bridging across cultures and other divides in society is as old as the social sciences and is of great urgency today. Auguste Comte first used the term "sociology" in 1838 to describe the study of the divide between prescientific (religious and metaphysical) stages of development and a scientific stage in societal development.[12] Elements of this divide are still with us in the current debates on the legitimacy of scientific findings that are ongoing and expanding. Around the same time that Comte was introducing sociology as a study of social divides, Herbert Spencer proposed the concept of the survival of the fittest to explain the divide between the successful and unsuccessful in society, while Karl Marx saw the same divide as a result of exploitation of those providing labor by those with accumulated capital.[13] A few decades later, Jane Addams founded the field of social work through her efforts to address the human impacts of these class- and economic-based divides (which are, of course, still with us).[14] Forms of collective action such as trade unions, civil disobedience, and social movements emerged in response to these divides. In some cases, these responses involved formal organizations, but they have often been preceded by consortia arrangements in which individuals and groups assembled, operating laterally, to accomplish together what they couldn't do separately. In this sense, the use of consortia to bridge across social divides is not new.

In our contemporary postindustrial era, the divides are expanding in at least three ways. First, divides across very different worldviews are becoming increasingly polarized, with diminishing instances of interactions among people who disagree.[15] In the United States some past equalizers, such as service in the military and public schools, have been having a less tempering impact. Worldviews rooted in economic systems (capitalism versus socialism), religion, political systems (democratic versus autocratic), urban versus rural, and others are not being tempered by various equalizing forces at local, national, and global levels. Second, divides between what are sometimes termed the Global North and the Global South are increasing as environmental and ecological change increases tensions and costs in the Global South (exacerbated by the history of colonial exploitation). Third, ubiquitous social media (and its misuse as a mis-/disinformation tool) and disparities in access to information technology have served to deepen digital divides and amplify divided views.

In this context of deepening divides, consortia do bring the promise of providing what are sometimes termed "slender bridges" across the divides, but they first must develop ways to operate in a context that is increasingly divided. The dilemma this creates is that as many consortia seek to be inclusive, it may be that bringing together such a diverse range of views stops forward progress. At the extreme, we know from countless peace and reconciliation efforts that an often insurmountable first step is even getting combatting parties to agree to be in the same room together. On the other hand, if only a subset of relevant stakeholders are brought together, then parties not included are likely to resent being added later.

To some degree, consortia can constructively engage the dilemma by having multiple separate gatherings of stakeholder clusters with worldviews that are different, but not wildly divergent. Then, as a second step, the clusters can be brought together. While the underlying differences will still persist, the central views of the clusters may be more compatible than the extremes within them. In a small way, this is what happened with the formation of the Council of Data Facilities presented at the beginning of Chapter 7, where there was a divide over whether to even launch this consortium among stakeholders with different underlying views. It was resolved by having those for and against the new council meet separately first and then the resolution was a new institutional arrangement that had an appropriately small institutional footprint.

Other mechanisms will also be relevant, such as process transparency, opt-out options on specific projects, social activities that enable person-to-person connections, storytelling narratives that humanize hopes and fears held by various individuals and groups, and other such activities. Key to this model is that active "aligning" and "advancing" needs to build in additional structures and processes that take into account that there may still be deep divides among stakeholders.

Universal policies, such as those in the vignette at the opening of this chapter, represent a productive way of bridging across deep divides. However, not all policies are self-implementing. Many require oversight or coordination through dialogue among representatives from different relevant stakeholders. In these settings, consortia that can bridge across the deep divides gain a measure of legitimacy. When this happens barriers shift to become drivers of change, but still not easily.

Legitimacy Crises

Core institutions in liberal democracies around the world are facing legitimacy crises. These crises involve challenges to the roles of the state and science in issues ranging from climate change to the COVID pandemic, to poverty and homelessness, to immigration, to gun violence, abortion rights, civil rights, LBGTQ+ rights, and more. Important as these issues are, actions to address them by legislative, judicial, and executive branches of government are undercut by a total rejection of the legitimacy of these social institutions. The same is true for the role of science and higher education, where efforts to increase understanding and action on these issues are undercut by a rejection of the societal legitimacy of those same institutions.

The German philosopher and social theorist Jürgen Habermas termed these dynamics a "legitimation crisis," one whose multiple dimensions suggest diverse, related crises.[16] Broad-brush attacks on what are being called "woke issues" serve to undercut constructive discourse on these matters, as well as threatening the institutions designed to foster what in Europe is termed "social dialogue." The effect is chilling for universities and other institutional arrangements that have long had a role in providing forums for open dialogue.

In this context, consortia will likely face legitimacy challenges, but we cannot lose sight of the unique roles that consortia play. They can convene diverse groups for focused dialogue even when these groups would not agree to be in the same hierarchical organization. Even where the interdependence is relatively low, consortia can bring parties together without threatening their independence.

Future Generations, Nature as a Stakeholder, and Complex Identities

Invariably, key stakeholders will be missing from the work of a consortium, including parties that are not well organized or that have historically been marginalized. Further, this includes unborn generations and may include nonhuman stakeholders (such as the natural environment).

During the formation of a consortium, it is essential to specify the stakeholders, as is outlined in Chapter 6. Once identified, the next challenge is to incorporate mechanisms to provide voice for those who are not easily represented. In steering committees and other governance structures, seats can be designated for missing parties who are represented by individuals who are best able to bring forward these voices. Once recognized, creative ways can be found to ensure that assumptions about what is in the interest of missing parties can be validated. As noted, a key stakeholder category not typically represented is future generations. There are advocates currently urging governing bodies to dedicate a seat to future generations; consortia might also consider this in their governing structure and operations.

Beyond future generations, advocates for biodiversity have filed court cases on behalf of rivers and fish in the rivers.[17] The World Economic Forum has argued that "nature is the most important stakeholder."[18] This may or may not be a useful extension of the concept of stakeholder for all consortia, but if we are to properly account for the interconnectedness of social, economic, and environmental systems, it is worth expanding one's view to consider a way to address nature as a stakeholder in governance structures and operations.

As we discussed in Chapter 3, Kimberlé Crenshaw introduced the term "intersectionality" in 1989 to describe the multiple identities that we all bring to discussions on race.[19] The concept transformed discussions on this issue, since the lived experience of an older, wealthy Black woman is not the same as that of a young, middle-income Black man, or a middle-aged nonbinary White person working a gig job, and so on. Looking ahead, this concept will be of increasing importance to consortia.

Consortia have always embodied diverse stakeholders. Typically, however, the stakeholders are treated as representative of one category or another. For example, when the Biomarkers Consortium was established, the stakeholder categories were pharma, biotech, FDA, NIH, universities, and patient advocacy organizations. Similarly, when the Minority Serving Cyberinfrastructure Consortium (MS-CC) was established, a clear distinction was made between historically Black colleges and universities (HBCUs), tribal colleges and universities (TCUs), Hispanic serving institutions (HSIs), other minority serving institutions (MSIs), predominantly White institutions (PWIs), commercial organizations, and others. If we bring an intersectional lens to these stakeholder categories, we quickly see that the classifications are more complex. Within the Biomarkers Consortium there are some biotech firms that have more in common with large pharma firms. Other biotech firms have been spun off from and have more in common with universities. The same can be said for countless other variations. Within MS-CC, there are some HBCUs that are large and research-intensive with many graduate programs, such as North Carolina A&T State University, while many are much smaller and primarily undergraduate institutions. Others have unique identities, such as Meharry, which is a medical school. This means that consortia need to operate with appreciation for the diversity within stakeholder categories, which will evolve and change over time.

Moreover, the individuals involved in consortia bring intersectional identities. These diverse identities are taking on increased meaning in society—in ways that are both positive and problematic. On the positive side, many consortia begin with an inclusive orientation. For example, when the Campus Research Computing Consortium (CaRCC) explored professionalization, the members wanted respect for the work they did, but didn't want to exclude or limit entry to the profession in the ways that they saw doctors and lawyers doing. On the negative side, identity-based politics are one of the deep divides that we noted above, which can bring social tensions into consortia operations.

Complex stakeholder and individual identities will be intersectional. On a practical level, this means that consortia may need to allow organizations, groups, and individuals to be in multiple membership categories. Moreover, leaders and members of consortia need to guard against assuming an individual, group, or organization will necessarily share an interest with others in the same category. Stakeholder maps that make visible the diverse combinations of interests in various categories can help to open dialogue on these differences and enable the identification of pathways forward that consider the complexity. By valuing complex identities, consortia reduce the risk of being superficial and are more likely to have greater legitimacy—again, with barriers that can become drivers if well managed.

Summing Up

Consortia face many operational and strategic dynamics, including superficial engagement, incomplete internal alignment, mission creep, leadership dynamics, insufficient resources, and poor timing of dissolution. We have documented these challenges throughout this book. As we look ahead, we see additional broader tensions and dilemmas associated with bridging deep divides in society, operating in the context of accelerating rates of change in technology, appreciating intersectional identities of individuals and organizations, utilizing ubiquitous data, and overcoming entrenched interests. In each case there are tactics and strategies that help to mitigate the risk, but success is never assured. Interestingly, by addressing the challenges, it is often more likely that a barrier, such as any of the challenges in this chapter, can be turned into a driver. For example, missing stakeholders may be a barrier to certain interests being taken into account, but, if addressed, they also represent potential that could be harnessed to become a driver. That will be key given the many societal needs for which consortia are essential.

Notes

1. See: https://www.whitehouse.gov/briefing-room/presidential-actions/2023/02/16/executive-order-on-further-advancing-racial-equity-and-support-for-underserved-communities-through-the-federal-government/.
2. U.S. Department of Agriculture. "Inflation Reduction Act (IRA) Assistance for Distressed Borrowers and Related Assistance." Farmers.gov. Accessed November 8, 2024. https://www.farmers.gov/loans/inflation-reduction-investments/assistance [farmers.gov].
3. U.S. Government. "Discrimination Financial Assistance Program 22007 Apply." Accessed November 8, 2024. https://22007apply.gov [22007apply.gov].
4. Powell, John. Targeted Universalism: Policy & Practice. Othering & Belonging Institute, University of California, Berkeley, 2019. Accessed November 8, 2024. https://belonging.berkeley.edu/sites/default/files/targeted_universalism_primer.pdf.

5. This vignette draws on the extensive experience of coauthor Kimberlyn Leary and the more limited experience of Joel Cutcher-Gershenfeld with this initiative.
6. The dynamic by which restraining forces become driving forces was first developed by Kurt Lewin with the concept of "force field analysis." See Kurt Lewin, *Field Theory in Social Science* (New York: Harper and Row, 1951).
7. See Gordon E. Moore, "Cramming More Components onto Integrated Circuits," *Electronics* (April 19, 1965): pp. 114–117.
8. There is increasing attention to what may be the physical limits of Moore's Law. See David Rotman, "We're Not Prepared for the End of Moore's Law," *MIT Technology Review*, February 24, 2020, https://www.technologyreview.com/2020/02/24/905789/were-not-prepared-for-the-end-of-moores-law/.
9. This analysis is adapted from Neil Gershenfeld, Alan Gershenfeld, and Joel Cutcher-Gershenfeld, *Designing Reality: How to Survive and Thrive in the Third Digital Revolution* (New York: Basic Books, 2017). This book lifted up digital fabrication as a third digital revolution, following digital communication and digital computation, and identified accelerating rates of change with each one based on the underlying logic of digital technologies.
10. See Erik Brynjolfsson and Andrew McAfee, *The Second Machine Age: Work, Progress, and Prosperity in a Time of Brilliant Technologies* (New York: Norton, 2014).
11. We thank coauthor Michael Maffie for these insights into collective action by rideshare drivers.
12. See Marcelline Block, "Comte, Auguste (1798–1857)," in *The International Encyclopedia of Revolution and Protest*, edited by Immanuel Ness, Wiley Online Library, https://doi.org/10.1002/9781405198073.wbierp0384.
13. See David Potter, *Disruption: Why Things Change* (Oxford: Oxford University Press, 2021), ch. 5, https://doi.org/10.1093/oso/9780197518823.001.0001.
14. See Patricia M. Shields, Maurice Hamington, and Joseph Soeters, eds., *The Oxford Handbook of Jane Addams* (Oxford: Oxford University Press, 2022), https://doi.org/10.1093/oxfordhb/9780197544518.001.0001.
15. For a research agenda designed to address these issues, see Timofey Agarin, Allison McCulloch, and Cera Murtagh, "Others in Deeply Divided Societies: A Research Agenda," *Nationalism and Ethnic Politics* 24, no. 3 (2018): pp. 299–310, https://doi.org/10.1080/13537113.2018.1489488.
16. For more legitimacy crises, see Jurgen Habermas, *Legitimation Crisis* (New York: Beacon Press, 1975); Edmund Husserl, *The Crisis of European Sciences and Transcendental Phenomenology* (Evanston, IL: Northwestern University Press, 1970); C.P. Snow, *The Two Cultures and the Scientific Revolution* (Cambridge: Cambridge University Press, 1959); Jean Francois Lyotard, *The Postmodern Condition* (Minneapolis: University of Minnesota Press, 1983); and Eduardo Batalha Viveiros de Castro, *Cannibal Metaphysics* (Minneapolis: University of Minnesota Press, 2014).
17. For arguments on nature having stakeholder status, see Johana Kujala et al., "Engaging with the Natural Environment: Examining the Premises of Nature-Inclusive Stakeholder Relationships and Engagement," Proceedings of the International Association for Business and Society 30 (2019): pp. 73–81, https://doi.org/10.5840/iabsproc20193010.
18. This is part of the shift from shareholder capitalism to stakeholder capitalism advocated by the World Economic Forum. See Tariq Al-Olaimy, "Why Nature Is the Most Important Stakeholder of the Coming Decade," January 7, 2020, accessed June 14, 2023, https://www.weforum.org/agenda/2020/01/why-nature-will-be-the-most-important-stakeholder-in-the-coming-decade/.
19. See Kimberlé Crenshaw, "Demarginalizing the Intersection of Race and Sex: A Black Feminist Critique of Antidiscrimination Doctrine, Feminist Theory and Antiracist Policies," *University of Chicago Legal Forum* 1989, no. 1 (1989): pp. 139–167.

Chapter 10
A Vision of Consortia for a Complex World

The Playing for the Planet Alliance is a consortium that builds on the massive popularity of video games. This consortium brings together 7 major gaming trade bodies spanning over 50 video game developers, gaming device manufacturers, and others. In order to join the consortium, members have to make specific environmental commitments.

The Playing for the Planet Alliance was launched in 2019. It was convened by the United Nations Environment Programme (UNEP), which was founded in 1972, and has a long track record of convening diverse stakeholders to advance its mission "to provide leadership and encourage partnership in caring for the environment by inspiring, informing, and enabling nations and peoples to improve their quality of life without compromising that of future generations." Implicit in this mission is an awareness that no one organization, even the UN, can address environmental challenges on its own.

As context, video games drive billions of hours of what the industry terms "lean-forward engagement" across the planet every week. It is one of the most powerful and impactful entertainment mediums, with revenues of $384 billion, exceeding movies, streaming services, and major league sports combined. Given such broad engagement, the Playing for the Planet Alliance is just one of a number of consortia harnessing the unique power of video games as a force for good in society.

As a result of follow-through on commitments by members of Playing for the Planet Alliance, themes around land or sea restoration have been built into video games that have reached over 130 million players, with 80% of these players responding positively to the themes. Console and PC manufacturers have committed to reduce their carbon footprint in manufacturing, distribution, and packaging operations. Over 60% of the commitments by members were goals to reach net zero or carbon negative operations by 2030. The commitments involve a mix of increasing the

> use of green energy, inserting "green nudges" into video games, offsetting emissions associated with business operations, promoting recycling of packaging and waste, and other ways to "achieve more together." Indeed, the Alliance emphasized that it "works together to create more visible, inspiring, catalytic change than any one organization could achieve on its own."[1]
>
> Although it was convened by the UNEP, the Alliance now operates as an independent entity under "Articles of Association" that were drafted in 2022. These articles incorporate a paid membership model, governance processes, dispute resolution procedures, and other formalization of operations. Beyond operational considerations, the articles indicate that "[t]he Alliance supports collaboration across the video game industry to help reduce its environmental impact.
>
> We envision a world where the video game industry serves in an expanding role in society for promoting positive dialogue and action on global environmental concerns."[2]

Imagine a world without consortia. There would still be government agencies, commercial organizations, nonprofit organizations, universities, community organizations, social movements, and others. There would still be collective action, enabled by these various organizational and institutional arrangements.

What would be missing, however, are the agile and adaptive ways that consortia enable diverse stakeholders to accomplish together what they can't do separately. Without the constraints of operating within formal hierarchies, but with the structures (and structuring processes) achieved through lateral alignment,[3] there is a sweet spot for these particular forms of collective action. Actions by consortia advance common interests across diverse individuals, groups, and organizations, while taking into account competing interests and respecting the separate identities of the various parties.

Global Challenges

Consider just a few of the global challenges where consortia are playing key roles and could play even greater roles. The challenges selected here are illustrative, not exhaustive. They were selected because one or more of us has direct experience with these issues and they map onto the UN sustainable development goals (SDGs) highlighted in Chapter 1. Selected challenges are addressed here include, in alphabetical order.

- Artificial intelligence
- Clean water
- Data sharing
- Geoengineering
- Green energy
- Social media
- Rising authoritarianism

In each, we will identify ways that a multilevel collaborative structure is possible, with an array of associated common and competing interests. These short thumbnail sketches of potential consortia illustrate both what is possible and the considerable challenges involved in realizing the potential in each case. Of course, these are just some of the challenges corresponding to the UN SDGs.[4]

Artificial Intelligence (AI)

AI technologies are increasingly embedded in everyday objects and systems (buildings, cars, roads, airplanes, medical devices, security systems, power plants, telecommunications, severe weather warnings, artwork, wrist watches, etc.). This includes what are termed large language models (LLMs). Most AI models draw on vast quantities of data in order to inform decision-making and action in ways that far exceed the capability of individuals or even groups. At the same time, the data utilized is biased in countless ways, often with highly consequential implications. Further, AI models bring additional fearful risks to society.[5] As futurist Ray Kurzweil comments:

> People are trying to figure out how to use the latest from AI such as LLMs and by the time they do, the next AI revolution will be here. It is not a one-time event.[6]

In this context, agile and adaptive institutional arrangements will be needed. Consortia are forming and more will form around specific applications. These may operate within national boundaries or span across national boundaries to match the broad use of the systems.

There are many common interests around reducing harmful bias, sharing liability, mitigating risk, and advancing the frontiers of the technologies. At the same time, there are competing interests around proprietary ownership of the technologies, enjoying the benefits of being a first mover in promising markets, and a lack of clarity on who is responsible for adverse impacts of the technologies. Since the AI technologies are often opaque, operating as what is often termed a "black box" or a "gray box," it is hard to know where responsibility resides or what responsibility even means. While progress with AI will continue without the relevant consortia, it will involve increased risk. As with any new technology, developing the associated social systems is easier early on since both the social and technical aspects have greater plasticity. Adding mechanisms for oversight, governance, shared decision-making, standard setting, and the like is harder after aspects of the technology are well established and the results are often less likely to fully consider the interests of those who are less powerful in society.[7]

The challenge is to now build collaborative arrangements for governance, standard setting, risk mitigation, and other aims that can coevolve with the technology. Some consortia are forming along these lines, but many more independent commercial enterprises, nations, and others are also racing ahead to set standards and define the technologies on a competitive basis. With AI there is an institutional race underway between collaborative governance, such as through consortia, and independent competitive actors in which the future of these associated technologies is at stake.

Clean Water

Water resource management drew the attention of Elinor Ostrom in her prize-winning work on public-private partnerships (recognized with the 2009 Nobel Prize in Economics). She observed that public-private partnerships were more effective than markets and regulation in governing common-pool resources.[8] What is particularly challenging about water resources is that nature doesn't typically observe city, county, state, and national boundaries, so consortia are key for public agencies as well as private organizations and other parties.

Many common interests center on not depleting or polluting water as a shared resource. Competing interests span diverse uses (agriculture, livestock, recreation, residential use, industrial use, etc.) as well as time horizons (current and future use) that can span generations. Given the breadth of interests, no one agency or organization is wide enough for governance of this issue. This insight led Elinor Ostrom to focus on public-private partnerships for the governance of common-pool resources, such as water.[9] We build on her findings here.

We envision one set of consortia for water resources organized around watersheds and aquifers—with social systems aligned with natural systems. Here the focus would be on balancing interests among agricultural, recreational, residential, and industrial uses. We also envision a second set of consortia in urban environments focused on clean water and water storage and delivery infrastructure. Current work on SDG 6, Clean Water and Sanitation, is illustrative.[10] In the case of both watersheds and urban settings, the consortia necessarily involve public, private, and nonprofit parties, with mechanisms to achieve sufficient alignment for action.

A challenge here is that some government entities at local, state, regional, and national levels are positively oriented around public-private partnerships and other reject the very concept. Further, some commercial enterprises embrace this idea and others reject it totally. Some in public and private sectors worry about transaction costs, but mostly this is a divide between pluralist and unitary mindsets, with clean water hanging in the balance.

Data Sharing

Virtually all global challenges depend on the sharing and reuse of data to enable collaborative problem-solving. We have studied many consortia associated with the sharing and reuse of research data, which has increased our appreciation for the ubiquitous role of data in this postindustrial digital era.[11] Not all data can or should be shared, but those fields and disciplines that are supporting increased data sharing are seeing considerable benefits. For example, the rapid developments of COVID treatments were only possible through data that had been shared through the Protein Data Bank (PDB), the Accelerating COVID-19 Therapeutic Interventions and Vaccines (ACTIV), and other consortia.

Looking ahead, data sharing will be of increasing importance to consortia. Equally, many types of consortia will be increasingly important to data sharing. Yet, proprietary views of data persist—scientists, commercial enterprises, and some governments hold onto data that could be integral to addressing global challenges. As we previously noted, one senior scientist stated to a doctoral student in the geosciences, "I am going to my grave with my disk drive in my cold dead hand."[12]

Despite the proprietary views of some, the collection, curation, and distribution of research data and many other forms of data, such as physical samples, is increasing in scale, with growing numbers of consortia needed to enable this work. Data often has value and meaning that crosses multiple organizational and institutional boundaries, which requires collective governance. Consortia are essential in this context. Further, consortia typically embody important data because they sit at the intersection of diverse types of stakeholders, which is a unique vantage point. When consortia conduct stakeholder maps or track indicators relevant to their mission, they do so as a bellwether for the changing aspirations of different stakeholders. Often, they are the only party with the associated data. Data generation is integral to the value proposition that consortia bring to their stakeholders.

The implications of the increasing importance of data are that most consortia need to have data collection, curation, and distribution capabilities. Even consortia that have data work as their mission don't always pay sufficient attention to how data might inform their own operation. Once a consortium focuses on its data, it will quickly encounter issues of data privacy, data storage, data security, data biases, and related matters requiring cooperation. When data is undervalued, it limits the operations of consortia; when data is widely incorporated and utilized it becomes an enabler of broader impacts.

The broad challenge in society is that data is increasingly understood to be strategic, but the work with data is generally seen as tactical. Risks associated with the potential misuse of data are elevating its importance, but many leaders in the public and private sectors still don't know how to fully value the data work that takes place within their enterprises. Consortia will be increasingly key in advancing data work in the current post-industrial digital era.

Geoengineering

Beyond carbon reductions through renewable energy, changes in consumption, and other means, there are many government labs, university researchers, and commercial enterprises (including entrepreneurial startups), all focused on what is often termed "climate geoengineering." This includes climate interventions in the atmosphere and near-Earth outer space (e.g., solar radiation modification [SRM] through stratospheric aerosol injection, marine cloud brightening, cirrus cloud thinning, and other options), in the oceans and land (e.g., carbon dioxide removal [CDR], through direct air capture coupled to durable storage, soil carbon sequestration, biomass carbon removal and storage, enhanced mineralization, ocean-based CDR, and others), and other technologies (such as afforestation) that are at very different stages of development. No single governing regime has the overall responsibility for ensuring that climate interventions are monitored and risks are mitigated.[13].

Potential geoengineering consortia will have two roles: First, for those willing to be subject to a voluntary compliance regime, there can be public-private consortia with mechanisms for representation and input into decision-making. Second, for those unwilling to be subject to such governance (potentially including private enterprises, some communities, and even some nations), there can still be consortia who oversee monitoring mechanisms to track interventions with visibility provided to relevant international bodies.

The common interests center on prioritizing carbon reduction and on mitigating the risks of unintended harmful impacts of interventions. The competing interests are many, including the view that even conducting research on climate interventions makes it more likely to be employed (with all the associated risks), the lack of transparency with proprietary commercial technologies, the sovereignty of nations (including First Nations), concerns that carbon reduction efforts will be undercut, the independence and autonomy of scientific researchers, and the concerns of those subject to unintended harmful effects. Developing consortia that are robust in handling this full range of common and competing interests is challenging, even though there is no one organization or institutional body that can do so in the absence of consortia. This is a case where the fate of the planet is literally at stake, though one participant in a stakeholder survey on geoengineering did comment, "Don't worry; Earth will survive climate change. We won't."[14]

Green Energy

At the community level, it will take public-private consortia to navigate key investment and operational choices around solar, wind, geothermal, hydropower, smart grid, and other key alternative energy considerations. These will need to connect to regional consortia that reinforce and extend community-level initiatives and that connect to global commons (commonly defined as outer space, atmosphere, high seas, deep seabed, and Antarctica). In all cases, data will be generated that will need to be treated as a shared resource for all parties (while still protecting privacy). Aggregating the data on performance and impacts at a national level is easier than aggregation across national boundaries, but this is possible with transnational consortia. Existing multilateral institutional bodies, such as the UN, intergovernmental organizations, the World Bank, and others, will play key roles, but there are additional stakeholders, such as commercial organizations, who will likely insist on broader, multiparty arrangements.

Common interests include reductions in global warming, allocations of carbon credits, job creation, public health, and other shared interests around sustainability. Competing interests involve the various providers of different technologies (with their associated supply chains), organizational change challenges (such as energy generators shifting to be energy distributors), noise and other mitigation challenges, jurisdictional boundaries for regulators, liability and risk responsibilities, and other potential points of contention. Designing consortia that can both advance the common interests and address the competing interests is a considerable challenge. At the same time, it is not clear that any one organization or institutional actor can do so otherwise. Clearly, we will need consortia that are not limited to areas of mutual agreement, but that also enable collective governance on matters in which deep conflicts need to be resolved.

Like water resources, some of the associated consortia for power infrastructure will follow the contours of grids, but may also depart when it comes to distributed local power generation capacity. Public utility governing bodies will have central roles, but the many independent parties who are not subject to governance by public utility bodies point to the need for public-private partnerships.

Green energy consortia will have to simultaneously navigate the technical complexity of the various green energy solutions, the complications centered on the existing embedded carbon-based infrastructure, and the increasing degree to which there are social divides deepening around these issues. This will require forms of consortia that are not just agile, but also robust enough to operate in contested terrains.

Social Media

Social media platforms are ubiquitous, beneficial, and problematic. These include software programs that foster interpersonal sharing, community building, communication, employment, health information, and more. Some aspects of these diverse digital ecosystems are governed by consortia or consortium-like arrangements, developers of open-source software, standard-setting bodies, and some user groups with specific software. Most of what happens in these ecosystems is only lightly regulated by governments and not subject to other forms of oversight or coordination. Although many of these bodies have consortium-like arrangements, some also behave with less collaborative forms of top-down control.

In social media ecosystems, particularly with respect to computer games, there is evidence that some forms of what might be termed "lightweight" governance are possible such as has been found with the use of "nudge" technologies to reduce highly objectionable online behaviors. It is possible that user groups and open-source developer groups could benefit from increased formalization as consortia with charters, shared visions, conflict resolution systems, and the like.

The common interests form around an increased sense of community, an improved ability to enjoy the positive benefits associated with social media, and the shared need to ensure cybersecurity. At the same time, there are competing interests including advancing self-interest at the expense of others, weakened social bonds, commercial incentives, weaponized social media, contrasting views of fairness, and more. These competing interests will not be handled well by either markets or regulation, nor can any single organization or institutional actor effectively address the competing interests. Challenging as it will be, consortia of various forms will need to play key roles to achieve meaningful and functional governance.

A core challenge centers on the opportunities for customers/participants themselves to be heard. Here there are loosely connected communities of hundreds of thousands or even millions of individuals who could be members of community consortia, having a collective voice in dialogue with social media companies. This will likely involve a tiered structure, such as the levels of editors associated with Wikipedia. Emergent consortia will likely raise challenging ownership questions for the technology companies providing the various social media platforms. It has taken hundreds of years to sort of the governance norms associated with constitutional democracies, town meetings, consumer cooperatives, and other participatory arrangements. How long will it take for such arrangements to take hold with respect to social media?

Rising Authoritarianism

There is a complicated history around whether or not consortia can form in response to rising authoritarianism. Sometimes there is collective action and sometimes there is inaction with various forms of appeasement. Currently, the Russian invasion of Ukraine in 2022 prompted a very different global reaction in comparison with Russia's annexation of Crimea in 2014. Not only was there a strong military response within Ukraine but also an international consortium came together to provide military support and impose a sanctions regime. In some respects, existing institutional arrangements were leveraged (NATO, UN, and others), but the mix of stakeholders and interests didn't fit within any one organization or institutional arrangement.

At the same time, authoritarian leaders make use of consortia. Hungarian president Victor Orbán was the opening speaker at the US Conservative Political Action Conference (CPAC) in August 2022 and called for the establishment of a global rightwing organization with the intent to destroy liberal democracy and establish Christian democracy.[15] He was proposing not just a social movement, but coordinated action that would likely take the form of a consortium.

Common interests among Western democracies include protecting the territorial integrity of established nations, combatting an expansionist agenda, and addressing war crimes. Competing common interests center on anti-immigrant policies, anti LGBTQ+ policies, misogynistic policies, and others. An underlying set of interests on both sides involves the contrast between more authoritarian and more democratic regimes as well as the contrast between liberal and illiberal democracies.[16] Conflicting interests on both sides of the Ukrane situation include contrasting views on how much and what type of military aid Western nations will provide to Ukraine, how much and what type of military aid nations such as China and North Korea will provide to Russia, how much and what type of sanctions will be imposed, different degrees of dependence on natural resources (from Russia, Ukraine, and other entwined nations).

Even if some form of peace is established in the region, there will be continuing questions about the ongoing role of the consortia forged during the conflict. This is a case where the world order itself is taking shape around various consortia and a core question will center on the degree to which sovereign nations cede expanded forms of control to consortia as the only way to mitigate further risks to the world order.

What Will It Take?

In addressing these and other pressing societal challenges, consortia will play pivotal roles in the years to come. In order to be effective, five key elements will be needed.

First, initial progress will take the formation of "minimum viable consortia." This will allow for early actions, as well as agile and adaptive development. It is important not to overspecify with too much bureaucracy nor underspecify with insufficient structures, processes, leadership, and resources. This builds on themes outlined in Chapter 4 and advanced in Chapters 6, 7, and 8.

Second, progress requires appreciation of both the common and competing interests as well as matters that involve various combinations of these interests. Failing to focus enough on the common interests can result in a lack of a shared vision. Focusing only on the common interests may lead to missing barriers that will undercut collaboration. Addressing both involves predicable tensions and dynamics. In each of the above thumbnail sketches, lists of common and competing interests were needed to create the full picture.

Third, internal alignment is needed for lateral alignment. On each of the issues listed above (and so many others), the stakeholders need to ensure (or work to achieve) sufficient internal alignment in order to engage together laterally. Further, it is not a one-time event, but a continuing alignment dynamic. Stakeholders need to be as interested and supportive in others addressing their "internals" as they are in achieving their own internal alignment.

Fourth, various forms of stakeholder maps are needed to visualize the array of different stakeholder types as well as the many interests (common and competing) that are "at stake." Further, these maps can illuminate points of alignment or misalignment within stakeholder groups as well as across them. These maps will be dynamic, since stakeholders and interests change over time. With these maps, progress on common interests is accelerated and the complexities of competing interests are anticipated and constructively engaged.

Fifth, mechanisms for review and adjustment must be built in to the way a consortium operates in order to ensure that the consortium's vision, structure, and processes continue to advance the interests of the consortium members.

Fit for Purpose

Consortia vary in structure, processes, and dynamics. There is a wide spectrum of structures ranging from loosely connected informal arrangements to groups with a charter and clear roles to entities with substantial funding and staff. Concurrently, the processes for determining membership, making decisions, overseeing staff and volunteers, resolving disputes, and other operational considerations vary as well. Further, there are dynamics over time that can include increasing formalization, adjustments in scale and scope, and even dissolution of the consortium.

Early design choices have subsequent implications. Given that the landscape of stakeholders and interests is dynamic, choices that allow for flexibility are key. At the same time, there is a need for sufficient stability to stay the course with the identified mission or missions. Even with preplanning, because multiple stakeholders are involved, the design process will be challenging. Typically, there is an individual or a small group of individuals involved in making initial design decisions. Invariably this leaves out some stakeholders (and the small group cannot always anticipate emergent interests). As a result, transparency in recording decisions and underlying assumptions is key, along with anticipating periodic review and adjustments.

Generative and Transformative Ecosystems

Consortia coexist with a full range of public and private organizations, as well as other types of institutional actors (education institutions, regulatory bodies, administrative processes, market dynamics, professional societies, etc.). In some cases, consortia are established to sidestep existing entities. More often, existing institutional or organizational leaders deliberately establish consortia to accomplish what they can't do alone. The critical issue is how all of these elements interact together in a given ecosystem.

Increasingly the world needs to be seen as being composed of ecosystems (natural and human-made), not just communities, sectors, industries, and other domains. Like ecosystems, consortia also span boundaries and involve diverse interacting stakeholders. In a world that is increasingly understood as being composed of ecosystems—social and technical—consortia will have central roles that interact with preexisting organizations and institutional arrangements.

Consortia can give voice and direction to groups with shared interests, while also concentrating efforts in ways that risk burnout and dynamics associated with the iron law of oligarchy. Both positive and negative aspects emerged with the National Data Service initiative, which pioneered a number of technological advances such as the use of "containers" to facilitate the exchange of software and data. At the same time, the concentrated effort did result in the burnout of some individuals and a fear of a form of oligarchy (though not stated that way) was behind the US National Science Foundation (NSF) not wanting to grant this initiative the status of being "the" national data service.

Consortia can complement and complicate regulatory agencies in multiple ways. As we saw with the Biomarkers Consortium, regulators valued knowing what scientific advances were coming their way and the private sector valued regulators having this information. The result has been better informed decisions by the regulators and enhanced regulatory review and approval. At the same time, regulators have to be careful regarding what is termed "policy capture" by those being regulated—ensuring that independent authority and perceptions of independence are maintained.

Consortia can extend the reach of commercial and nonprofit organizations, while also constraining them in multiple ways. Organizations are increasingly finding their members entangled in consortia of various types. For example, as discussed in Chapter 8 university-based cyberinfrastructure professionals are increasingly affiliated with the Campus Research Computing Consortium (CaRCC), the Minority Serving Cyberinfrastructure Consortium (MS-CC), and dozens of others. This places individuals in boundary-spanning roles where they need to simultaneously align themselves with the consortium's goals and internally align with the needs of their home organization. The advantage is bringing new ideas back to the home organization, but a negative is added complexity. For example, members of the various research computing and data consortia not only bring new ideas with software and hardware applications but they now expect their universities to have better defined career paths and improved opportunities for professional development. They are also more aware of job opportunities beyond their home institution and more valuable on the job market as they have transferable knowledge and skills.

Ultimately, consortia and ecosystems will coevolve in the 21st century in anticipated and also surprising ways—for better and sometimes for worse.

Return to the Video Game Industry

As we noted in Chapter 1, any new institutional arrangement needs to deliver on creating value, mitigating harm, or a combination of the two. We began this chapter with the Playing for the Planet Alliance, a consortium centered on harnessing video games to have a positive collective impact. There are also serious concerns about screen times, inappropriate content, toxic cultures, and other potential harms of the medium.

A second consortium, the Thriving in Games Group (formerly Fair Play Alliance), is focused on sharing real-world insights and research on reducing the toxicity and creating healthier cultures within the communities of popular video games. In this case, the mitigating harm is not with respect to an external issue, but a focus on a central negative impact that the industry itself was having in society and its ability to attract new and more diverse gamers.[17]

> Founded in 2017 as the Fair Play Alliance, this group now has over 300 members, a diverse mix of gaming companies, with additional links to player communities, researchers, and others. The Alliance has presented itself as "a global coalition of gaming professionals and companies committed to developing quality games... provid[ing] a forum for gaming professionals and companies to work together to develop and share best practices in encouraging healthy communities and awesome player interactions in online gaming." The Aliance has added that they "envision a world where games are free of harassment, discrimination, and abuse, and where players can express themselves through play."

In defining the problem that needs to be addressed, the Alliance has stated "[p]art of what makes online games so great is playing with other people! Today, however, players are overwhelmingly telling us that they're frustrated by how often games are disrupted, for example by in-fighting on the same teams, or by harassment and hate." Many online gaming environments have problems with racism, sexism, and homophobia. As Alliance cofounder, Kimberly Voll commented:

> The focus of the Alliance, now the Thriving in Games Group, is to equitably empower game developers to address issues of disruptive and harmful behavior with the goal of ensuring player and community well-being, which extends to existing and future players. The issues we see are in part because of games themselves, but also in large part because games are where people are today (hence bringing the complexity and problems of people at scale) and the need for games and online spaces more generally to function as social infrastructure despite not being designed or often even recognized as such.

In response, the Alliance has highlighted five guiding principles:
- Intentionally evolve how games are made
- Facilitate learning and coordination
- Prioritize inclusivity and safety
- Uphold the spirit of the game
- Promote the value of player dynamics

Methods advanced by Alliance have included a combination of moderation, shielding, and nudging in the live games, as well as upstream approaches such as safety by design and player dynamic design. All of these methods are relevant for reducing toxicity in society. Nudging, for example, involves simple messages such as "Teammates perform worse if you harass them after a mistake." Behavioral economist Richard Thaler received the Nobel Prize for his scholarship on what is now termed nudge theory[18]—emphasizing how small practical guidance can shift behaviors. In video games, the impact of nudges was documented in a 2016 *Scientific American* article, "Can a Video Game Company Tame Toxic Behavior?" by Brendan Maher.[19] The focus was on *League of Legends*, which had a community of 67 million players, grossed an estimated $1.25 billion in revenue, and had a reputation for toxic behaviors. Riot Games, the platform for *League of Legends*, saw these behaviors as a threat to its business. Over 200 different types of nudges were tested. The sample nudge listed above (on teammate behavior) was found to have "reduced negative attitudes by 8.3%, verbal abuse by 6.2% and offensive language by 11% compared with controls."

Kimberly Voll cofounded the Alliance while working at Riot Games. As she recalls:

> We were increasingly noticing more individuals focusing on these problems at gaming companies, but a lack of support and a lack of best practices (and even active misinformation in some cases) was holding them back. After numerous conversations with such colleagues, we realized it made sense to start a community of practice to support one another. We all felt that best practices in this domain should be equitably shared with a philosophy of "a rising tide floats all boats"; ultimately no one should compete on the health and wellness of one's community, but instead all players deserve to feel safe and welcome in gaming spaces to the best of our ability.

Kimberly Voll adds:

> The Alliance, now the Thriving in Games Group, today exists as a space in the industry for the work that individual companies may struggle to prioritize or support given a myriad of constraints, and a way to amplify and share best practices equitably around the world so that we can better hold ourselves accountable to healthier outcomes.

Both the Playing for the Planet Alliance highlighted at the beginning of this chapter and the Fair Play Alliance/Thriving in Games Group emphasize shared global governance involving diverse stakeholders, public engagement, ethical considerations, and continuous monitoring of impacts. Both are new enough that is not yet possible to discern whether they can be agile in response to changing circumstances. Together they are illustrative of the combination of creating value and mitigating harm.

Summing Up

A broad cross-section of global challenges that may benefit from consortia are addressed in this chapter: artificial intelligence, clean water, data sharing, geoengineering, green energy, social media, and rising authoritarianism. In each case, the current presence of and future potential for consortia is clear, spanning diverse stakeholder types. A list of illustrative common and competing interests helps to show what consortia could advance and also what needs to be addressed in order for them to be viable in the long term.

Not all consortia will be the same, with variation in formality, scale, scope, and time horizons. Further, consortia will not operate in a vacuum—they will emerge from social groups, interact with government agencies, private organizations, nonprofit organizations, social movements, and other existing organizational and institutional arrangements—both complementing and competing with others in their respective ecosystems. Because social challenges are increasingly understood in the context of ecosystems (rather than communities, organizations, sectors, or industries), consortia play key boundary-spanning roles.

Ultimately, agile and adaptive consortia will be the defining institutional arrangement of the 21st century—not because consortia are easily established and sustained (which they are not), but because they enable parties to accomplish together what they cannot otherwise do separately.

Notes

1. See https://playing4theplanet.org/members.
2. We thank Sam Barratt and Alan Gershenfeld for their insights as we developed this vignette. Of course, the responsibility for the text is entirely ours as coauthors.
3. We add "structuring processes," building on the work of Giddens and Bourdieu, each of whom highlighted how institutions are a product of interactive processes—structuring, not just structures.
4. For more information on the current efforts around the UN SDGs, see https://sdgs.un.org/2030agenda. In this context, the UN states the "[a]ll countries and all stakeholders, acting in collaborative partnership, will implement this plan." What is not spelled out sufficiently are the collaborative institutional arrangements enabling such partnerships, which is the focus of this book.
5. For a set of ethical standards (including a summary of many others) for AI/ML, see "AGU—NASA Ethics in AI/ML," *AGU: Advancing Earth and Space Science*, accessed June 14, 2023, https://data.agu.org/ethics-ai-ml/.
6. Personal correspondence with coauthor Joel Cutcher-Gershenfeld.
7. This is a core argument made in Neil Gershenfeld, Alan Gershenfeld, and Joel Cutcher-Gershenfeld, *Designing Reality: How to Survive and Thrive in the Third Digital Revolution* (New York: Basic Books, 2017).
8. See Elinor Ostrom, *Governing the Commons: The Evolution of Institutions for Collective Action* (New York: Cambridge University Press, 1990).
9. There are many consortia organized around common-pool resources. See, for example, https://globalcommonsalliance.org/global-commons/.
10. See, for example, Tal Septon, Nidhi Nagabhatla, Angela Min Yi Hou, and Fan Yang, "BRICS Consortium: Toward Implementing Sustainable Development Goal 6," in *Partnerships for the Goals: Encyclopedia of the UN Sustainable Development Goals*, edited by W. Leal Filho, A. M. Azul, L. Brandli, A. Lange Salvia, and T. Wall (Cham: Springer, 2020), pp. 1–16, http://doi-org-443.webvpn.fjmu.edu.cn/10.1007/978-3-319-71067-9_108-1.

11. See, for example, Stakeholder Alignment Collaborative, Joel Cutcher-Gershenfeld et al., "Five Ways Consortia Can Catalyse Open Science," *Nature* 543 (2017): pp. 615–617, https://doi.org/10.1038/543615a.
12. Quoted inCutcher-Gershenfeld et al., "Five Ways Consortia Can Catalyse Open Science." p. 615.
13. There are relevant bodies and initiatives, including the United Nations Convention on the Law of the Sea (UNCLOS) which has responsibility for aspects of CDR in the ocean, the Montreal Protocol on Substances that Deplete the Ozone Layer, the Convention on Biological Diversity, the London Convention on the Prevention of Marine Pollution, and others that point to the need for a consortium of consortia. For more information on climate intervention ethics, which can be a foundation for such governance, see "Ethical Framework for Climate Intervention," *AGU: Advancing Earth and Space Science*, accessed June 14, 2023, https://www.agu.org/Learn-About-AGU/About-AGU/Ethics/Ethical-Framework-for-Climate-Intervention.
14. Joel Cutcher-Gershenfeld, Chris Guillot, Monica Morrison, and Billy Williams, "Navigating Three Fundamental Challenges Facing Geoengineering Ethics," Working Paper, 2024.
15. Heather Cox Richardson, "March 10, 2023," *Letters from an American*, accessed June 14, 2023, https://open.substack.com/pub/heathercoxrichardson/p/march-10-2023?utm_campaign=post&utm_medium=web.
16. See Fareed Zakaria, "The Rise of Illiberal Democracy," *Foreign Affairs* 76, no. 6 (1997): pp. 22–43, https://doi.org/10.2307/20048274.
17. We thank Kimberly Voll for her insights as we developed this vignette. Of course, the responsibility for the text is entirely all of ours. We draw here on information from https://fairplayalliance.org/.
18. See Richard Thaler and Cass Sunstein, *Nudge: Improving Decisions about Health, Wealth, and Happiness* (New Haven, CT: Yale University Press, 2008).
19. Brendan Maher, "Can a Video Game Company Tame Toxic Behavior?," *Scientific American* 531, no. 7596 (March 31, 2016), retrieved from: https://www.scientificamerican.com/article/can-a-video-game-company-tame-toxic-behavior/.

Epilogue

At its best, science fiction both anticipates the future and informs the present. Too often this is done in dystopian ways. *The Ministry for the Future* by Kim Stanley Robinson is compelling both in looking ahead with respect to climate change and in reflecting on the insufficient responses in the present.[1] Moreover, it manages to combine both utopian and dystopian threads. It is the utopian threads that draw our attention here.

In chapter 85 Robinson lists 200 actual and hypothetical consortia centered on ecological regeneration from around the world. These include proposed reports from Australia's Yarra Yarra Biodiversity Corridor, Belize's Coral Reef Restoration, Cameroon's Bafut Ecovillage, China's Zhejiang Green Rural Revival Program, Denmark's Vitsohus Permakultur, Eritrea's Manazares Mango Regeneration, and so on throughout the world, with imagined entries for many countries, each with names beginning with every letter of the alphabet.

The point is clear—the repair of the planet will not just happen with the top-down hypothetical UN agency that gives the book its title. Robinson adds to the picture this bottom-up outpouring of collective effort. Not fully spelled out in the novel—and the motivation for our book—are the mechanisms for lateral alignment among these many collective initiatives. This aspect of social change—lateral rather than top-down or bottom-up—is suggested by some of the ways that the "Ministry of the Future" operates in the novel, but can go further. Lateral alignment is not instinctive, but it will be at the heart of what we anticipate will be the consortia century.

Lateral forums could be regional agglomerations or collections of initiatives with a similar focus. This will involve leaders in boundary-spanning or linking-pin roles, bringing forward interests from among the laterally connected groups and integrating them into a combined strategy. Invariably, there will be competing as well as common interests, so the lateral forums will involve constructive negotiations.

In our aspirational scenario, aligning and advancing will interweave. It will be important to get the diverse stakeholders aligned on the same page with respect to shared visions, charters, and metrics. It will be equally important for leadership and resources to be advancing common interests, mindful of separate interests.

Ultimately, the needed change will be institutional—codifying broad, constructive patterns of interaction in society. Institutionalized norms that anticipate and expect lateral alignment for collective action honor Martin Luther King's words in his 1963 Letter from Birmingham Jail:

We are caught in an inescapable network of mutuality, tied in a single garment of destiny. What affects one directly, affects all indirectly.[2]

Notes

1. Kim Stanley Robinson, *The Ministry for the Future: A Novel* (New York: Orbit; Hachette Book Group, 2020).
2. For a recording of Martin Luther King reading the full letter, see https://www.youtube.com/watch?v=Di05SvJ8utI.

Acronyms

3DEM	Three-dimensional electron microscopy
ACTIV	Accelerating COVID-19 Therapeutic Interventions and Vaccines
AFSCME	American Federation of State, County, and Municipal Employees
AGU	American Geophysical Union
AI	Artificial Intelligence
AIHEC	American Indian Higher Education Consortium
AQPC	American Quality and Productivity Center
ARPANET	Advanced Research Projects Agency Network
AU	Australia
BC	Biomarkers Consortium
BMRB	BioMedResBank
BNL	Brookhaven National Laboratory
CaRCC	Campus Research Computing Consortium
CCDC	Cambridge Crystallographic Data Centre
CDF	Council of Data Facilities (within the NSF EarthCube Initiative)
CDR	Carbon Dioxide Removal
CHW	Community Health Worker
CI	Cyberinfrastructure
CIO	Chief Information Officer
CLB	Consortium Leadership Board (within MS-CC)
CLC	Consortium Leadership Council (within MS-CC)
COMECON	Council for Mutual Economic Assistance
CoP	Community of Practice (within RDA)
COVID	Coronavirus disease
CPAC	Conservative Political Action Conference
DMZ	Demilitarized Zone for sensitive data
DoC	US Department of Commerce
DoD	US Department of Defense
DoE	US Department of Energy
DoT	US Department of Transportation
EDI	Environmental Data Initiative—Streamlining Data Curation to Accelerate Scientific Inquiry
EIS	Environmental Impact Statement
EMDB	Electron Microscopy Data Bank
EPA	US Environmental Protection Agency
EU	European Union
FAA	US Federal Aviation Administration

FACA	Federal Advisory Committee Act
FAIR	Findability, Accessibility, Interoperability, and Reusability (for data)
FDA	US Food and Drug Administration
FDC	Finance and Development Committee (within MS-CC)
FNIH	Foundation for NIH
FPA	Fair Play Alliance
GPS	Global Positioning Satellites
H2O	Health Outcomes Observatory
HBCU	Historically Black Colleges and Universities
HSIs	Hispanic Serving Institutions
IAAC	Institute for Advanced Architecture of Catalonia
IBT	International Brotherhood of Teamsters
ICANN	The Internet Corporation for Assigned Names and Numbers
IETF	Internet Engineering Task Force
IG	Interest Group (within RDA)
ILWU	International Longshore and Warehouse Union
IMT	Institute for Market Transformations
ISOC	Internet Society
IUCr	International Union of Crystallography
IUOE	International Union of Operating Engineers
JPDO	Joint Planning and Development Office
KPI	Key Performance Indicators
KPNAA	Kaiser Permanente Nurse Anesthetists Association
LGBTQ+	Lesbian, Gay, Bisexual, Transgender, and Queer or Questioning, plus additional related identities
LEO	Low earth orbit
LERA	Labor and Employment Relations Association
LLM	Large Language Model
LMP	Labor-Management Partnership (Kaiser Permanente, Coalition, Alliance)
LTER	Long Term Ecological Research Program
MNC	Membership and Nominating Committee (within MS-CC)
MoU	Memorandum of Understanding
MQWLC	Michigan Quality of Work Life Center
MS-CC	Minority Serving Cyberinfrastructure Consortium
MSI	Minority Serving Institution
NACHW	National Association for Community Health Workers
NAE	National Academy of Engineering
NASA	US National Aeronautics and Space Administration
NATO	North Atlantic Treaty Organization
NCSA	National Center for Supercomputing Applications
NDS	National Data Service
NIH	US National Institutes of Health

NEON	National Ecological Observatory Network
NextGen	Next Generation Air Transportation System
NIH	National Institutes of Health
NIST	National Institute of Standards and Technology
NMR	Nuclear magnetic resonance
NOAA	US National Oceanic and Atmospheric Administration
NRDC	Natural Resources Defense Council
NSF	US National Science Foundation
NTIA	US National Telecommunications and Information Administration (within US Department of Commerce)
OFNHP	Oregon Federation of Nurses & Health Professionals
OPEC	Arab Petroleum Exporting Countries
OPEIU	Office and Professional Employees International Union
PA	Physician Assistants
PCC	Patient Care Collaborative
PCORI	Patient Centered Outcomes Research Institute
PDB	Protein Data Bank
PDCA	Plan, Do, Check, Act (or Adjust)
PPC	Program and Priorities Committee (within MS-CC)
PPE	Personal Protective Equipment
PPP	Public-Private Partnership
PWI	Primarily White Institution
R&D	Research and Development
RCSB	Research Collaboratory for Structural Bioinformatics
RDA	Research Data Alliance
RN	Registered Nurses
SAC	Scientific Advisory Committee (within PDB)
SDGs	UN Sustainable Development Goals
SDSC	San Diego Supercomputer Center
SEIU	Service Employees International Union
SEIU-UHW	Service Employees International Union - United Health Workers
SRM	Solar Radiation Management
TCUs	Tribal Colleges and Universities
UCAR	University Corporation for Atmospheric Research
UFCW	United Food and Commercial Workers
UN	United Nations
UNEP	UN Environment Programme
UNITE HERE	Union of Needletrades, Industrial, and Textile Employees (UNITE) and Hotel Employees and Restaurant Employees Union (HERE).
US	United States
USW	United Steelworkers
WHO	World Health Organization
WIA	Work in America Institute
WG	Working Group (within RDA)
wwPDB	World-Wide Protein Data Bank

Glossary

Bottom-Up Change: Decentralized initiatives operating without depending on a hierarchical structure to achieve a desired aim by an acting party or parties.

Boundary Spanners: Individuals with roles and knowledge that spans multiple groups, functions, or organizations, enabling them to serve as intermediaries.

Collective Action: Initiatives advanced together by a group of people in order to enhance their condition and achieve a common objective.

Consortia: Self-governing collaborative arrangements among individuals, groups, and organizations that are independent and interdependent, so they can accomplish together what they cannot do separately.

Ikamva Labantu: "The Future of the People" in isiXhosa (South Africa)

Institutions: Stable, valued, recurring patterns of behavior that form the social order in society.

Interested Parties: Individuals, groups, organizations, and other parties with interests relative to a given issue, initiative, or organization.

Interests: Hopes, fears, concerns, and other underlying considerations. In contrast with stated positions (such as in a negotiation), interests are the underlying considerations that motivate the positions and that can prompt the generation of alternative options.

Lateral Alignment: The dynamic, iterative, negotiated process by which sufficient understanding or agreement is reached horizontally across individuals, groups, and organizations to enable coordinated action toward achieving common goals.

Middle-Out Change: Initiatives operating horizontally across individuals, groups, and organizations to achieve an aim desired by multiple acting parties.

Minimum Viable Consortium: Consortia having the minimum necessary structure and processes needed to generate positive early results, together with the ability to adapt and adjust as needed.

Mixed-Motive Assumption: Assuming that interacting parties will have a mixture of common and competing interests.

Organizations: Individuals and groups operating within a formal unitary structure guiding action.

Rights Holders: Individuals, groups, organizations, and other parties with legal rights relative to a given issue, initiative, or organization.

Social Movements: Connected individuals and groups with a shared vision and a commitment to action.

Stakeholders: Individuals, groups, organizations, and other parties with substantive interests in a given issue, initiative, or organization.

Stakeholder Alignment: Lateral connections among individuals, groups, and organizations that are sufficient to enable collective action.

Stakeholder Engagement: One party's systematic efforts to identify and influence or motivate others whose views and actions provide a potential benefit for that party's initiatives and operations.

Stakeholder Management: One party's systematic efforts to identify and influence or control others whose views and actions pose a risk for that party's initiatives and operations.

Top-Down Change: Centralized initiatives operating within the authority and responsibility of a hierarchical structure to achieve a desired aim by an acting party or parties.

Index

For the benefit of digital users, indexed terms that span two pages (e.g., 52–53) may, on occasion, appear on only one of those pages.

21st century, 9, 31, 45, 68, 94, 150, 178, 182, 183, 185, 208, 211

Accelerating COVID-19 Therapeutic Interventions and Vaccines (ACTIV), 77–78, 199
Accelerating rates of change, *see* Change
Accomplishing together what can't be done separately, 11–12, 30–31, 57–58, 70, 74, 88, 138, 161
Actor mapping, 94
Adams, Julia, 54
Addams, Jane, 69–70, 188–189
Advanced Research Projects Agency Network (ARPANET), 55–56
Agile/agility and adaptive, 9, 11, 15–16, 36, 40, 46, 68, 72, 73, 76–77, 89, 145, 173, 184–186, 196, 197, 205, 211
Aircraft noise and emissions, 25–26, 112, 114
Alignment
    A continuing accomplishment, 38, 55, 76, 82
    Equity teams, 103–105, 181
    Internal, 38, 40, 42, 44, 46, 54, 64–65, 74–75, 88, 98, 114, 163–164, 182, 193, 205
    Lateral, 3, 15–16, 34, 40, 44, 46, 54, 75, 88, 114, 163–164, 182, 196, 205
    Sufficient for action, 2, 16–17, 37–38, 40, 42–45, 46, 70, 74–75, 88, 162, 199
American Quality and Productivity Center (AQPC), 60–61
Americas Partnership for Economic Prosperity, 36
Arab Petroleum Exporting Countries (OPEC), 56
Arctic Council, 82
Area Labor-Management Committees (ALMC), 60–61
Artificial intelligence (AI), 7, 10, 157, 181–182, 185–186, 197–198
Assumption wrangling, 60
Authoritarianism, 204–205

Balanced scorecard, 38, 74–75, 154
BHP Billiton, 106–109
Biomarkers Consortium (BC), 14, 16–17, 23–24, 53, 68, 72–73, 75–78, 80–84, 163, 166–167, 187–188, 192, 207
BioMedResBank (BMRB), 157
Blalock, Hubert, 57
Blank, Steven, 72
Boundary
    Condition, 109
    Objects, 12–13, 17
    Space, 79–80
    Spanners/Spanning, 18–19, 147–148, 164–165, 187–188, 207–208, 211
Bottom-up, *see* Change
Brandeis, Louis, 62
Brave Hearts, 19, 21–22
Bridges, William and Susan, 101
Brookhaven National Laboratory (BNL), 156

Cambridge Crystallographic Data Centre (CCDC), 156
Campus Research Computing Consortium (CaRCC), 164–165, 192, 207–208
Carbon Dioxide Removal (CDR), 200–201
Center for Bits and Atoms (CBA), 160–161
Century of Aviation Reauthorization Act (H.R. 2115, Public Law 108-176), 112
Change
    Accelerating rates of, 46, 184–186, 193
    Bottom-up, 34, 38–39, 76, 98–99, 101, 163
    Culture, 30, 170
    Drivers of, 190
    Environmental, 72
    Leading, 96–98, 103–104, 108
    Management, 98, 103–104
    Middle-out, 15–16, 38–39, 76
    Organizational, 202
    Resistance to, 110, 173
    Social, 10, 34
    Stakeholders, 119, 165–166

Change (*Continued*)
  Top-down, 34, 38
  Technological, 9, 88
  Transformational, 37–39, 163
Charter/chartering, 12, 17, 30–31, 45, 68–69, 75–77, 79–80, 105, 114, 132–150–154–157, 165–170, 173, 175–177, 186, 206
Clean water, 34, 198–199
Climate Mayors, 1–2, 27
Climate change, 1–2, 9, 30–31, 113, 132, 190, 201, and Epilogue
Collective action, 2, 13–15, 33–34, 37–38, 45, 49–59, 61–65, 68, 69–71, 75, 88, 103, 105, 135, 163–164, 183, 188–189, 196, 204
Collective impact model, 15–16, 81
Common and competing interests, *see* Interests, common and competing
Community Health Worker (CHW), 24, 85, 86–87
Community of Practice (within RDA) (CoP), 84, 185–186
Comte, Auguste, 188–189
Conflict resolution, 56, 72, 135, 153–154, 188, 203
Conservative Political Action Conference (CPAC), 204
Consortia
  Agile and adaptive, 68, 170, 172
  Alignment for, 37–38
  Boundaries, 188, 207
  Century, 3, 27–28, 66, and Epilogue
  Challenges, 196–205
  Characteristics of, 69, 71–72
  Charter, *see* Charter/Chartering
  Common and conflicting interests within, 38, 66, 71
  Consortia-like, 36–37, 55, 160, 181
  Consortia of consortia, 88
  Continual accomplishment, 55
  Contrast with hierarchical control, 68–69
  Defined, 11–12, 31–32
  Defining institutional arrangement, 31, 35, 46
  Different ways of knowing within, 59–60
  Disbanding, 174–176
  Diverse stakeholders, 75, 192, 196
  Dynamic, 72
  Ecosystems/context/landscape, 82, 124, 185–186
  Earlier forms, 60–61
  Eastern and Western views, 50
  Engagement, 102
  Facilitating, 34
  Governance through, 33–34, 145–146, 186, 191, 198
  Incorporation/nonprofit, 146–147, 167
  Increasing importance/formation, 32–33, 182
  Independent and interdependent stakeholders in, 81–82
  Interests within, 40
  Launch and sustainment, 88, 121–122, 147, 162
  Legitimacy, 98, 190
  Limits/legal/institutional, 105, 187
  Membership, 150–151
  Minimum viable, 74, 205
  Mitigating harm, 58–59
  Monopolistic, 56
  Network structure, 54, 57–58
  Power/standing, 70
  Rates of change, 184–185
  Resources, 166–170
  Rights within, 42
  R&D, 35–36
  Roots, 31
  Shift in mindset, 69
  Sustainment, *see* Launch and Sustainment
  Underrepresented parties/tokenism, 57
  Value propositions, 80–81
  Varieties of, 37, 68, 206
  Volunteers/tragedies of the commons, 52
Consortium Leadership Board (within MS-CC) (CLB), 144–149
Consortium Leadership Council (within MS-CC) (CLC), 144–145, 149–150
Council for Mutual Economic Assistance (COMECON), 35
Council of Data Facilities (within the NSF EarthCube Initiative) (CDF), 25, 43, 85, 132, 133–134, 138
COVID Coronavirus disease, 23, 77–78, 162, 172, 174, 190, 199
Creating value, 3, 36–37, 71–72, 208, 210
Crenshaw, Kimberlé Williams, 18, 191–192
Cutcher-Gershenfeld, Joel, 63
Cyberinfrastructure (CI), 30–31, 34, 83, 85, 118, 123, 125–128, 136, 138, 140, 142–143, 154, 207–208, *see also* Minority Serving Cyberinfrastructure Consortium

Data sharing, 84, 127–128, 132, 199–200
Davids, Ishrene, 21

INDEX   221

Decision making, 24, 64, 79, 100, 104–105, 148, 152, 198, 201
Demilitarized Zone for sensitive data (DMZ), 30, 171
Deming, Edwards, 82, 101, 102
Digital divides, 9–10, 25–26, 41, 49, 116, 172, 189
Digital technologies/Digital era, 3, 10, 32, 36–37, 52, 73, 185–186, 199, 200
Disbanding/Dissolution, 72, 77, 174–178, 183, 186–187, 193, 206
Dodge City, Kansas, 25–26, 49, 59, 127
Donelan, Karen, 100
Dynamic, 11, 15–17, 37–39, 46, 50–51, 60–61, 63–65, 70, 72–74, 76, 77–78, 88, 100, 104, 117, 119, 121–122, 128, 139, 163–166, 177, 182, 184–185, 193, 205–207

EarthCube, 25, 85, 127–128, 132
Ebola, 27, 93
Ecosystems, 9, 12–13, 26, 33, 82, 89, 203, 206–208, 211
Electron Microscopy Data Bank (EMDB), 173
Emanuel, Rahm, 1
Engels, Frederick, 69–70
Environmental Data Initiative (EDI), 177
Environmental Impact Statement (EIS), 25–26, 106, 107–108
Environmental Justice, 170
Equity, 27, 44–45, 103–105, 136, 143, 181–182
European Union, 119

Fab
  Academany, 160–161
  All In, 160–161
  Cities, 26, 160–161
  Foundation, 26, 160–161
  Labs, 23, 26, 138, 160–161
Fallahq, Mosoka, 93
Fair Play Alliance (FPA), 26–27, 208, 210, see Thriving in Games Group
Federal Advisory Committee Act (FACA), 133
Finance and Development Committee (within MS-CC) (FDC), 146–147
Findability, Accessibility, Interoperability, and Reusability (FAIR), 43, 175
Fiscal agent, 72–73, 146–147, 172
Fissurization, 51, 60–61
Follett, Mary Parker, 71
Foucault, Michel, 57
Foundation for NIH (FNIH), 77–81
  Finance and Audit Committee, 167

Governance Committee, 167

Geoengineering, 196–197, 200–201
Gershenfeld, Neil, 160
Global challenges, 10, 34, 196–197
Global Positioning Satellites (GPS), 128
Global North, 189
Global South, 86, 189
Governance, 12, 33–34, 40, 53, 56, 94–95, 132, 139, 144–148, 167, 175–177, 186, 191, 196, 198–200, 202, 203–204, 210
Green energy, 195–197, 201–202, 210–211
Green, Steven, 108
Guiding values, 143–144

Hardin, Garrett, 52
Health Outcomes Observatory (H2O), 73
Hierarchical organization, 9, 15, 35–37, 46–47, 68–69, 89, 163, 191
Hispanic Serving Institutions (HSI), 24–25, 30–31, 114, 116, 119, 122–126, Ch 6 Appendix, 142, 144, 150, 192
Historically Black Colleges and Universities (HBCU), 24–25, 30–31, 62, 83, 114, 116, 119, 123–126, Ch 6 Appendix, 136–137, 141–142, 144, 150, 166, 192
Huggins, Charlie, 63

Identifying interests, 39, 77–78, 114, 117–122, 128
Ikamva Labantu, 19, 21, 22, 26
In group/out group, 51, 58–59
Independent and interdependent, 37–39, 72, 81–82, 109–110
Indo-Pacific Economic Framework for Prosperity, 36
Industrial democracy, 62
Industrial Relations Research Association (IRRA), 60–61
Influence, 17, 33–34, 95, 96, 98, 99, 103, 107–108, 163
Integration, 71–72, 101
Institute for Advanced Architecture of Catalonia (IAAC), 160–161
Institute for Market Transformations (IMT), 1
Institutions/Institutional/Institutionalization
  Arrangements, 2, 11–13, 31–32, 36–37, 68, 74, 88, 101–102, 161, 184–185, 197, 204
  Defined, 2
  Dynamic, 161
  Organizations and, 35, 182, 185–186
  Legitimacy, 190

Institutions/Institutional/Institutionalization (*Continued*)
  Work, 12–13
Internet Engineering Task Force (IETF), 56
Internet Society (ISOC), 56
Interest group (within RDA) (IG), 84, 185–186
Interests
  Common and competing, 1–2, 12, 17, 37–39, 66, 69–72, 79–80, 88, 103, 119, 121–122, 128, 153, 165, 170, 177, 197, 205–206
  Separate, 77, 161, 170–172
  Shared, 11, 36, 38, 77, 161, 170, 184, 202, 207
Interested parties, 12, 14–15, 33–34, 40, 69
Internal alignment, *see* Alignment
International Union of Crystallography (IUCr), 173
Internet Corporation for Assigned Names and Numbers (ICANN), 55
Internet2, 30–31, 72–73, 145–146, 155, 166, 172, 176
Iridium, 174–175
Iron law of oligarchy, 51, 55–57, 173, 175–176, 187, 207

Joint Planning and Development Office (JPDO), 113

Kaiser Permanente, Coalition, Alliance, 20–22, 65, 138–139
Kanter, Rosabeth Moss, 57
Kaplan, Robert, 74–75
Keidel, Robert, 18–19
Key Performance Indicators (KPIs), 74–75, 154, 155, 158
Keystone XLPipeline, 98
King, Mel, 160
Knowledge boundaries, 51, 60
Kotter, John, 96
Kuübler-Ross, Elisabeth, 101
Kurzweil, Ray, 197

Labor and Employment Relations Association (LERA), 60–61
Labor-Management Partnership (LMP), *see* Kaiser Permanente, Coalition, Alliance
Large Language Model (LLM), 197
Lassiter, Sherry, 160–161
Lateral alignment, *see* Alignment
Lateral thinking, 69
Lawrence, Paul, 59–60

Lax, David, 71–72
Lesbian, Gay, Bisexual, Transgender, and Queer or Questioning, plus additional related identities (LGBTQ+), 204
Lewin, Kurt, 51
Liberia, 93
Linking pins, 147–148
Long Term Ecological Research Program (LTER), 25, 176
Lorsch, Jay, 59–60
Low earth orbit (LEO), 174
Lyft, 26, 187

Maher, Brendan, 209–210
Marx, Karl, 69–70, 188–189
Max M. and Marjorie S. Fisher Foundation, 170
McKersie, Robert, 71–72
Membership (within MS-CC), 149–150
Membership and Nominating Committee (within MS-CC) (MNC), 145–146
Membership meeting (within MS-CC), 134
Memorandum of Understanding (MoU), 55–56
Michels, Robert, 55–56
Michigan Quality of Work Life Center (MQWLC), 60–61
Microelectronics and Computing Consortium (MCC), 12–13
Middle-out, *see* Change
Minimum Viable Consortium (MVC), 17, 40, 45–46, 72, 74, 88, 172, 205
Minority Serving Cyberinfrastructure Consortium (MS-CC), 13–14, 23, 24–25, 30–31, 62, 75, 83, 109–110, 114, 116, 118, 119, 122, 123, 125, 126–127, Ch6 Appendix, 134–136, 138, 140–144, 146–155, 163, 166, 170–173, 176
Minority Serving Institution (MSI), 24–25, 30–31, 114, 119, 124, 126, Chapter 6 Appendix, 142, 150, 192
Mitchell, Bill, 160
Mitigating harm, 3, 36–37, 58–59, 208, 210
Mixed-motive assumption, 71–72, 77
Montesinos, Deborah, 63
Moore, Gordon, 185
Motorola, 174–175

National Academies, 117
National Academy of Engineering (NAE), 34
National Association for Community Health Workers (NACHW), 87

National Center for Supercomputing Applications (NCSA), 175
National Data Service (NDS), 35–36, 162, 164, 175
Natural Resources Defense Council (NRDC), 1
Neil, Garry, 163
NextGen Next Generation Air Transportation System (NextGen), 25–26, 114
Nin, Anaïs, 61–62
North Atlantic Treaty Organization (NATO), 204
Norton, David, 74–75
Nuclear magnetic resonance (NMR), 173

Olson, Mancur, 52
Olympic Dam, 25–26, 105, 106–109
Organization/organizational, 2, 8–22, 27, 31–40, 43, 45–46, 51, 54–55, 57, 59–60, 68–69, 72, 74–75, 77–78, 80–81, 84, 86, 88, 93–94, 96, 99, 103–104, 109, 116, 119, 133–134, 144, 146–147, 150, 154, 158, 161, 163, 164, 166–167, 175, 176, 182, 184–189, 191, 192–193, 195–196, 198–204, 206–208, 211
Organization of Arab Petroleum Exporting Countries (OPEC), 56
Ostrom, Elinor, 33–34, 52, 74, 198–199
Otani, Akiko, 7–8

Patient Advocacy Organization, 7, 16–17, 23–24, 53, 75–78, 80–81, 119–122, 166, 192
Patient Care Collaborative (PCC), 24, 44–45
Patient Centered Outcomes Research Institute (PCORI), 24, 99–100
Personal Protective Equipment (PPE), 23
Piore, Michael, 36–37
Plan, Do, Check, Act (or Adjust) (PDCA), 82, 101
Playing for the Planet Alliance, 26–27, 195–196, 208, 210
Pluralism/Pluralist assumption, 10, 13, 17, 34, 69–70, 94, 98, 102, 110, 184, 199
Power, 8, 16–17, 23, 26–27, 35, 50–51, 55–62, 68–72, 75–76, 98, 99, 108, 157, 163, 184–187, 198
Principal/agent dilemmas, 51, 54–55
Primarily White Institution (PWI), 141, 192
Primary Care Collaborative (PCC), 24, 44–45
Program and Priorities Committee (within MS-CC) (PPC), 146

Protein Data Bank (PDB), 23–24, 154–158, 162, 173–174, 199
Protocol of Peace, 62
Public-Private Partnership (PPP), 7, 9, 11–12, 25–26, 31–32, 55–56, 73, 109, 113, 119, 198–199, 201–202
Putnam, Robert, 60–61

Quilt, 176

Racism, 58–59, 103–104, 209
Regan, Dave, 64–65
Research and Development (R&D), 7–8, 35–36, 174
Research Collaboratory for Structural Bioinformatics (RCSB), 156, 173
Research Data Alliance (RDA), 43, 84, 185–186
Rights holders, 14–15, 33–34, 40, 69
Rogers, Everett, 18–19
Roloff, Julia, 94–95
Rutgers University, 156

Sabel, Charles, 36–37
San Diego Supercomputer Center (SDSC), 175
Sandman, Peter, 95, 98
Scientific Advisory Committee (within PDB) (SAC), 156–157
SEMATECH, 35–36
SDG, see UN Sustainable Development Goals
Sebenius, James, 71–72
Self-governance/Self-governing, 9, 11–13, 22, 35
Service Employees International Union - United Health Workers (SEIU-UHW), 63–65
Seul, Jeffrey, 61–62
Shared governance, 12, 33–34
Shared vision, 12–13, 40, 42–44, 46, 61–62, 76–77, 79, 80–81, 132, 134–138, 141–142, 158, 170, 177, 203, 207–208
Situational leadership, 98
Slender bridges, 58–59
Social media, 10, 37, 101–102, 185–186, 189, 196, 203–204, 210–211
Social movements, 10, 13–14, 19–22, 101–102, 161, 188–189, 196, 211
Social networks, 101–102
Societal challenges, 2, 10, 11–13, 17, 116
Sociotechnical theory, 72
Solar Radiation Management (SRM), 200–201

Spencer, Herbert, 188–189
Stakeholder(s)
  Alignment, 2–3, 14–18, 24–28, 34, 37–41,
    44, 46, 55, 69, 82, 93–94, 100, 105,
    109–110, 114, 117, 118, 128, 134, 155
  Alignment Model, 15–16, 76–77, 115, 135,
    162
  Baggage, 14–15
  Defined, 14–15
  Differences among/Diversity of, 16–17, 40,
    45, 57, 58–59, 61–62, 69, 70–71, 75, 137,
    181, 187, 192–193
  Engagement, 16, 24, 25–26, 38–39, 93, 94,
    (defined), 98–109–110, 181
  Future generations as a, 184, 191–193, 195
  Management, 16, 25–26, 38, 93–98, 99,
    102–110, 181
  Mapping/Survey, 30–31, 42, 49, 116,
    122–124, 127–128, 172, 201
  Marginalized, 191
  Multi, 12–13, 26, 37–38, 44–45, 52, 55, 76,
    113–114, 124–125, 139, 175, 182, 185–186
  Nature as a, 184, 191–193
  Specify, 40, 46
  Value propositions, 76–77, 79, 80–81, 109,
    124–126, 128, 141, 143–144, 149, 200
Stewart, Douglas Bitonti, 170
Sufficient alignment for action, see Alignment
Superficial engagement, 114, 182, 193
Sustainable Development Goals, see UN
  Sustainable Development Goals
Sustaining phase (Stakeholder Alignment
  Model), 161

Takeda, 7–8, 22, 23–24, 55, 73, 109, 114, 119
Tansley, Arthur, 39
Targeted universalism, 182
Technological change, 9, 88
Thaler, Richard, 209–210
Three-dimensional electron microscopy
  (3DEM), 156, 173
Thriving in Games Group, 208–210
Tokenism, 51, 57–58
Top-down, see change
Tragedies of the commons, 51–53
Transforming/Transformational, 7, 21, 25, 30,
  37–39, 109, 136, 138, 160–161, 163,
  176–178, 206–208
Tribal Colleges and Universities
  (TCU), 24–25, 30–31, 83, 114, 116, 119,
  123, 124–126, 136, 142, 144, 150, 166, 170,
  192

Trump, Donald, 1

Uber, 26, 187
United Nations
  Environment Programme
    (UNEP), 195–196
  Sustainable Development Goals
    (SDGs), 10, 34, 196–197, 199
United States
  Department of Commerce (DoC), 55–56,
    79–80, 113
  Department of Defense (DoD), 112–113
  Department of Energy (DoE), 113, 172
  Department of Transportation (DoT), 113
  Environmental Protection Agency
    (EPA), 113
  Executive Order 13985, 103–104, 181–182
  Executive Order 14901, 27, 103
  Federal Aviation Administration
    (FAA), 25–26, 112–114
  Food and Drug Administration (FDA), 14,
    16–17, 75–81, 163, 167, 192
  Foundation for NIH, 77–78, 80–81, 167
  National Aeronautics and Space
    Administration (NASA), 112–113, 133
  National Institutes of Health (NIH), 14,
    16–17, 75–81, 163, 192
  National Institute of Standards and
    Technology (NIST), 156
  National Oceanic and Atmospheric
    Administration (NOAA), 133
  National Science Foundation (NSF), 30–31,
    83, 85, 116, 127–128, 132, 133, 137, 141,
    146, 147, 160, 164, 172, 177
  National Telecommunications and
    Information Administration within US
    Department of Commerce) (NTIA), 172
US-EU Trade and Technology Council, 36
Unitary, 12–14, 69, 75–76, 94–96, 98, 102, 106,
  110, 199
University Corporation for Atmospheric
  Research (UCAR), 12–13

Value Propositions, 76–77, 79, 80–82,
  124–126, 128, 141, 143–144, 149, 200
Voll, Kimberly, 209–210

Waitz, Ian, 112–113
Walton, Richard, 71–72
Webb, Sydney and Beatrice, 69–70
Weak signals, 32
Weil, David, 60–61

Wholley, David, 81
Wiggins, Urban, 62
Work in America Institute (WIA), 61–62
Working Group (within RDA and MS-CC) (WG), 30–31, 84, 145–147, 185–186

World Economic Forum (WEF), 160–161, 191
World Health Organization (WHO), 93
Worldview, 51, 61–62, 189–190
World-Wide Protein Data Bank (wwPDB), 156–157, 173